FLORIDA STATE
UNIVERSITY LIBRARIES

JUN 14 2001

TALLAHASSEE, FLORIDA

CONTEMPORARY ECONOMIC THEORY

Also by Andriana Vlachou

THE SOCIALIST TRANSFORMATION OF CHINA (*co-author, in Greek*)

ENVIRONMENTAL CRISIS (*co-author, in English and in Greek*)

NATURE AND SOCIETY: A Debate over Ecology, Marxism and Knowledge (*editor, in Greek*)

Contemporary Economic Theory

Radical Critiques of Neoliberalism

Edited by

Andriana Vlachou
Associate Professor
Athens University of Economics and Business

First published in Great Britain 1999 by
MACMILLAN PRESS LTD
Houndmills, Basingstoke, Hampshire RG21 6XS and London
Companies and representatives throughout the world

A catalogue record for this book is available from the British Library.

ISBN 0-333-75362-3

 First published in the United States of America 1999 by
ST. MARTIN'S PRESS, INC.,
Scholarly and Reference Division,
175 Fifth Avenue, New York, N.Y. 10010

ISBN 0-312-22324-2

Library of Congress Cataloging-in-Publication Data
Contemporary economic theory : radical critiques of Neoliberalism /
edited by Andriana Vlachou.
  p. cm.
Includes bibliographical references and index.
ISBN 0-312-22324-2 (cloth)
1. Radical economics—Congresses. 2. Neoclassical school of
economics—Congresses. 3. Liberalism—Congresses. 4. Free
enterprise—Congresses. I. Vlachou, Andriana.
HB97.7.C66   1999
330.15'7—DC21   99-12195
                                                                     CIP

Selection and editorial matter © Andriana Vlachou 1999
Chapter 1 © Andriana Vlachou and Georgios K. Christou 1999
Chapters 2–10 and Discussions © Macmillan Press Ltd 1999

All rights reserved. No reproduction, copy or transmission of this publication may be made without written permission.

No paragraph of this publication may be reproduced, copied or transmitted save with written permission or in accordance with the provisions of the Copyright, Designs and Patents Act 1988, or under the terms of any licence permitting limited copying issued by the Copyright Licensing Agency, 90 Tottenham Court Road, London W1P 0LP.

Any person who does any unauthorised act in relation to this publication may be liable to criminal prosecution and civil claims for damages.

The authors have asserted their rights to be identified as the authors of this work in accordance with the Copyright, Designs and Patents Act 1988.

This book is printed on paper suitable for recycling and made from fully managed and sustained forest sources.

10 9 8 7 6 5 4 3 2 1
08 07 06 05 04 03 02 01 00 99

Printed and bound in Great Britain by
Antony Rowe Ltd, Chippenham, Wiltshire

Contents

List of Figures and Tables	vii
Preface	ix
Acknowledgements	xxii
Notes on the Contributors and Discussants	xxiii
List of Abbreviations	xxix

1 Contemporary Economic Theory: Some Critical Issues
  Andriana Vlachou and Georgios K. Christou — 1

PART I THE CRITIQUE OF THE NEOLIBERAL ECONOMIC PARADIGM

2 Privatization: Theory with Lessons from the United Kingdom
  Ben Fine — 41

  Discussion
  Stavros Mavroudeas and Lefteris Tsoulfidis — 67

3 Limiting the State vs. Expanding it: A Criticism of the Debate
  Richard D. Wolff — 72

  Discussion
  Anwar M. Shaikh — 86

4 Explaining Inflation and Unemployment: An Alternative to Neoliberal Economic Theory
  Anwar M. Shaikh — 89

  Discussion
  Thanassis Maniatis and Nikos Petralias — 106

5 Revisioning Socialism: The Cherry Esplanade Conjecture
  David Laibman — 113

Discussion
Richard D. Wolff 133

Discussion
Dimitris Milonakis 137

PART II EUROPEAN MONETARY AND ECONOMIC UNION

6 The Single Currency: Prospects and Problems
Georgios Katiphoris 145

7 Financial Governance and Democratic Consolidation: The Dual Challenge of the EU
Louka T. Katseli 159

8 Capitalist Globalization and Economic and Monetary Union
Guglielmo Carchedi 173

Discussion
George Liodakis 195

Discussion
John Milios 200

9 Central Bank Independence: Problematic Theory and Empirical Evidence
Costas Lapavitsas 205

10 Is There any Alternative to the Current EMU Project?
Jörg Huffschmid 220

Discussion
Panos Tsakloglou 245

Discussion
Guglielmo Carchedi 250

Index 253

List of Figures and Tables

Figures

4.1	OECD growth and unemployment, 1964–91	95
4.2	OECD inflation vs. unemployment, 1965–91	95
4.3	OECD inflation vs. growth, 1965–91	97
4.4	US profit rate and accumulation rate, 1947–95	101
4.5	US inflation vs. throughput coefficient, 1947–95	101
D4.1	GDP growth and unemployment, 1960–94	109
D4.2	GDP growth, unemployment and inflation, 1960–94	109
D4.3	Greek inflation rate and throughput coefficient, 1959–94	110
D4.4	Greek inflation rate and throughput coefficient, 1959–94	110
5.1	The π curve	119
5.2	The δ curve	120
5.3	Early socialist development	121
5.4	The Cherry Esplanade Conjecture	123
5.5	Stages of socialist development	124

Tables

D4.1	Output, unemployment and inflation in the Greek economy, 1960–94	108
7.1	Unemployment rates and GDP at 1990 market prices, 1961–97	161
7.2	Growth of financial activity, 1980–2000	163
7.3	Maturity of net global foreign exchange transactions, April 1992 and April 1995	163
7.4	European FDI flows and their distribution, 1985–94	168

Preface

The papers drawn together in this volume were presented and discussed at the conference on '*Contemporary Economic Theory: Critical Perspectives*', held at the Athens University of Economics and Business, Athens, Greece, on 6–7 October 1997. The purpose of the conference was to discuss critically major aspects of Neoliberalism and present alternative theoretical viewpoints. The conference also assessed and questioned the current project for the monetary and economic union (EMU) of Europe which was at the time (and still is) of major concern in view of the evaluation of the European Union (EU) members for participating in the monetary union. The current project for the EMU has been convincingly presented by critics as the application of Neoliberalism in the European economies.

Neoliberal theory and policies have dominated contemporary economic thinking. They are often presented as the only valid analysis and policy recommendations of our time. The sophisticated mathematical analyses and techniques used by many neoliberal economists, based on aptitude that requires a long and painful training, supposedly grant their arguments and policy proposals a high scientific status. 'The lure of technique', the obsession with 'rigor and precision at the expense of relevance' almost precludes any discussion of economic questions that can not be formulated in and solved by advanced mathematical analysis.[1] In the process, however, economic issues that have been the subject of investigation have been trivialized. For example, today, 'the cry is to get growth started again', as it was twenty years ago. However, 'here we come upon the greatest of all economic questions, but one that in fact is never asked: what is growth for?'.[2] At the same time, the explanatory power of economics has been diminished to such an extent that not only important neoclassical economists like Mark Blaug express their dissatisfaction, but also even students question the usefulness of economics proper and turn to some more 'practical' training like finance, banking, business and so forth to be able to earn a living.

Travelling through contemporary economics, any sense of history, variability, change and transcendence of economic systems and theories is lost. Slavery or feudalism seem as if had never existed. One does not get even informed that the economic system to which modern economics directs its analytic investigation is capitalism. One has the impression that modern economic inquiry searches for some sort of eternal 'natural laws' of economic behaviour. Given the proclaimed scientificity of the dominant economic theory, colloraries which, for example, attribute economic problems to the impairment of the operation of market forces and propose their reinforcement appear to be of a natural order to which all economies should adjust. The thought that such a 'truth' suits today's global capitalism could come only from the perverse mind of some radicals, not from an ideologically neutral scientist. However, this is what conservatives do all the time: they try to demonstrate that the world in which we live is the best of all possible worlds. For this, in the words of Joan Robinson, 'the conservatives are compensated by occupying positions of power, which they can use to keep criticism in check'.[3]

Radical economists share a critical perspective towards capitalism as an economic system and towards its many unpleasant consequences and injustices. They also typically share a commitment to socialism in some form, though, in many cases, have been critical of the former Soviet system. Many of them trained in prestigious universities and equipped with sophisticated analytical skills, oppose the dominant theory on its assumptions, its methods of analysis and on its conclusions. Within the radical tradition, Marxist economists in particular have offered major critiques of the orthodox economics. Their notable knowledge of history of social systems and ideas enables radical economists to draw from the dynamics of the rise and fall of systems and theories in order to challenge the nirvana of the neoliberal proponents of capitalism. The unsettling realities of capitalism are on their side. Radical economists, at the same time, are also compelled to be in a continuous dialogue with the orthodoxy: they read and evaluate its new developments and assess its policy recommendations. Interestingly, it is the persuasive power of the radical explanations of economic phenomena – compared with the diminished relevance of neoclassical theory – which keeps the radical tradition and the discussion alive and vibrant.

Nevertheless, radical perspectives never attained a dominant position within the economics profession. As far as they oppose capitalism, they will keep being subordinate to neoclassical economics. There are many and complicated factors that combine to produce such an outcome. Among them, one should include 'the rigid and hierarchical organization' of the economics profession itself, headed by those who hold positions at the few 'top' universities, as Heildroner and Milberg have already argued.[4] In particular, echoing Ward's similar points,[5] the power inherent in the system of quality control within the economics profession makes young economists to soon realize that they cannot expect to be hired by leading universities, publish in prestigious academic journals, and be granted research funds unless they do approvingly mainstream 'scientific' work. Ward also tells us that 'consciences are not much troubled by such practices because the ideologically unconventional usually appear to appointment committees to be scientifically incompetent'.[6] These insights are certainly very telling about the way of thinking and practice of contemporary neoliberals placed at 'top' universities but they do not come as a surprise to radical economists. After all, the economics profession is embedded in capitalism and may well secure conditions for its existence; at the same time, the various social aspects of capitalism condition personal choices and development.

The book opens with an introductory essay by Andriana Vlachou and Georgios Christou which provides a summary of the theoretical foundations of neoliberal policies. In particular, it sketches the basic microeconomic concepts and the New Classical macroeconomic contributions upon which the Neoliberal theory rests. The introductory paper also discusses major economic theories in competition with Neoliberal theory. It sketches the differentia specifica of New Keynesian theory and Marxist economic theory in comparison to Neoliberal theory. The paper also examines the influence of Neoliberal theory on European unification. It provides an initial critical discussion of the major potential effects of the completion of the internal market and the current project for the Economic and Monetary Union (EMU).

The essays of the first part of the book focus on the critique of fundamental concepts, theoretical arguments and major policy recommendations of Neoliberalism today; they also discuss alternatives to them. In Chapter 2, Ben Fine critically reviews the conventional theory for analyzing privatization and finds it to be sorely inadequate, not least for narrowing the understanding of what constitutes industrial policy, for its undue separation or simple understanding of the relationship between economics and politics, and for its lack of historical specificity. The main conclusion reached by Fine is that a general theory of privatization is not appropriate; the latter must be situated within a certain socioeconomic and historical context. The experience of privatization in the UK is examined by Fine against this analytical background. He concludes that privatization in the UK has in some respects represented continuity with policies of the past, rather than a fundamental break, thereby further signifying and consolidating the weakness of the British economy.

In their comment, Mavroudeas and Tsoulfidis concur with Fine on several major points. However, they disagree with Fine's conclusion that a general theory of privatization is not suitable. They contend that such a general theory could be grounded in the postwar conditions of accumulation, and, in particular, in the reduced profitability and capitalist restructuring to restore it. In this context, they argue that privatization was the outcome of two general trends: the search of abundant financial capital for profitable investment and the defeat of workers' movement in the late 1980s.

The essay by Richard Wolff (Chapter 3) criticizes neoliberal theories and economic policies as diagnoses and cures for modern capitalism's problems. It likewise criticizes neoliberalism's traditional enemies: welfare statists, Keynesians, and most Marxists. Moreover, Wolff argues that, in their disputes over markets versus state allocation and over private versus collective property, both sides remain trapped within capitalism's periodic oscillations between its private and state forms. Thus, both sides base their contesting arguments on a common 'efficiency calculus' that is highly problematic and questionable, according to Wolff. Likewise he argues that both sides missed Marx's focus on class as the production, appropriation and distribution of surplus labour. In contrast to both, Wolff sketches a diagnosis and policy response to capitalism's problems that avoids the pitfalls of the efficiency calculus and foregrounds issues of class structure and class transformation in surplus labour forms.

Anwar Shaikh, in his comment, supports many of the central points made by Wolff. With respect to the efficiency calculus, he emphasizes that although we can not exist without making evaluations of outcomes, nevertheless, we should be wary of the way we make them. Moreover, although Shaikh shares Wolff's commitment to the importance of class, he stresses the need to put equal emphasis on Marx's 'beloved economics', that is on class as the element that structures the economic behaviour of capitalism, not just as a political and social structure.

In Chapter 4, Anwar Shaikh first discusses the treatment of inflation and unemployment in orthodox economic theories (Keynesian and Neoliberal), as they arose historically in the face of challenges from reality. He concludes that the presumed trade-off between inflation and unemployment, which has been a central concern over the postwar period, is not supported as a general historical pattern by empirical evidence. He then presents an alternate approach, based on a classical marxian framework, to address the question of inflation. He argues that the ratio of the actual growth rate of accumulation to the normal profit rate, which he calls the throughput coefficient, can be viewed as an index for inflationary pressure. The differential dynamics of the two variables involved provide the key to explaining inflation. Using data for the US economy for the postwar period, Shaikh is able to show a strong connection between the throughput coefficient and the inflation rate. Maniatis and Petralias, in their comment, use data for Greece to test Shaikh's hypothesis. They conclude that, despite some data difficulties, the movements of the throughput coefficient can satisfactorily explain inflationary pressures, especially over longer time periods (approximately 3 to 5 years), in Greece.

David Laibman in Chapter 5 argues that the recent monumental changes in the former Soviet Union and other East European countries have given rise to a new interest in rethinking socialism, which still remains the only *coherent* alternative to neoliberal capitalism. However, he contends that current thinking about socialism – whether market socialist, communitarian, anarchist, or traditional Marxist – has failed to envision societies that truly embody human growth and potential. In particular, recent socialist experience suggests an inverse relation between productivity and autonomy (both broadly defined). The 'conjecture' that Laibman presents in his essay is that the productivity–autonomy curve eventually bottoms out and then rises. The possibility thus emerges of an advanced socialism in which spontaneous individual activity deepens principled behaviour and collectivity, rather than leading to selfishness, alienation, polarization and domination. According to Laibman, this activity has aspects of both plan and market, suggesting a need to transcend the plan–market dichotomy in socialist thought.

In his comment on Laibman's paper, Wolff argues that Laibman cannot legitimately proceed his analysis as if the definitions of capitalism, socialism and communism, as well as the notions of productivity, democracy, autonomy, socialist consciousness and so forth were resolved and universally agreed matters. Laibman ought to address this problem, even in a preliminary way. Wolff also underlines the absence of any discussion of the class dimensions of the relation between autonomy and productivity in Laibman's essay.

He also criticizes Laibman for inadequate use of dialectics in discussing autonomy and productivity. According to Wolff, a more dialectical approach towards these issues would have led Laibman in examining the social conditions which would make more autonomy *and* higher productivity possible. Milonakis, in his comment, also concludes that Laibman's proposals for an inspirational and sophisticated socialism should be complemented by a discussion of the specific social forms and institutions that will make such a project workable. Milonakis welcomes Laibman's rethinking of socialism at a time when much of the current theory on the left has been influenced by neoliberal arguments, as happens to be the case with the market socialism school, the proposals of which he reviews briefly. Nevertheless, Milonakis finds Laibman's analysis very abstract, not grounded in present-day capitalism, and not connected with a concrete social transformation and with social or political forces that would make the proposed socialism possible. However, one should keep in mind that these are monumental problems facing not only Laibman but all socialists today.

The essays in the second part of the book concentrate on the Economic and Monetary Union (EMU) of Europe. In Chapter 6, George Katiphoris, drawing from an 'unashamedly old-fashioned political economy', discusses the problems and prospects of the single currency. He considers two large categories of problems: problems of acceptance by public opinion in general and in relation with the financial markets; and problems of a technocratic-economic nature. The second category covers, in particular, the fulfilment of the conditions of nominal convergence, the economic impact of the fulfilment of these conditions on member-states, the selection of member-states which qualify for single-currency membership, the relations between early entrants and non-entrants (the 'ins' and the 'pre-ins') and the procedures of introducing the new currency. As to prospects, Katiphoris focuses on three big topics: the internal economic implications (internal market, demand/supply shocks), the foreign implications ('hard' or 'soft' currency, reserve role, international monetary system) and the management of monetary policy. He argues, normatively rather than positively, that the integrated internal market and the single currency will create the possibility for a new Keynesian-type macro-economic policy without the distortions and deformations and difficulties of the past.

Louka Katseli, in Chapter 7, argues that the two most important challenges for the European Union are the strengthening of financial governance and the consolidation of democracy, to which growth and employment performance are intimately tied. She first looks at the dynamics of European integration and shows that low growth and unemployment are structurally related to the process of integration and the policy agenda that shaped it. Furthermore, she attributes the 'policy deficit' that has emerged to the prevalent inadequate distribution of competencies across national and community institutions. She concludes that the risks of prolonged stagnation, of increased fragility and of democratic deconsolidation could undermine the process of European integration, unless mitigated by concerted action; the latter, however, would require a major restructuring of competencies across national and Community institutions which would enable the use of policy instruments to affect growth, income distribution and financial stability.

In Chapter 8, Guglielmo Carchedi, following a Marxist approach, takes a more critical stance towards capitalist globalization and the EMU of Europe. He argues that the different aspects of the notion of globalization emphasize some real changes (e.g. rapid technical change, greater internationalization of capital, and so forth) but that these changes are seen through a distorting lens, through an aggressively ideological frame. He further submits that these real developments can be best understood as elements of a new stage of imperialism and as such can not bring generalized employment and welfare, as often promised by the globalization theorists. To illustrate his point, he discusses the impact of technological innovation (TI) and argues that TI results in unemployment and in a fall in the average rate of profit. He then focuses on the effects of globalization on Europe. He argues that the European nations have to aggregate in an economic and monetary union in order to compete with the two other major blocks, the United States and Japan. This process, however, takes place under the leadership of Germany. He suggests that this integration is accepted, and actually welcomed, because it allows for a common advantage for European capital, the extraction of greater surplus value. In order to explain how this takes place concretely, Carchedi discusses the workings of the European Monetary System (EMS), the precursor of the Economic and Monetary Union (EMU). He concludes that both systems (EMS and EMU) force technological laggards to renounce inflation and devaluation in order to safeguard their competitiveness and income, and to resort to the extraction of greater absolute surplus value at the point of production; on the other hand, they make possible for Germany, as well, to raise its absolute surplus value as German capitals demand and achieve more 'freedom' to deal with labour.

In his comment, George Liodakis shares many of the arguments put forward by Carchedi. However, he finds Carchedi's analysis inadequate in terms of the method used. He discusses, for example, Carchedi's arguments regarding technological innovation in the era of globalization and finds them not adequately dialectical. He also argues that while Carchedi sufficiently demonstrates the negative effects of the fulfilment of the requirements for the EMU, it is misleading, however, to focus on the restricted use of inflation and devaluation by the less developed countries. According to Liodakis, inflation and the determination of exchange rates in these countries are more or less structural phenomena resulting from the production-determined structure of competitive advantages, and not so much an intended policy. Emphasizing the significant negative effects of EMU on labour, Liodakis would expect from Carchedi suggestions for a specific strategy for labour to oppose the current EMU project and for a radical unification of Europe. John Milios, in his comment, concurs with Carchedi that current economic problems are due to a fall in the average rate of profit in capitalist economies. However, he argues that the thesis that technological innovation may cause a fall in the rate of profit is not complete. A more concrete analysis could reveal that since the end of the 1970s capitalist restructuring through micro-electronic innovation aimed not only at increasing productivity but also at economizing constant capital. The latter could result after all in an increase in the rate of profit. Milios also argues that the effects of the EMS on unequally developed capitals (economies) should be analyzed in terms of the movement of *real*, not nominal, currency parities. For example, he argues, in the 1970s and 1980s, when inflation differentials among the EC countries were significant, what appeared as a gradual nominal devaluation might well have been a real revaluation.

The essay by Costas Lapavitsas (Chapter 9) focuses on the issue of central bank independence. In this essay, Lapavitsas claims that the large and still expanding literature which presumably establishes the welfare benefits and superior inflation performance resulting from central bank independence suffers from a major conceptual weakness: it refers to a social planner in command of monetary policy rather than a central bank. Thus, according to Lapavitsas, two sets of problems emerge. First, it is not clear why a monetary planner improves social welfare compared to the complete absence of monopoly over legal tender. Given a planner, furthermore, there is no reason why the theory's own first-best solution cannot be achieved in preference to the typically advocated second-best. Finally, the goals of a monetary planner need not be limited to price stability alone. Second, according to Lapavitsas, for a central bank, wedded as it is to the financial system and the state, the notion of independence has little meaning. This considerably limits the persuasiveness of the empirical work. The article finally outlines the components of an explanation of the actual trend toward central bank independence with reference to the financial instability of the post-Bretton Woods world. The essay concludes with the argument that since central bank holds an organic position in the financial system as a private institution that necessarily acquires the mantle of a public one, it cannot be independent either of the private sector or of the state.

Jörg Huffschmid, in the final essay of the book (Chapter 10), tries to answer the question 'Is there any alternative for Europe to the current EMU project?' Huffschmid argues that the current project for EMU is wrongly propagated as the only way to promote economic welfare and political unity in Europe. The current deflationary strategy of EMU, leading to high unemployment and social polarization in Europe, has been a political choice which has been taken under the pressure of problems related to economic development and after a change in the balance of social interests and forces. According to Huffschmid, at the heart of an alternative strategy for Europe lies a policy for full employment which would increase economic and social welfare and strengthen the position of the working class. The economic policy measures which he proposes to achieve such an alternative are: a loosening of macroeconomic monetary and fiscal policy, reduction of working time, structural, regional, social and welfare policy, complemented by protective measures against external shocks and attacks. He also discusses the implementation problems of such an alternative. He claims that in the short run it requires strong social movements and a change in the balance of power in member states and the EU. In a long-term perspective, it must be based on a new institutional framework of democratic decisions and political control of the main directions of economic development.

Panos Tsakloglou, in his comment, considers some of Huffschmid's ideas rather utopian, at least in the present political climate. In particular, he questions Huffschmid's proposals for the creation of some sort of central European government and a fivefold increase in the EU budget in order to realize an alternative to the current EMU project with full employment as its primary objective. Tsakloglou argues that the governments of the member-states do not seem to be even remotely willing to transfer some powers to EU bodies. Similarly, the recommended increase in EU budget seems totally unrealistic, even in the medium to long run. In addition, Tsakloglou reminds us that the recommended policy measures are likely to increase costs and lead to lower competitiveness and stagnation. His conclusion is that the whole alternative project for the labour movement in Europe has to be redrafted in a far less ambitious scale. On the other hand, Guglielmo Carchedi, in his short comment, although in appreciation of Huffschmid's position that *there is an alternative* to the current EMU project, hopes for a more radical unification of Europe than that proposed by Huffschmid. He contends that to argue for more employment and greater social justice within a theoretical scheme that stresses the rationality of capitalism and the market which generate social evils (that is, within neo-classical economics) – as Huffschmid does – cannot but be self-defeating.

Although almost a year has passed by since the conference, the concerns, questions and arguments presented at it continue to be very opportune and interesting. The increasing unemployment and relative poverty have resulted in a growing public dissatisfaction with dominant economic arguments and policies. Current policies have not yet brought forth the promised growth and prosperity. Nevertheless, neoliberals keep dogmatically insisting on their theories and policy recommendations to tackle unemployment: cut taxes, reform social-security systems and above all deregulate labour market.[7] Intensified competition at the global scale – the desired outcome by neoliberals of unleashed market forces – creates worldwide instability and deepens unequal development.

The present crisis of global financial markets causes an unprecedented international turmoil. It has been increasingly recognized as a systemic crisis – it arises from within the ordinary workings of global capitalism. In particular, in a recent article which appeared in *The Financial Times* (7 October 1998), Paul Volcker, chairman of the Federal Reserve from 1979 to 1987, attributes the current crisis to the combined workings of two factors: the huge and volatile financial flows around the world and the small emerging financial markets opened up as a result of the ideology of free and open markets which has swept over virtually the entire word in the last fifteen years. As the crisis worsens, George Soros, chairman of Soros Fund Management, warned that it would be regretable if America remained complacent just because most of the trouble is occurring beyond its border: 'There comes a point when distress at the periphery cannot be good for the center', he added.[8] Today, many leading policy makers share the fear that what began as an emerging markets problem might now turn into a global recession, while a number of bankers consider the treat of a global credit crunch seriously. Alan Greenspan, chairman of the Federal Reserve, indicated recently that there is a very dramatic change in investors' sentiment away from risk and he warned that companies were finding it more difficult to raise fresh capital as banks and other lenders grew more concerned about risk. He added that this will dampen US growth to an unknown extent, worsening the problems in the international economy.[9] Greenspan, who has been monitoring the US policy on a daily basis for the last fifty years, warned that he had never seen anything like the present financial crisis.

In order to deal with the current crisis the companies seek to increase their size and to differentiate. This trend is evidenced in the surge of mergers and acquisitions within the industrialized world and in the increased foreign ownership in the emerging markets. Emerging markets also retreat into exchange controls. At the same time, the crisis renewed the questions about 'all that is holy and good: the sanctity of markets and their unfailing ability to adjust, the freedom of capital and trade'.[10] The communiqué of the International Monetary Fund's ministerial committee released on 4 October 1998, reflected the change of mood: references to the merits of 'liberalizing' capital were missing. Several experts have persistently argued that there is an urgent need to recognize that financial markets far from tending toward equilibrium, are inherently unstable. All sorts of proposals for dealing with current crisis and for creating a crisis-proof system have been made. They include the establishment of some sort of supervision over global financial markets, controls on short-term capital flows and reduction in the interest rates.

A few months before the launch of monetary union of the first eleven member-states, Europe has not been immune from the current crisis. Since the memories of the 1987 stock market crash and the subsequent forced decrease in interest rates are still fresh, there has been speculation of a reversal of the much praised monetary policy of the European Central Bank due to the current crisis, although such an outcome is not considered very likely at the present.[11] European unification is not only strongly questioned but also uncertain.

Against the background of the current crisis, the criticism and recommendations presented in this collection of papers are more than ever relevant and persuasive. At the end, it will be proved that neoliberal policy 'is just as much a policy as any other.'[12] The reported 'death' of Marxism, and of socialist thought more generally, might have been greatly exaggerated. In the current era of 'globalization', a spectre may still haunt Europe – and the whole globe – if the history of all hitherto society is the history of class struggles, as Marx believed.[13]

Athens   ANDRIANA VLACHOU
October 1998

Notes

1. Mark Blaug also speaks very critically of the 'formalism' of modern economics, which gives top priority to the formal structure of modelling irrespective of its content. See Mark Baug, 'Why I am Not a Constructivist: Confessions of an Unrepentant Popperian', in R. Backhouse (ed.), *New Directions in Economic Methodology* (London: Routledge, 1994), p. 131.
2. See Joan Robinson, 'What are the Questions?', *Journal of Economic Literature*, December 1977, 1318–39, p. 1337.
3. Ibid, p. 1318.
4. Robert Heilbroner and William Milberg, *The Crisis of Vision in Modern Economic Thought* (New York: Cambridge University Press, 1995), p. 100.
5. Benjamin Ward, *What's Wrong with Economics?* (New York: Basic Books, 1972), pp. 29–30. Ward has also been approvingly quoted by Joan Robinson in her work mentioned earlier.
6. Ibid, p. 38.
7. *The Economist*, 29 August–4 September 1998, p. 67.
8. *The Wall Street Journal Europe*, 16 September 1998.
9. *The Financial Times*, 8 October 1998.
10. Paul Volcker, *The Financial Times*, 7 October 1998.
11. *The Financial Times*, 1 September 1998. Hans Tietmeyer, president of the Bundesbank, also consented that it might be necessary to cut interest rates (*The Financial Times*, 6 October, 1998).
12. The words of Joan Robinson (p. 1318) speaking of *laissez-faire*. She adds '[economic] questions involve the whole political and social system

of capitalist word; they cannot be decided by economic theory, but it would be decent, at least, if the economists admitted that they do not have an answer to them' (p. 1337). Joan Robinson, 'What are the Questions?', *Journal of Economic Literature*, December 1977, pp. 1318–1339.
13. Karl Marx and Friedrich Engels, 'Manifesto of the Communist Party' in Karl Marx and Friedrich Engels, *Selected Works* (Moscow: Progress Publishers, 1969), p. 108.

Acknowledgements

I am deeply indebted in many ways to the contributors to the Conference on 'Contemporary Economic Theory: Critical Perspectives' from which this collection of papers is drawn. I also wish to thank the Athens University of Economics and Business and especially the Economics Department under the auspices of which the conference was organized. I gratefully acknowledge the financial contributions of the General Bank of Greece, the Commercial Bank of Greece and the Athens University of Economics and Business.

I want to thank Georgios Christou, Kyprianos Prodromidis, Georgios Samaras and Anastasia Mouriki for working to organize the Conference. I wish to extend my thanks to Demetra Demakou, Olga Bati and Athanasios Aliferis for their hard work in preparing the book. I am also grateful to Sunder Katwala, the publishing editor, for his cooperation, and to Keith Povey for his editorial assistance. Finally, I would like to thank many other individuals – translators, the administrative staff and students of the Athens University of Economics and Business and friends – who contributed in many ways to make the conference a great success.

ANDRIANA VLACHOU

Notes on the Contributors and Discussants

CONTRIBUTORS

Guglielmo Carchedi teaches at the University of Amsterdam, Faculty of Economics and Econometrics. He is the author of several books and articles. His two most recent books are *Frontiers of Political Economy* (1991) and, with A. Freeman (eds), *Marx and Non-Equilibrium Economics* (1996).

Georgios K. Christou is Professor at the Department of Economics, Athens University of Economics and Business Science. He graduated with a degree in Economics from the Athens School of Economics and Business Science and received his Master's and PhD degrees from North Carolina State University. He teaches Econometrics, Principles of Economics, Trade and Economic Integration. He has previously taught at the University of New Orleans, the University of San Francisco, and he has published articles in the *Journal of Common Market Studies*, the *Journal of Developing Areas*, the *Journal of Latin American Studies*, and others. He has also published in Greek textbooks in econometrics and principles of economics.

Ben Fine is Professor of Economics at the University of London and Director of the Centre for Economic Policy for Southern Africa, SOAS; formerly Professor of Economics at Birkbeck College, University of London, he received his BA in Mathematics and his BPhil in Economics from Balliol College, Oxford, and his PhD in Economics from the University of London. His main research interests include the British economy and industrial policy, energy economics and the British coal industry, the South African economy, especially the minerals–energy complex, on which he completed a research project funded by the ESRC with research officer Zavareh Rustomjee. His more recent books are *Diet, Health and Food Policy* (forthcoming); *Labour Market Theory: A Constructive Reassessment* (1998); *The Political Economy of South Africa: From Minerals–Energy Complex to Industrialization* (1997, with Z. Rostonjee). He has published articles in the *Cambridge Journal of Economics, Development and Cultural Change, Capital and Class, Metroeconomica*. He served as an expert advisor to the year-long South African Presidential Labour Market Commission which published its report in July 1996.

Jörg Huffschmid is Professor of Political Economy and Economic Policy at the Institute of European Economy and Economic Policy of the University of Bremen. He studied in Freiburg, Paris and Bremen. He is a research visitor in London, Moscow and Madrid, visiting Professor at the New School for Social Research in New York, a member of the German Arbeitsgruppe Alternative Wirtschaftspolitik and of the working group 'European Economists for an Alternative Economic Policy'. He has published books and articles on corporate strategies and economic policy in Germany and Europe, including *Wem gehört Europa? Kapitalstrategien und Wirtschaftspolitik in der EU* (1994, 2 vols).

Georgios Katiphoris is Economist and Senior Lecturer at University College London. He served as Economic Advisor to Prime Minister, Andreas Papandreou (1987–9 and 1993–4). He is a member of the European Parliament (since 1994) and First Vice-Chairman of the Economic, Monetary and Industrial Policy Commission of the European Parliament. His main publications include *Introduction to Marxist Economics* (1989); *Value Exploitation and Growth* (with M. Morishima, 1978).

Louka T. Katseli is chair and Professor of Economics at the Department of Economics, University of Athens. Before that, she taught at Yale University (1977–85). She received her PhD in International and Development Economics from Princeton University. She is the author of more than 40 articles in refereed journals while her most recent book is *Foreign Direct Investment and Trade Linkages in Developing Countries* (1993). She has recently served as a member and rapporteur for the UN Committee for Development Planning as well as member of the 'Comité des Sages' of the European Commission.

David Laibman is Professor of Economics at the Brooklyn College and Graduate School, City University of New York. He is the Editor of *Science & Society* (an interdisciplinary Marxist journal, published quarterly in New York). He is the author of *Value, Technical Change*

Notes on the Contributors and Discussants xxv

and Crisis: Explorations in Marxist Economic Theory (1992), *Capitalist Macrodynamics: A Systematic Introduction* (1997).

Costas Lapavitsas is Lecturer in Economics at the University of London, SOAS. He received his PhD in Economics from Birkbeck College, University of London. He has published articles in the *Cambridge Journal of Economics*, *Capital and Class*, *Keizaigakuronshu* (*The Economic Journal*), *Contributions to Political Economy*, and others. His most recent book (co-authored with Makoto Itoh) is *Political Economy of Money and Finance* (1998).

Anwar M. Shaikh is Professor at the Department of Economics at the Graduate Faculty of Political and Social Science of the New School for Social Research, New York, USA. He received his PhD in Economics from Columbia University (1973). His fields of teaching and research include Political Economy, Development Economics, International Trade, Mathematical Economics, Growth and Cycle Theory, National Economic Accounts, History of Economic Thought, and Macroeconomics. His most recent book (co-authored with E. Ahmet Tonak) was *The Political Economy of National Accounts: An Alternate Approach to the Measurement of the Wealth of Nations* (1994). He is currently working on the long-term determinants of the exchange rates of OECD countries, and on the dynamics of money and credit, and of the stock market, in the United States.

Andriana Vlachou is an Associate Professor of Economics at the Athens University of Economics and Business. She received her PhD in Economics from the University of Massachusetts (1983). Her fields of teaching and research include Environmental and Natural Resource Economics and Marxian and Neoclassical Economic Theories. She has published articles in *Rethinking Marxism*, *Capitalism, Nature, Socialism*, *Southern Economic Journal*, *Energy Economics*, *Environmetrics* and others. She has edited *Nature and Society: A Debate over Ecology, Marxism and Knowledge* (1995, in Greek).

Richard D. Wolff is Professor of Economics at the University of Massachusetts. Before that he taught economics at the City University of New York and at Yale University. With co-author Stephen Resnick he has published many books and articles on Marxian economic theory and its applications in many fields. Most recently, he co-authored (with H. Fraad and S. Resnick). *Bringing it All Back Home: Class, Gender, and Power in the Modern Household* (1994). He is currently completing, with S. Resnick, a class analysis of the rise and fall of the USSR.

DISCUSSANTS

George Liodakis is Associate Professor at the Technical University of Crete. He received his BA from the University of Athens (1975), and his PhD in Economics (Economic Development, International Economics) from the American University (1980). His areas of research interest are: Political Economy, Economic Development and Technology, Agricultural Development, International Economic Relations, Environment, and Philosophy of Science. He is the author of *International Division of Labor and Greek Agriculture* (1991), *Ground – Rent. Interest Rates and Agricultural Prices* (1994), editor of *Society, Technology and Restructuring of Production* (1993), and author of articles in *The Review of Radical Political Economics, Innovation, Plus Valore, Sociologia Ruralis, Review of Agrarian Studies, The Social Science Tribune, Utopia*, and others.

Thanassis Maniatis is a Researcher at the Centre for Planning and Economic Research Athens, Greece. He received his PhD in Economics from the New School for Social Research (New York, 1992). He has taught Marxian economic theory at the Graduate Faculty of the New School for Social Research and the Department of Economics of the University of Athens. He has published on Marxist economics in *Capital and Class* and the *Encyclopedia of Political Economy* and he is co-author of the forthcoming book *Issues of Political Economy: The Case of Greece* (1998, in Greek).

Stavros Mavroudeas is an Assistant Professor of Political Economy at the University of Macedonia. He received his PhD from Birkbeck College, University of London (1990). His teaching and research fields include Political Economy, History of Economic Thought and Development Economics. He has published articles in the *Journal of Applied Business Research, Science and Society, Research in Political Economy* and others.

Notes on the Contributors and Discussants

John Milios is Associate Professor of Political Economy and the History of Economic Theories at the National Technical University of Athens. He is the Director of *Thessis*, a quarterly journal of economic and political theory published in Greek since 1982. His fields of interest are Marxist theory, the study of the process of capital internationalization, in relation to international trade and the changing currency parities and with emphasis on the process of European integration, and the analysis of the role of public institutions and state policies to economic development, employment and the distribution of the net product. His most recent books are *Marxism as a Conflict among Schools of Thought* (1996, in Greek), *Theories of Global Capitalism. A Critique* (1997, in Greek), *Modes of Production and Marxist Analysis* (1997, in Greek). He has also edited the collected volume *Social Policy and Social Dialogue in the Perspective of the Economic and Monetary Union and of the 'Europe of Citizens'* (1996).

Dimitris Milonakis is currently a lecturer in Economics at the University of Crete. He received his PhD in 1990 from Birkbeck College, University of London. His teaching and research fields include Comparative Economic Systems, Political Economy, Theory of Economic and Social History, History of Economic Thought. He has published articles in *Science & Society*, *Journal of Research Studies*, and others. He is co-editor of the book *Marx Revisited* (1996, in Greek).

Nikos Petralias is Professor of Political Economy at the Department of Economics of the University of Athens. He received his PhD in Economics from the University of Heidelberg (1971). He has served as Rector of the Panteion University and he is currently President of the Board of Trustees of the Sakis Karageorgas Foundation. His teaching and research interests include growth and cycles theory and the methodology of economic theory.

Panos Tsakloglou is Assistant Professor at the Department of International and European Economic Studies, Athens University of Economics and Business. He received his BA from the Department of Economics, University of Thessaloniki, Greece, and his MA and PhD from the Department of Economics, University of Warwick, UK. He previously taught at the University of Bristol, UK and served as an expert in poverty statistics at Eurostat,

Luxembourg. He has recently published articles in the *Economic Journal*, *Journal of Development Economics* and *Review of Income and Wealth*. His research interests are economics of welfare comparisons, inequality, poverty and social exclusion and development economics.

Lefteris Tsoulfidis is Assistant Professor of Economics at the University of Macedonia. He received his PhD from the New School for Social Research (New York, 1989). His teaching and research fields include History of Economic Thought, Political Economy and Mathematical Economics. His most recent publications include 'Alternative Theories of Competition: Evidence from Greek Manufacturing', *International Review of Applied Economics*, 'The Relationship of Saving and Finance in EU Countries', *Research in Economics*. He is a co-author of the forthcoming book *Issues of Political Economy: The Case of Greece* (1998, in Greek).

List of Abbreviations

ARP	average rate of profit
CAP	Common Agricultural Policy (EU)
CPI	Consumer Price Index (average rate of inflation)
EC	European Community
ECB	European Central Bank
ECJ	European Court of Justice
EcoFin	Economic and Financial Council (EU)
ECSC	European Coal and Steel Community
ECU	European Currency Unit (now euro)
EEC	European Economic Community
EMI	European Monetary Institute (now ECB)
EMS	European Monetary System
EMU	Economic and Monetary Union
ERM	Exchange Rate Mechanism (EU)
FDI	foreign direct investment
GDP	gross domestic product
GNP	gross national product
IT	information technology
JIT	just-in-time
JV	joint venture
LDC	less-developed country
M & A	merger and acquisition
ME	Marxian economics
MU	monetary union
NAIRU	non-accelerating inflation rate of unemployment
NC	New Classical
NK	New Keynesian
NTB	non-tariff barrier
NUR	natural unemployment rate
R & D	research and development
SCP	structure–conduct–performance
SEA	Single European Act
TI	technological innovation

1 Contemporary Economic Theory: Some Critical Issues

Andriana Vlachou and
Georgios K. Christou

INTRODUCTION

Neoliberal theory has become very influential today. Several factors have contributed to its wide spread, among them the persistent decline in economic development since the mid-1970s and the rising dissatisfaction with Keynesian explanations and prescriptions. The analytical tensions and inadequacies of Keynesianism became particularly apparent in dealing with the concurrent problems of unemployment and inflation. Moreover, the continuing internationalization of economic relations in terms of trade, investment and finance gave rise to the concept of 'globalization' – that is, to the idea that national economies and cultures are dissolving into global processes. Global economic activity appears to be dominated by market forces; multinational companies can render national fiscal and monetary policies ineffective. Neoliberalism, with its strong support for market forces, is thus well suited to this international environment.

Popularized versions of Neoliberal theory attribute economic slowdown and increased unemployment to the impairment of market forces. It is claimed that the main responsibility lies with state intervention, which obscures market signals and also distorts the incentives of economic agents. In addition, organized labour also contributes to price rigidities and to misallocation of productive resources by setting wage rates and job tasks and by shaping working conditions. Naturally, Neoliberals advocate cuts in taxation and government spending, privatization, and reinforcing market relations by deregulating, for example, capital and labour markets or by liberalizing foreign trade. Thus, the free market mechanism is celebrated by Neoliberals as a sufficient mechanism for achieving economic growth and welfare.

This paper is organized as follows. The next section discusses the theoretical foundations of Neoliberal policies, in particular the basic microeconomic concepts and the New Classical macroeconomic contributions upon which the Neoliberal theory rests. The following section discusses the economic theories in competition with Neoliberal theory; it presents the *differentia specifica* of New Keynesian (NK) theory and Marxist Economic (ME) theory in contrast with Neoliberal theory. We then examine the influence of Neoliberal theory on European unification, providing an initial critical discussion of the potential effects of internal market and the project for Economic and Monetary Union (EMU). The final section provides a summary of the major conclusions.

NEOLIBERAL THEORY

Neoliberal theory rests upon the microeconomic basis of neoclassical theory, developed in the legacy of Adam Smith, Leon Walras and Alfred Marshall[1]. At the macroeconomic level, Neoliberalism has embraced the developments advanced by the New Classical (NC) approach. In this section we briefly sketch out the neoclassical microeconomic foundations and those of the New Classical theory.

The Microeconomic Basis

The starting point of microeconomics is the individual behaviour of economic agents. The *individual* is taken as the foundation, the conceptual core of modern economics. Microeconomic theory involves some essential ideas about human nature. It is assumed that it is part of the nature of human beings to pursue their self-interest and to be able to make rational choices; it is also assumed to be in the nature of each human being to optimize – and, in particular, to maximize – her pleasure while satisfying her needs, subject to some constraints such as income or resource endowments (Barro 1993, p.18). Utility is a central concept for neoclassical economics. Moreover, needs, tastes, preferences and rational and productive abilities all belong to the innate nature of individuals. Significantly, human nature is treated as a given by neoclassical theory; it may change, but this change is caused by factors exogenous to economy

– that is, by the factors exogenous to economic variables that neoclassical theory focuses on (Rowthorn 1974; Wolff and Resnick 1987). Utility is the common property of commodities for neoclassical theory. Individual demand and supply for final goods – derived on the assumption of optimizing behaviour under the constraints of income or endowments and technology – jointly determine the quantities produced and consumed. These are optimal decisions for economic agents since they satisfy the efficiency criterion – that is, they maximize the net benefits from any economic activity.

Employment and wages are determined by the interaction of demand and supply of labour. The supply of labour for any individual is determined by the choice between real income and leisure (pertaining to human nature), the given real wage and the given initial endowment of labour time. The demand for labour is a function of the marginal productivity of labour and the price of the commodity produced.Thus the ultimate determinants of the supply and demand for labour are preferences, production functions and resource endowments. For any given technology and initial endownment of non-labour resources, wage income depends on the individual's preference for work rather than leisure. In this case, low or high income is a matter of individual choice.

On the other hand, the supply of capital by its owner depends on the preference between present and future consumption, the given real rate of return, and the initial endowment of current real income. The demand for capital depends, as in the case of labour, on the price of output (ultimately based on preferences for the commodity), the marginal product of capital and the initial endowment of resources.

Demand and supply of goods and factors act together to determine prices and quantities produced and consumed. Given the optimizing behaviour of consumers and producers, general equilibrium conditions follow. In this framework, *efficiency* is the accepted criterion for optimality as defined by Pareto.[2] Significantly, the 'invisible hand', the competitive market mechanism, can satisfy the optimal conditions for general equilibrium. Competitive markets require that no individual has any power to control prices or quantities so that buyers and sellers take prices as given. They also require that information is abundant and freely available to market agents. Competitive markets thus become the optimal social institution for the attainment of social welfare. However, this conclusion is the result of an important value judgement – that is, the acceptance of

Pareto-optimality as representing social optima (see also Henderson and Quandt 1971, p. 264).

In the neoclassical framework, the distribution of income is achieved through the workings of the markets for factors of production. The same markets determine the level of factor employment, including labour. In a certain economic configuration, each factor of production receives what it contributes to production – that is, the value of its marginal product. In fact, individual preferences, technology and initial resource endowments are the ultimate determinants of wages and employment. Income distribution does not thus involve any kind of coersion or exploitation; it is determined by scarcity as captured by the given resource endowments, production function and by preferences – that is, in the last instance, by physical or human nature. In a similar fashion, the equalization of demand and supply for production factors determines the level of employment. If, for example, there is unemployment at the equilibrium wage, it is considered to be voluntary and thus is not a social problem. As Blinder (1987, p. 131) puts it:

> in Lucas' view, a person laid off from a job can, presumably, shine shoes in a railroad station or sell apples on a street corner. If he is not doing any of these things, he must be *choosing* not to do so.

Microeconomic analysis thus celebrates competitive markets. As Smith argued, the pursuit of self-interest, without any government assistance or interference, could lead society to allocate resources efficiently and attain maximum welfare. Limiting the state and *privatizations* of state enterprises are grounded today on this microeconomic notion of efficient resource allocation. Moreover, for many neoclassical economists, private property and competitive markets are mutually supportive. It is argued, for example, that since state-owned enterprises do not face bankruptcy or risk takeover, they do not encounter market competition, and that is why they do not operate in an efficient way. A society which establishes and protects private property and competitive markets, often called a capitalist society, offers its members the best environment to gain the maximum wealth possible.

So, from the microeconomics' point of view, government intervention is justified only in the cases of market imperfections, externalities and public goods. However, Neoliberal theory seems to assign little importance to these phenomena while it advocates the reinforcement of market relations based on the assumption that agents form expectations rationally (to be discussed below) and markets adjust instantaneously so that equilibrium is by assumption guaranteed. No wonder why for the Neoliberals the role of the state should be limited to securing private property and competitive markets.

The Macroeconomic Basis

The Neoliberal theory embraces many of the macroeconomic developments that constitute the New Classical (NC) approach. We will discuss the NC theory through the major points of its departure from traditional Keynesian theory.

For many critics of Keynesianism, its most important analytical difficulty was the lack of *microfoundations*. New Classical economics attempts to rebuild macroeconomics, beginning with the specification of a microeconomic basis, similar to the one presented on pp. 2–4. New Classical economists maintain that the rational agents (individuals or firms) always optimize and, furthermore, that macroeconomic outcomes are the (consistent) aggregation of the acts of all such agents. In addition, they assume that markets clear instantaneously. NC economists thus assume that there is no price or wage stickiness in their models. The idea that markets clear is closely related to the notion that markets function efficiently (McCallum 1989; Barro 1993).

Significantly, the *rational expectations* hypothesis is an essential ingredient of the NC approach. The hypothesis of rational expectations is the concept that individuals make estimates or forecasts of unknown variables in the best possible way, utilizing all information currently available. The hypothesis implies that people do not make systematic mistakes in forming their expectations. New Classicals maintain that, on average, rational expectations are accurate estimates of the dynamics of unknown variables.[3]

Following Friedman (1968a), the New Classicals consider *inflation* as primarily a monetary phenomenon. Inflation is caused by (anticipated) monetary growth. Governments can thus cause inflation by increasing the supply of money. Real disturbances, such as supply shocks, are considered quite unimportant for chronic inflation. In the market-clearing macroeconomic model, assuming perfect foresight about future price levels and constant output, an increase in the growth rate of money results in the long run in equiproportonial increases in the inflation rate, the nominal interest rate and the growth rate of nominal wages. This conclusion follows from the important result of the New Classical model that anticipated changes in the quantity of money have no effect on real variables (real wage rate, real interest rate, output and employment).[4] Only unanticipated changes of money and inflation have real effects.[5] However, rational expectations imply that unexpected inflation will not exhibit a systematic pattern of errors over time (Barro 1993).

The New Classical microeconomic model maintains that adjustments in real wages clear the labour market. However, as Barro (1993) recognizes, this model cannot explain why unemployment and vacancies change over time. To allow for some friction in the labour market, New Classicals have embraced a job search model. Since jobs and workers are not identical, to find a job and to hire a worker takes time and involves costs for workers and firms, respectively. When rates of job separation (dismissals and quits) and job finding do not change, the rate of unemployment is constant and the economy has reached the *natural unemployment rate* (*NUR*).[6] The important determinants of the NUR are unemployment insurance, the minimum wage and labour unions. Generous unemployment insurance programmes are considered to be responsible for the large amount of long-term unemployment in Western Europe. A high minimum wage reduces the incentive of employers to hire low-productivity workers, resulting in reduced employment. Labour unions can raise real wage rates and also the acceptance wage and thus reduce the level of employment. Policies to reduce unemployment should therefore be based on these important determinants of the NUR.

New Classicals recognize that disturbances that lead to recession can cause unemployment. Supply shocks (such as energy crises and shifts in technology) and shifts in preferences may result in sectoral shifts and seasonal fluctuations and thus have important effects on employment in the short run.

However, an important characteristic of the NC theory is the hypothesis of the *non-accelerating inflation rate of unemployment* (*NAIRU*), as defined by Lucas (1972b, cited in McCallum 1989), that unemployment cannot be kept permanently low (or output permanently high) by any monetary policy. This assumption, offered previously by Friedman, is in sharp contradiction with traditional Keynesian theory which maintained that there is a trade-off between inflation and unemployment, captured by the negative slope of *Phillips curve*. The critics of the Phillips curve maintain that there is a natural rate of unemployment, as explained above, and that the Phillips curve would be vertical at this point in the long run. This is, they argue, because the level of unemployment is not related to the nominal but to the *real* wage. Thus, in the case of monetary policy which affects nominal wages, there would be a period of quantity adjustment (of 'money illusion') but after this period a specific relation between unemployment and inflation would be re-established (Heilbroner and Milberg 1995, p. 53).

Interestingly, NC theory has focused on the issue of *real business cycles* (Stadler 1994). The theory advanced the new assumption that there are large, random fluctuations in the rate of technological change. In particular, many models explain recessions as periods of declines in the technological capabilities of society. Because these exogenous shocks lead to fluctuations in relative prices, individuals rationally change their labour supply and consumption. The labour input happens to be procyclical because, in the case of temporary shocks, the intertemporal substitution effect tends to be stronger than the wealth effect. This means that when wages fall, the incentive for work declines (the demand for leisure increases as its price falls), increasing (voluntary) unemployment. This theory actually supports the notion of 'optimality' for business cycles, since they are the natural and efficient response of the economy to exogenous technological changes in the production function (Mankiw 1990, p. 1653). Significantly, real business cycle theorists assume that monetary policy is irrelevant for economic fluctuations, given that there is no substantial long-term effect of monetary policy on output and employment. This leads, as expected, to laissez-faire policy recommendations for business cycles (Blinder 1988, p. 285).

The *effectiveness of fiscal policy* is also limited in the NC model. Economic agents form rational expectations about their future path and that is why they will take into consideration the after-tax real variables in their decision-making. Thus a higher tax rate has an adverse effect on the incentives to work and to invest, leading in the long run to lower levels of production and consumption. This limits the ability of government to raise tax revenues. The government may then try, for a given level of expenditure, to cut taxes and substitute a corresponding increase in its interest-bearing debt. The theorical findings of New Classicals suggest that this fiscal policy has no real effects and thus it can not stimulate economic activity.[7]

By the same logic, if government monetizes the deficit by printing money instead of increasing taxes it will have no real effects on the economy; however, monetization will cause inflation. In short, monetary and fiscal policies are more or less ineffective. This ineffectiveness property obviously has significant implications for governmental role. Since neither monetary nor fiscal policy, if anticipated, can have any significant long-run real effects on employment and output, a reduction in macroeconomic intervention by the government is justified.

Closely related to the ineffectiveness proposition is another important characteristic of NC economics; the belief in the superiority of *policy-making by way of rules* rather than discretion. This belief is related to another problem regarding a government's policies, generally referred to as the 'time inconsistency of optimal policy' (Kydland and Prescott 1977; Mankiw 1990). The NC solution to this problem suggests depriving the government of its discretionary power by binding it to a fixed policy rule.

Within the framework of international economics, the microfoundations of NC theory imply that international trade in goods and credit promote the efficient allocation of resources by exploiting comparative advantage, scale economies and product differentiation. In addition, international credit allows for growth as a country is able to finance expenditure greater than its current income, relaxing the liquidity constraint. The basic NC theory also has important implications for European integration: the current project for the Economic and Monetary Unification of Europe (EMU) in fact puts New Classical policy recommendations into practice.

Concluding this section, it seems that five critical questions for the Neoliberal theory are:

- Are the basic assumptions about human nature, and about individual and social decision-making, in particular, satisfactory?
- Do markets clear instantaneously?
- Do they face rigidities, and what is their nature?
- What is the nature of unemployment and inflation today?
- Is governmental policy ineffective indeed in dealing with unemployment and inflation?

ECONOMIC THEORIES IN COMPETITION WITH NEOLIBERAL THEORY

The New Keynesian (NK) theory and Marxist Economic (ME) theory challenge Neoliberal theory on several major issues. In this section, we attempt to present the *differentia specifica* of these theories in comparison to Neoliberal theory.

New Keynesian Theory

New Keynesians accept the *microfoundations*, the *general equilibrium* models and (many of them) the *rational expectations hypothesis* of the New Classical approach. However, they depart from the latter by maintaining that there are market imperfections which prevent market clearing. In this sense, involuntary unemployment is not eliminated by assumption, but it can result from market imperfections. NK theory also considers institutional rigidities that may cause market imperfections; because of these imperfections, New Keynesians still see a role for government to play.

In particular, according to NK theory, there are a number of imperfections that can lead to sticky wages and prices. These include monopolistic competition, 'menu costs', labour contracts, efficiency wages, 'hysteresis' and information asymmetries. *Monopolistic competition* would result in an equilibrium in which output (and employment) are generally below socially optimal levels. Moreover, in monopolistic competition, when firms face fixed costs of changing nominal prices (often called 'menu costs', price rigidities can be encountered and result in declines in aggregate demand, thus leading to the old Keynesian position of insufficient demand (Mankiw 1990, p. 1657). In this case, monetary policy seems to be effective in increasing aggregate demand.

New Keynesians have also turned to the workings of the labour markets in order to explain the sluggish adjustment of wages. Labour contracts and efficiency wages are used to account for rigidities in the labour markets. *Labour contracts* that specify nominal wages in advance may lead to unemployment as the labour market fails to clear. If nomimal wages cannot adjust to economic disturbances, then monetary policy may be used to affect the real wage and thus reduce unemployment and stabilize the economy, even when rational expectations are assumed. Again, monetary policy may not be ineffective, after all[8] (Mankiw 1990, p. 1656).

Efficiency wages can also give rise to real wage rigidities. The basic assumption of this theory is that higher wages enhance productivity (Shapiro and Stiglitz 1984). As a result, firms may not reduce wages in the face of persistent unemployment because they do not want to reduce productivity. If the productivity effect is sufficiently strong, the labour market does not clear and unemployment may persist. However, the efficiency wage theory explains real wage rigidities, which do not relate to nominal price rigidities and thus give no role for money or aggregate demand management to deal with unemployment. Efficiency wages have to be combined with fixed costs of changing prices (and wages) – which do cause nominal rigidities – to explain fluctuations in employment and output and to call for Keynesian solutions (see Blinder 1988, p. 290; Mankiw 1990, p. 1659).

Insider-outsider theories attempt to explain unemployment and wage rigidities, even though there are outside workers willing to work at a wage lower than the prevailing insider wage (Shaked and Sutton 1989; Solow 1985; Gordon, 1990; Greenwald and Stiglitz 1993). The theories assume that there are turnover costs (hiring, training, negotiation, litigation and firing costs) so that untrained inside workers are not a perfect substitute for trained outside workers. Thus it becomes costly for firms to replace insiders with outsiders, and once hired and trained, the outside workers may also demand higher wages. These theories may also extend to include the behaviour of unionized insiders.

The *hysteresis* thesis maintains that the economy's equilibrium depends on what came before – or, in other words, it depends on the path the economy follows to get there. The hysteresis models thus preserve a role for aggregate demand management in raising employment and output permanently. One mechanism is through human capital. Assuming that human capital increases when in use (for example, learning-by-doing), a demand-induced increase in economic activity will build human capital and hence increase potential GNP for the future while the opposite happens in a recession. The hysteresis proposition is thus in sharp contradiction with the natural rate of unemployment hypothesis by claiming that one-time disturbances affect the path of the economy. In such a case, there is no 'natural' rate of unemployment.

The *cost of gathering information* questions the assumption of complete information, closely related to rational choice. It has been argued that there is a link between information and the degree of centralization in a market (Grahl and Teague 1990). In decentralized markets, communication between potential buyers and sellers, or workers and employers is costly. As a result, they try to establish long-term relationships between them – for example, by signing long-term contracts. A degree of inertia and internal rigidity may then be experienced in decentralized markets because of costly information which renders the process of trying to match up idiosyncratic preferences, skills and needs costly. Since this process is not instantaneous, wage reductions, for example, may not clear the labour market.

Under conditions of uncertainty, the risk-averse nature of firms may lead to market failures in capital and labour markets. Greenwald and Stiglitz (1993), for example, present a model for economies with imperfect information and incomplete contracts. The model contains three basic elements: risk-averse firms; a credit allocation mechanism in which credit rationing by risk-averse banks plays a central role; and new labour market theories, including efficiency wages and insider–outsider models.[9] In this framework, as the economy goes into a recession, the perceived risks increase, while the willingness and the ability (reduced cash flow from lower profits) of the firm to bear the risk of maintaining the same level of activity is also decreased. Each firm's supply curve, and hence the aggregate supply curve, shifts to the left. In addition, the firm's demand for investment may shift down considerably, leading to a decrease in aggregate demand – which is a very Keynesian situation. Moreover, if hiring is considered as an investment in human capital, new hires are reduced and hence unemployment rises. As Greenwald and Stiglitz emphasize, they reach these results even with complete flexibility of wages and prices – an assumption maintained in theory by New Classicals. In this case, aggregate demand management and/or monetary policy can facilitate equilibrium.

On the other hand, Blinder (1987, p. 133) strongly supports the short-run Phillips curve. He maintains that Lucas' critique was 'wildly incorrect' because the Phillips curve, once modified to allow for supply shocks, has been one of the best-behaved empirical regularities in macroeconomics.[10]

Interestingly, empirical evidence provided by new (and old) Keynesians challenge several of the hypotheses of the New Classicals, including voluntary unemployment. Blinder (1987, pp. 1310–12) observes for the United States that when the unemployment rate rises, it is layoffs, not quits, that are rising while consumption falls rather than rises. He also points out that unemployment is heavily concentrated among the long-term unemployed; in addition, the unemployed accept their first job offer, and those who are looking for work spend an average of only 4 hours per week on search activity. He concludes that Lucas' view that the unemployed are engaged in job search or purposeful intertemporal substitution between labour and leisure is not substantiated. He also argues that unemployment insurance (a government intervention) does not seem to lead workers to unemployment. This is supported by evidence which shows that insurance replaces only about 40 per cent of lost earnings and, at the time he wrote, only about one-third of the unemployed collected it.

In conclusion, New Keynesians challenge the market-clearing model on the ground of many market imperfections which may result in insufficient aggregate demand and unemployment. Fiscal and monetary policies can be employed to produce the desired results.

Marxist Economic Theory

Marxian Economics (ME) constitutes a radical break from neoclassical economic theory.[11] Despite the current intellectual swing to the disadvantage of Marxism, Marxian Economics still constitutes a very important challenge to Neoliberalism. Marx, himself, and Marxists, deploying a materialist standpoint, take society – in particular, the class process – as the point of return and departure of their analysis, not the individual. For them, it is human labour in interaction with nature that has always sustained societies, and thus individual human lives. Means of production are also 'dead' labour – the products of labour in the past. Commodities produced are useful – they fulfil human needs – but, more importantly for the act of exchange, they are the product of labour; their exchange value is determined not by utility but by the amount of socially necessary labour for their production.

Social labour is performed within class relations in class societies. *Class* is a central concept for Marxist theory. The class process is the extraction and appropriation of unpaid surplus labour in different forms.[12] In capitalism, the appropriation of surplus value by the capitalists – that is, the appropriation of the values of commodities produced by surplus labour – is complexly determined by many natural, economic, political and cultural conditions. Among these is the private property of the means of production, the existence of labour power as a commodity, the generalized market relations and the assurance of political freedom for the individual.[13] It is the *dialectical method* of Marxist analysis (as captured, for some Marxists, by the concept of overdetermination) that enables Marxist economists to describe the complex interaction and the mutual constitution of the class process and the other social processes, thus avoiding, at least, crude reductionism.

Marxist theory does not attribute social inequalities and injustices to personal choices, that is to 'innate' human nature, as Neoclassical theory does. Human nature, for Marxist theory, is neither exogenously given nor reduced to some unchanged natural constants; it is socially shaped and therefore ever changing. The rational and productive abilities of individuals are developed within social contexts. Subjectivity takes social reality as its condition of existence – for example, individual freedom, so celebrated by the Neoliberals, can be realized only when the enabling conditions are secured. Marxist theory, being very concerned with social and individual well-being and freedom, comes into investigating the economic (including class) and social conditions of existence in order to secure them. This, for Marxists, sounds like a more promising path for achieving a better and self-determined society in comparison to the neoliberal naturalization of social virtues and miseries.

Marxist theory recognizes the importance of *competition*, but conceptualizes it very differently from neoclassical economics. Competition among capitalist firms takes many forms; it is not simply related to the number of firms in a market or to the power to control prices or quantities. Competition takes places over the production, appropriation and distribution of surplus value. In the production site, for example, capitalists strive for more control over their workers and also for cost-reducing innovations. The first innovators increase the efficiency of their workers over the average efficiency of the industry and thus they appropriate extra profits, enabling them to accumulate and foster further growth. On the other hand, innovation may also be a defensive strategy for many industrial firms to secure their reproduction threatened by the offensive strategy of their competitors. Competition becomes a structural requirement of capitalism imposed upon individual firms. In Marxian terms, this is the basic logic behind the necessity for the 'modernization' of contemporary capitalism. Actually, very little of modernization is new, since technical restructing was always a necessity for the survival and growth of capitalist firms. Moreover, capitalist firms tend to prefer labour-saving cost-cutting technical change – that is increased mechanization of production – as a result of intracapitalist struggle and of the continuous struggle of capital against labour. Technical change thus leads to persistent *involuntary unemployment* – in sharp contrast with the neoliberal notion of voluntary unemployment. Moreover, these arguments about competition and innovation point out the endogeneity of technical change and thus underline a critical difference between Marxist economists and real business cycle theorists.

The quest for profit, as manifested in the competition among capitalists and in the struggle between capital and labour, drives the ceaseless but oscillating capitalist growth. Accumulation out of the increasing mass of profits (concentration of capital) and buying out existing firms (centralization of capital) increase the cost-efficient scale of production, leading to large capitalist enterprises – monopolies or oligopolies. It is the higher efficiency of these large enterprises that primarily enables them to appropriate surplus profits. These firms may also appropriate monopoly rents as long as they control the access to conditions of production and realization of a commodity. However, their profits and monopoly rents are constantly threatened by prospective competitors. The question whether concentration and centralization of capital has eliminated competition among capitalists (and thus the process for equalizing the profit rate among them) has for long troubled the Marxist tradition. In these debates, many convincing arguments have been developed which support the view that large enterprises do not stand above competition (see, for example, Semmler 1982). On the contrary, competition has been intensified in contemporary capitalism and has dramatic implications for smaller, less competitive firms.

The issue of *crises* is very critical for capitalism as it engenders many negative social and economic results (including unemployment), but at the same time creates the possibility for radical change. For Marxists, economic crises are grounded in the dynamics of capitalism: crises can emerge out of the contradictions of the capitalist economy. Marxists have actually provided different explanations of crises by singling out a certain contradiction as being more essential than others – in particular, crises have been explained by reduced profitability which results from the tendency of capitalist expansion either (1) to use labour-saving technologies; or (2) to create an excess demand for labour; or (3) to create underconsumption, or (4) to exhaust the productivity gain. In addition, some Marxists have attributed the decline in profitability to the increased power of labour in its struggle against capital.[14] Wolff and Resnick (1987) explain crises as the overdetermined effects of the contradictions of capitalism, without privileging some essential cause or mechanism: any of the above-mentioned mechanisms could trigger a crisis. Marxists of all persuasions, however, consider crises as embedded in the structural aspects of capitalism so that crises cannot be avoided by government intervention (Keynesianism) or the lack of it (Neoliberalism). Importantly, for Marxists, it is the unemployment and the decreases in real wages which occur during crises that renew the incentives for capitalist accumulation. This line of thinking is in total disagreement with Neoliberal explanations and prescriptions. Marxist theory does not see austerity programmes, cuts in wages and the dismantling of labour market regulations as a solution to the problem of crises; these policies tend to reinforce the forces at work during crises in order to restore capitalist incentives (Fine and Harris 1979): the elimination of crises requires radical social changes.

Workers organized in *trade unions* could wage a better struggle against capitalist pressures to increase the rate of exploitation. In times of increasing productivity, organized labour could even advance its position by getting a share of the benefits of increased productivity. In the eyes of Neoclassicals, however, organized labour creates 'rigidities' in the labour market that block its efficient workings and thus should be eliminated. Since this cannot be easily achieved, capitalists can benefit from *inflation* which reduces the real wages of workers and redistributes the surplus value produced to capitalists through the realization process, as long as there is no full income indexation. In the era of Keynesianism, a moderate rate the of inflation was accepted to mediate the struggle between labour and capital. However, inflation creates problems for capitalists themselves; it creates instability in the markets and tends to discourage investment because of the uncertainties involved in the calculation of benefits and costs of the future projects. Neoliberals thus propose a more direct change in the terms of surplus value extraction and distribution – that is, they propose deregulation of the labour market, itself, called labour flexibility.

Given that the role of the *state* is heavily debated today, the question then is whether the Marxist tradition has anything to offer to a better understanding of the state's role. For Marxists, the state is not above, beyond, or neutral with respect to the society. It is involved in various processes that secure the reproduction of capitalism. A share of the surplus value appropriated by industrial capitalists is distributed to the state in the form of taxes and the state in return secures the conditions of existence of private capitalists, including private property, infrastructure to increase private capitals' efficiency, public security, and so forth. The state also receives personal taxes from working people and provides collective goods and services to them in a cheap and reliable way.[15]

Importantly, the state can use revenues from personal taxes to finance policies that directly favour private capitalists (such as subsidies to industrial firms or increased public security expenditures) while, at the same time, it may cut the provision of collective goods and services. Such a policy may be combined with reductions in corporate and personal taxation, given a general dissatisfaction with taxes. This shift of the tax burden back from firms on to working people results in a redistribution of income from labour to capital.[16] Current Neoliberal policies to reduce taxes and state expenditures certainly support such Marxist insights.

In capitalism, for a number of reasons (Vlachou and Maniatis 1997), the state may also operate enterprises to produce commodities which are consumed by capitalist firms and working people. State firms are involved in capitalist extraction – that is, although they are owned by the state, they produce and appropriate surplus value. The state may distribute the appropriated surplus value not only to secure the reproduction and growth of state-owned firms, but also to satisfy other objectives relating to the reproduction of private capitals or labour in general. Operating a state firm may thus become a very contradictory process that may strengthen the growth of private capitals in some periods but block it in others. Therefore, *privatizations* become the outcome of such a contradictory process as well as the outcome of changing technical, economic and social conditions that no longer require state ownership and operation of certain activities.

Competition among capitalists and the struggle of capital against labour for increased profitability eventually lead to the *internationalization* of capital in the form of international trade, flows of financial capital, direct investments in other countries and labour migration.[17] International trade can increase profitability by cheapening labour power and providing constant capital. Moreover, since capitalist growth needs enlarged markets for realization, international trade expands markets in which capitalists sell their commodities and thus secure profitable realization. International movements of finance capital help the establishment of capitalist firms, while it gets in return, in the form of interest, a share of the surplus value extracted by these firms. Direct investments create industrial firms which directly appropriate surplus value in the host country.

The international competitiveness of domestic industrial capitalists depends both on the internal conditions of value production and realization and the exchange rate between the prevailing international currencies and the national currency. Devaluation of the national currency, for example, can compensate for low productivity and thus can preserve the competitive position of domestic firms in the short and medium run. On the other hand, in the case of fixed exchange rates and anti-inflationary state policies, domestic producers have to resort (even in the short run) to an increase in the rate of exploitation of labour and to cost-cutting in the realization process in order to preserve or improve their competitive position. Firms of low efficiency that cannot 'adjust' go out of business. International competition based on efficiency can thus mean only one thing: low-cost capitals drive high-cost ones out of business. Increased unemployment and poverty follow as the outcome of both the adjustment process and the collapse of firms. This is the logic that lies behind the combined and unequal development in capitalism. The precedence of low-cost capitals over high-cost ones is not easy to overcome.

European unification is embedded in this fundamental Marxian account of international economic relations. From its outset, European unification intended to consolidate and secure capitalism in Western Europe, which was perceived to be threatened by the social unrest in Europe and by the strengthening of the Soviet Union after the Second World War (Busch 1978). European integration was expected to promote capitalist growth by enlarging the market for capitalists, following the pattern of the United States, and by enjoying the benefits of unfettered international trade within the common European market. At the same time, member states were able to sustain important relations with their former colonies, by redressing these relations through new agreements between these countries and the Community and by granting them financial aid. The '1992' programme to create an internal market and the treaty for Economic and Monetary Union (EMU) are in line with the initial goals of European unification. However, the path of European unification has been, and is currently being, shaped by complex and interacting economic, political and cultural processes. This complex determination has produced significant shifts in orientation, goals and measures, reflecting different conjunctures of predominant forces and interests. For many Marxists, the current EMU project reflects the influence of Neoliberalism. It is also very telling for them that the current EMU project is mainly being supported by the business world, especially the large international units of industrial and financial capital, which cluster in, or originate from countries such as Germany, Japan and the United States and lead competition on a world scale.[18]

Concluding this section, it should be mentioned that almost every Marxist feels compelled to study socialism and communism. This is because it is not enough for Marx and Marxists alike to explain the contradictions, tensions and miseries embedded in a class society; an equally important task for them is to change society. Yet there are many disagreements among Marxists over the nature of, and the road to, a classless society.[19] For many Marxists, communism is defined as a collective form of production, appropriation and distribution of surplus labour. A number of economic, political and cultural conditions should develop during socialism and combine in order to bring communism into existence; socialism is then understood as the transition from a capitalist social formation to a communist one. Current debates over socialism and communism include the issues of democratic political decision-making, of forms of property of the means of production, of the market vs. planning mechanisms for the allocation of inputs and outputs, of the priority given to the development of productive forces (productivity), and so forth (Laibman 1992; Vlachou 1993).

In summary, Marxist theory challenges Neoliberalism on almost every major economic issue. Marxism sees economic and social problems as interwoven with the class structure of capitalism; the elimination of social inequalities and injustices can be achieved only by changes in the class structure and other enabling social processes of capitalism.

THE ECONOMIC AND MONETARY UNIFICATION OF EUROPE

The (1992) programme for completing the internal market was a significant change in policy in the European Community established in 1957. The 1986 Single European Act (SEA) was followed in 1991 by the Maastricht Treaty for Economic and Monetary Union, a Treaty which also brought dramatic changes for Europe. The Treaty of Amsterdam (1997) made minor amendments to the Maastricht Treaty, mainly concerning unemployment policies. To a great extent, these developments could be considered as the application of the Neoliberal theory in practice. Critical evaluations have been mainly advanced from within the Neoclassical tradition, especially from a New Keynesian perspective. Marxists have also offered a number of critical insights. In this section, we provide an initial discussion of the major potential effects of these developments on the course of European integration and on the economies of member countries.

The Internal Market

The goal of the Single European Act (SEA) of 1986 was to complete a single market in goods, services, labour and capital by 1 January 1993 in the European Community (EC). The Maastricht Treaty also committed EC members to the completion of an internal market.[20] The single market, as described in a White Paper of 1985 (Commission 1985), was expected to provide new opportunities for growth in Europe. Recent efforts toward completing the internal market extend their scope to energy and other utility services, harmonization of key provisions in social welfare and social security policy, and to the development of a common environmental policy. These areas, however, have been traditionally experiencing market failures, calling for state intervention.

The programme for completing the internal market is under the strong influence of Neoliberalism, both in its objectives and its methods (see also Cutler et al. 1989; Grahl and Teague 1990) The emphasis has increasingly been against government and in favour of private economic activity and market forces. The completion of the internal market is oriented to permit market forces to operate where they were previously absent, and also to increase the facility with which private firms can operate across national frontiers.

In particular, the completion of the internal market presupposes the elimination of all non-tariff barriers (NTBs) (for example, different taxes, different technical standards and regulations, and so on) to trade within the Community because they adversely affect competition among firms of different member countries. Restrictions to market access applied to firms from other Community countries were also targeted for elimination. Of significant importance are restrictions (specifications, direct contracting practices, and so on) on public procurement which account for approximately 10 per cent of the national product in most member countries (Grahl and Teague 1990, p. 34). Huge markets in equipment and services for water, energy, telecommunications, transportation and construction sectors will be opened up to suppliers from other countries, mostly to multinational corporations; it will not be possible any longer to favour national suppliers. This is expected to increase competition and efficiency in resource allocation.

Gains are also expected to come from increased labour and capital mobility. Restrictions on capital movements are in the process of being fully eliminated while banks and other financial institutions are free to locate in all EC countries. Financial liberalization is also going ahead impressively fast. However, this rapid deregulation of the financial sector has not yet been followed by an institution at the Community level vested with the responsibility of supervision. The European Central Bank (ECB) acts as a lender of last resort but it is not responsible for the prudential supervision of the banking system in the Community.

Another major set of reforms concerns labour market regulation. Measures taken or still debated are designed to increase labour market flexibility. Several barriers to labour movement across member states (equivalence of university degrees, passport controls, and so forth) were targeted for elimination. However, language and cultural differences are still expected to limit labour movement. Significant changes concerning the social security system, minimum wages, limits on dismissals by firms, temporary employment, and so forth have also been proposed in order to increase labour market flexibility; these proposals have met strong opposition from labour.

In Marxian terms, the '1992' programme attempts to remove any obstacles to 'genuine' international competition between capitalist firms – that is, obstacles to accumulation and innovation, and thus to capitalist expansion. In particular, the liberalization of financial markets may increase the realized surplus value for industrial capitalists and the profits of financiers by increasing the turnover of capital, reducing circulation expenses and the cost of borrowing. Labour market flexibility affects the terms of surplus labour extraction and constitutes a direct attack in vested-by-struggle labour rights and interests.

It is important to note that member states are to a great degree responsible for the ways in which harmonization of policies will be achieved. The Commission made and continues to make an increasing use of Directives to outline what should be achieved, leaving the choice of means to the member states. Importantly, the Single Market programme is actually based on the markets' disciplinary role: countries that establish regulatory regimes that are bad for business will lose business. Competition between types of regulation (tax systems, social security policies, and so on) will drive member countries to converge on systems of regulation which are favourable to business.

The Gains

The completion of the internal market is expected to lead to cost and price reductions (Cecchini Report 1988). The elimination of NTBs should lead to cost reductions and should thus increase the scope for exploiting comparative advantage. Moreover, the single market may increase the two-way trade between countries in the same industry. Intra-industry trade stems from scale economies and product differentiation; on the completion of the internal market firms previously selling to small and fragmented national markets may take advantage of the big Community market to exploit economies of scale further. The elimination of NTBs barriers and increased flexibility actually mean deregulation or lower regulation of relevant markets, thus increasing the scope of the working of markets and competition. In addition, competition could be intensified as a greater number of firms have access to a country's market.

However, the estimates of gains were not impressive. In particular, the Cecchini Report (1988) estimated that the static benefits of the '1992' programme would amount to a one-off rise in EC income of 2.5–6.5 per cent. Baldwin (1989) finds the mismatch between the radical nature of the liberalization and the modest nature of the estimated gains by the Cecchini Report to be striking. He then makes an effort to show that the greatest benefits of internal market come from its dynamic effects: more innovation, faster productivity gains, greater investment and higher output growth – he shows, for example, that simply taking account of the medium-run growth effect would double the Cecchini estimates of benefits in terms of EC income increase.

Neven (1990) investigated the very controversial issue of the distribution of gains among member countries. He concluded that the main beneficiaries of the '1992' programme would be the Southern European countries (Greece, Portugal and Spain). These countries can better exploit their comparative advantage in labour-intensive industries (especially clothing and footwear) and can also gain from unexploited scale economies. On the other hand, the Northern countries have already exploited scale economies and although they have a comparative advantage in goods which are intensive in human capital, they do not stand to gain much since Southern markets for these goods are relatively small. That is why, Neven concludes, it is the Southern countries which stand to gain.

Some Critical Questions

The benefits from completing the internal market were based on the existence of market competition and, in particular, on its intensification. This assumption, however, has been heavily questioned by several authors from within the Neoclassical tradition. The background of the SEA was that large number of economic interactions were not direct market exchanges but were transfers of goods and services within transnational companies. In addition, the boom of mergers, takeovers and joint ventures (JVs) experienced in Europe in response to the '1992' programme will tend to preserve or increase market power. Franks and Mayer (1990) provide some impressive figures for cross-border takeovers of UK, French, and German firms during the first years of SEA implementation. This concentration may be an act of defence on the part of firms; by regrouping and increasing size, firms might reduce the uncertainty and instability they face due to more intense competition. On the other hand, firms may be restructuring to better exploit comparative advantage and scale economies. Whatever the reason, if – by mergers and acquisitions (M&As) – firms increase their size in the market, assumed gains from increasing market competition after completing the internal market will be dissipated (see also Helm 1993). It should be noted that these developments are compatible with the Marxist notion of competition; concentration and centralization are the outcome of competition and may increase profitability through the redistribution of surplus value extracted.

On the other hand, scale economies can lead to natural monopoly and this has been the principal reason for significant state intervention in the case of utilities. In these activities, issues of 'vital national interest' are also often encountered. The Treaty of Rome (Article 92) made provision to limit the impact of competition policy on areas of national interest and, consequently, governments intervened, often in the form of state ownership. The Commission, applying the Treaty of Rome as amended by the SEA and by the Maastricht Treaty, attempts today at extending the internal market in the energy, transport, and telecommunications sectors through a series of Directives. Deregulation and privatizations in these areas have again raised issues of monopoly pricing and its social and distributional effects, issues of access to networks which affect competition and issues of efficiency in the development of production and distributional networks.

Significantly, assumed intensified competition by the completion of the Single Market will have adverse distributional effects. Higher-cost producers, if they can not improve themeselves, will lose business to low-cost competitors. In this case, income will be squeezed out from the less advanced countries (where the less competitive firms cluster) to the advanced ones. Improving competitiveness in a relative short time is not an easy task; the process depends heavily on differences in the initial conditions between firms and member countries. This problem becomes particularly intense because the EC lacks a community-wide system of fiscal transfers to achieve some income redistribution as it happens within the national states. The EC structural funds, often considered as a compensatory mechanism, cannot be considered as a solution because they are very limited in comparison and are mostly related to long-term infrastructure, and not to short- or medium-run income distribution.

The gains from further exploiting comparative advantage are also susceptible to serious qualifications. Current-account imbalances in the late 1980s and in the 1990s indicate that the Southern European countries have not experienced an improvement in competitiveness. The comparative advantages identified are considered to be ambiguous owing to aggregation problems (Jacquemin 1990). Importantly, the existing division of labour between Northern and Southern Europe is taken as given, which may not be acceptable from a dynamic perspective. Greece, Spain and Portugal may not find a comparative advantage in labour–intensive commodities satisfactory, because they compete for a market share in the Community with the less developed countries, which typically have the same comparative advantage in labour-intensive goods: a trade liberalization between the EC and the rest of the world significantly jeopardizes their competitiveness within the EC. Prudently, the Southern countries may want to undertake strategies to modify their comparative advantages over time (Jacquemin 1990, p. 49). In a dynamic setting, policies to increase investments in physical and human capital is the typical way of shaping a new dynamically viable comparative advantage. It is in this spirit that Fitoussi (1997, p. 38), following Krugman (1990), speaks in support of a necessary protectionism in certain production lines that would help a country to establish a dynamic comparative advantage. Preventing some industries from closing down, a country may also preserve some know-how and human capital that can affect the development of future technology and of human capital which would help the establishment of a new comparative advantage.

The assumed significant benefits from the dynamic effects of an internal market have also been questioned. The long-run positive effects depend on the ability of the programme to encourage investment in physical and human capital. But these effects on investment are quite ambiguous (Grahl and Teague 1990; Helm 1993). In many member countries, unemployment rates have substantially increased, while the average rate of unempolyment for the 15 European member states increased from 8.3 per cent in 1991 to 10.9 in 1996 (Eurostat, *Yearbook 1996*). Firms seem to be disturbed by uncertainty and instability, both being aggravated by intensified oligopolistic competition; thus they are discouraged from financing new undertakings. Firms are actually interested more in investments which reduce the cost of the current levels of output rather in investments which expand it.

Taking all the above into consideration, it is not surprising that, in an initial assessment of the consequences of the competition of the internal market, Helm (1993) indicates that the initial promises were grossly exaggerated. The margin of error is extremely large and depends on the author's theoretical construct, reflecting fundamental disagreements about the nature of microeconomic behaviour in general and models of oligopolistic competition in particular. Interestingly, with regard to the laissez-faire approach of the '1992' programme, Helm points out that ultimately the notion that markets are inherently better than governments is an argument by assumption, an act of faith.

Let us offer a final remark from a Marxist perspective. These arguments reflect the Marxian thesis of the combined and unequal development of capitalism. European unification as part of the global capitalist expansion cannot change this structural feature of capitalism.

Monetary Union (MU)

The Delors Report on European monetary unification, published in 1989, provided the framework for the intergovernmental negotiations in 1991 which resulted in the Maastricht Treaty at the end of that year. The Treaty of Amsterdam (1997) made minor amendments to the Maastricht Treaty, mainly concerning unemployment. The Maastricht Treaty lays down the preconditions under which individual countries can enter the monetary union and the timetable for the unification. It also describes the institutional structure and the operational objectives of the European Central Bank (ECB) which will formulate and execute the Union's monetary policy while the national central banks will be subordinate to it.

The Maastricht Treaty specifies four preconditions for participating in monetary union. The first is that the average rate of inflation (CPI) over the preceding 12 months should not exceed the inflation rates of the three lowest-inflation member rates by more than 1.5 percentage points. Participating members should run very similar inflation rates. The second precondition requires that qualifying members must have maintained their exchange rates within the normal EMS fluctuation bands (2.25 per cent at the time of the Maastricht Treaty negotiations, and 15 per cent today) and should not have realigned them for the two years prior to joining the union. In this way, nominal exchange rates will be stabilized. The third precondition is that long-term interest rates over the preceding year must not have been more than two percentage points above the average of the three best performing – in terms of inflation – member states. Given that exchange rates and inflation are stabilized, this precondition aims at minimizing the risk of default which seems to be the main reason why interest rates vary across economies (risk premium). The fourth precondition is that the budget deficit of a qualifying country must be no larger than 3 per cent of GDP and gross public debts no larger than 60 per cent of GDP. These figures corresponded to the Community averages when the Maastricht Treaty was negotiated; their purpose seems to be to avoid inflationary pressures in the union as a whole. These last preconditions allow for some exceptions if an 'excessive' deficit is temporary, or an 'excessive' deficit and/or debt ratio is declining at a 'satisfactory' pace.

We can discern a Neoliberal imprint on the preconditions for admittance to the union in the fact that preconditions relating to the convergence of unemployment or GDP growth rates were not embodied in the Maastricht Treaty. Obviously, the Treaty is not designed to promote convergence of the real economies of the participating members, but only to secure 'nominal' convergence.

With respect to the timetable, the Maastricht Treaty describes a monetary union to be accomplished in three stages. Stage I (1 July 1990–31 December 1993) was to be characterized by the completion of the internal market. Member countries were to strengthen the independence of their central banks and follow economic programmes that adjusted their economies to the preconditions for entry into the monetary union. Stage II (1 January 1994–31 December 1996 or at the latest 31 December 1998) was to be marked by further convergence of national economic policies and by the creation of the European Monetary Institute (EMI), a temporary entity to coordinate monetary policies and facilitate the transition to a single currency. In stage II, it was to be assessed whether or not the majority of member countries met the preconditions for the monetary union to move to the final stage. On 2 May 1998, eleven countries entered the monetary union only by using the discretionary element regarding fiscal preconditions. From the remaining four (Denmark, Greece, United Kingdom and Sweden), only Greece was involuntarily left out of the euro zone. Stage III begins on 1 January 1999 (if no other date is set by the end of 1997), and is characterized by fixed exchange rates and by the replacement of the EMI by the ECB which will assume responsibility for unionwide monetary policy.

The primary objective of the ECB is price stability. The institutional structure of the ECB provides it with independence from political pressure for financing a government's deficit and/or debts – ECB officials will enjoy long terms in office, for example. Members of the ECB's Governing Council are also prohibited from assuming other political responsibilities or receiving instructions from their national governments.

Expected Benefits of MU

A single currency is expected to reduce cross-border transaction costs, in terms of time and resources used in changing money. However, this cost saving is not expected to be significant; the direct welfare gain from eliminating currency conversion has been estimated to be around 0.4–0.5 per cent of GDP for the EC as a whole (Bean 1992; Eichengreen 1993).

One argument frequently heard is that a common currency would reduce exchange rate volatility and uncertainty, which discourages international trade and cross-border investment. Empirical studies do not seem to conclude that the benefits of this type are considerable; this outcome may be explained by the existence of forward markets in foreign exchange which permit traders and investors to hedge against currency risk at low cost.

Compared to a regime of fixed exchange rates across multiple currencies, an important advantage of the single currency often claimed is that it establishes the credibility and longevity of monetary union. As long as national currencies are retained, there remains the possibility that a government may be tempted to use the exchange rate as a policy instrument and thus leave the union. On the other hand, a single currency involves sunk costs (creating legal and constitutional arrangements) that deter any escape.

Fixed exchange rates between national currencies or a single currency regime seem to be the necessary corollary of factor and product market integration, the target of the SEA. The European Monetary System (EMS) of the pegged but adjustable exchange rates was undermined once controls on capital movements were abolished. Exchange rate swings are considered incompatible with integration not on efficiency but on political economy grounds, because they affect competitiveness. National industries under pressure from the removal of barriers to intra-European trade find their competitive position further undermined by a sudden exchange rate appreciation. The completion of the internal market would then be resisted due to the distributional effects of exchange rate changes, while exchange rate stabilization would prevent 'exchange dumping' (Eichengreen 1993, pp. 1329–31).

The Maastricht Treaty, by creating a central bank dedicated to price stability and independent from political control, removes from the authorities the incentive to renege on their low-inflation promises; the Treaty thus establishes credibility in such policies. The Treaty also sets ceilings on budget deficits, which further reinforces the commitment that EC monetary policy will primarily fight inflation. In other words, inflation is mainly explained as the result of governmental mismanagement since governments with big budget deficits and increasing debts are tempted to resort to the central bank for financing their deficits or buying up their debts. In this way, they tend to increase the money supply and create inflation which tends to reduce the real value of outstanding debt. The structure and the workings of the ECB should prevent such inflationary finance.

Expected Costs of MU

An important cost of monetary union is the loss of exchange rate changes and monetary independence as instruments of macro-economic management. In the case of an economic shock, altering the exchange rate may be a useful tool for adjusting the nation's terms of trade in order to restore its competitiveness when domestic wages and prices adjust sluggishly (Mundell 1961). More analytically, since competitiveness depends not only on nominal exchange rates but also on relative domestic and foreign prices, it can also be improved by changes in domestic prices. If nominal prices and wages adjust swiftly, market forces will provide a rapid adjustment mechanism for restoring competitiveness. If, on the other hand, domestic wages and prices move slowly, it could take a long time for the trade balance to adjust while causing a recession in the meantime. In this case, an exchange rate realignment can quickly accomplish the adjustment without the painful period of recession.

Whether abandoning monetary autonomy is costly or not depends crucially on two factors: (1) the significance of rigidities and the usefulness of monetary policy for facilitating adjustment; and (2) the nature of the shocks (symmetric vs. asymmetric) that member countries experience (see also Bean 1992; and Eichengreen 1993). In New Classical models labour and product markets adjust instantaneously so that by assumption rigidities are non-existent. To the extent that rigidities do in reality exist, the completion of the internal market is designed to establish the desired market flexibility. So, if nominal rigidities are insignificant, the cost of abandoning exchange rate realignment is also insignificant. In addition, if monetary policy cannot affect output and employment, as the New Classicals argue, then abandoning monetary autonomy is also costless. But if movements of nominal variables exhibit rigidities, as the New Keynesian critics of Neoliberal theory maintain, then monetary policy matters and forsaking its independence involves costs. Eichengreen (1993, p. 133), for example, mentions that 25–75 per cent of a price increase is passed on to nominal wages in Europe, which means that there remains some real wage responsiveness to the price level and hence to monetary policy. The cost of forsaking monetary policy seems to be negligible in the case of symmetric disturbances because then the same policy response is appropriate for all the members of the monetary union and can thus be taken at the union level. However, when shocks are asymmetric, a country-specific monetary policy would be appropriate, but this is unattainable when monetary independence is lost. In this case, adjustment occurs through factor and product markets. If, as mentioned above, markets display limited flexibility (in terms of both mobility and price movements), the loss of monetary independence will be costly. The lack of labour mobility and the limited wage flexibility in Europe are often singled out to emphasize the difficulty of adjusting to region-specific shocks; country- and region-specific or idiosyncratic shocks are still expected to occur in a monetary union because the completion of the internal markets may lead European countries to greater specialization, scale and consolidation of production.

Another cost of monetary union is a loss of seigniorage in high-inflation countries. Seigniorage is the revenue that accrues to a government when it finances its budget deficit through printing money rather than selling debt. At constant employment, this financing leads to inflation which reduces the real value of outstanding debt and acts as a tax on holders of circulating money balances. Since monetary union will establish converging and low rates of inflation, high-inflation countries will lose this privilege.

The workings of the ECB seem to increase the 'democratic deficit' – that is, the insufficient accountability to the constituency they represent within the Community. In addition, although the Maastricht Treaty puts forward some provisions for ECB accountability, these are deemed inadequate compared to those that apply to independent national central banks. The latter may be independent of the government in power but are not independent of politics as they are ultimately under parliamentary control.

Moreover, the ECB is not responsible for the prudential supervision of the banking system in the Community; this responsibility is left with the national central banks. The same is true for the oversight of Community-wide payments which are settled daily by banks by using accounts held at the central bank. This lack of some Community-level institution vested with regulatory responsibility when combined with deregulation of the capital markets may cause serious problems for the Community as a whole. In particular, the completion of internal capital markets will intensify competition between banks, driving some of them out of business and creating financial instability. This instability will adversely affect product and factor markets, including decisions for investment.

The fiscal rules set by the Maastricht Treaty limit fiscal flexibility, thus imposing further costs for the participating countries. The fiscal preconditions for joining the union have been justified by the need to avoid externalities from national fiscal policies, given the purported tendency of governments to overborrow (Bean 1992). These fiscal rules are also expected to continue to operate after joining the union, thus limiting the fiscal options for the member countries. This premium on fiscal flexibility reinforces the constraints imposed on fiscal policy by high capital mobility established by the SEA and the single currency. If capital and labour are freely moving within the union, a particular government cannot increase taxes on these production factors in order to finance its spending or serve its debt, because they could just flee to lower-tax countries (tax competition).[21] It should be also noted that the erosion of the tax base as captured by 'voting with the', affects a government's ability to borrow today because it cannot raise taxes in the future from a limited tax base.

Having abandoned monetary independence and facing serious limitations to their fiscal policies, national governments that confront a domestic economic disturbance may be forced to leave the adjustment mainly to market forces. This is especially true for the European Union since there is no federal or cross-state fiscal system comparable to that of the United States. A federal fiscal system attempts to redistribute income, and thus addresses the cohesion problem of the European Union; it also tries to provide mutual insurance via income tax and social security provisions. In the case of a country-specific shock, for example, a union-wide system of federal taxes and transfers could automatically shift resources from prospering countries and regions to the less well off ones. However, the EC's budget is very small and proposals to increase it significantly, made mainly by the low-income countries, have run into resistance.

In conclusion, the benefits of the internal market and EMU have been seriously challenged and it is one of the objectives of the chapters in Part II of this volume (Chapters 6–10) to investigate them further. These critical accounts of EMU might help in formulating a more promising alternative for the European unification

– an alternative that would also be supported by working people in Europe. These critical accounts might also reflect back on the Neoliberal Theory itself, and improve its ability to explain and solve economic problems.

EPILOGUE

In this introductory, we have presented the conflicting explanations of unemployment, inflation, recession and poverty provided by different economic theories. Explanations depend crucially on the basic concepts and assumptions, and the way of reasoning of each theory. This is the reason why we first summarized the theoretical foundations of Neoliberal theory, the most influential economic theory today. We have seen that the theory's reliance on market forces is mainly justified by the microeconomic conclusion that perfectly competitive markets satisfy the conditions for Pareto-optimality, defined only in terms of efficiency. From a macroeconomic point of view, privileging market forces stems from the conclusion of the New Classical school that government policies are ineffective.

These findings are based on several critical assumptions and a particular reasoning which has been challenged by New Keynesianism and Marxism. Given that the current EMU project for European unification is influenced, to a great extent, by Neoliberal recommendations, it is very important today for critics of Neoliberalism to sharpen their analyses and develop alternative solutions.

In this spirit, it seems to us that the most critical questions for the economic theory today are the following:

- Are the basic assumptions of Neoliberal theory about human nature and about (individual and social) decision-making, satisfactory?
- In particular, do individuals form expectations rationally?
- Do markets work efficiently?
- Is efficiency a satisfactory criterion for the determination of social optima?
- Are market deregulation and privatization adequately justified?
- Is governmental policy ineffective indeed in dealing with unemployment and inflation?
- What is the nature of EMU?
- Is there any alternative to the current EMU project for European unification?

32   Contemporary Economic Theory

- Can a class analysis offer a better explanation of social inequalities and injustices?
- Is socialism still desirable and feasible today?

The chapters included in this collection make a serious effort to answer some of these questions.

Notes

1. For expositions of contemporary Microeconomics see, for example, Varian (1984, 1990); Ricketts (1988); Wolff and Resnick (1987); Fine and Morris (1979).
2. An allocation is Pareto-optimal if no reallocation can improve the position of one or more individuals without undermining the position of others. Pareto-optimality is defined only in terms of efficiency and accepts the prevailing income distribution, that is the prevailing factor endowments. Pareto-optimality is thus a certain ethical belief.
3. Rational expectations depart significantly from Keynes' view of uncertainty and forecasting. As Blinder (1987, p. 130) points out:

    > Keynes, though no stranger to probability theory, was nonetheless unequivocal in his denial that expectations are what we now call rational.

4. The neutrality of money is limited only by the fact that monetary changes affect the demand for real balances, the nominal interest rate and the volume of transaction costs.
5. This assumption was first featured in a model built by Lucas (1972a). Two empirical studies by Barro (1977, 1978) suggested that anticipated changes in US money growth had exerted insignificant effects on output and employment over the post-war period, while unanticipated changes had strong effects, thus supporting the ineffectiveness property.
6. The hypothesis of the natural rate of unemployment (NRU) is incompatible with the Keynesian notion of involuntary unemployment. In Keynes, involuntary unemployment results from insufficient effective demand, and can coexist along with system-wide equilibrium.
7. This conclusion is basically the Ricardian Equivalence Theorem on public debt which views as equivalent a current aggregate tax and a current budget deficit of an equal amount. The theorem implies that a shift between them would not affect the aggregates of consumer demand and work effort.
8. A number of qualifications are in order. Contracts are sometimes theorized as optimal risk-sharing arrangements between firms and workers. If this holds, the resulting stickiness is not non-optimal. Moreover, labour contracts are always under the pressure of the unemployed.

Significantly, the observation of some stickiness does not necessarily imply that the allocation of labour is not efficient. If the workers hold lifetime jobs, the wage paid at any given period need not be equal to the product of labour; it may be like an instalment payment of a lifetime income. From these and other arguments, the labour contract proposition has not been very convincing for explaining unemployment (Mankiw 1990, p. 1656).
9. Imperfections in the equity markets imply that it is important for firms whether finance comes from equity or debt. Firms are assumed to be risk-averse if they do not have easy access to equity finance (in which they share risk with the share holders), and are, therefore, pushed to debt financing. The decisions of firms (prices, employment, production, and so forth) are affected by their perceptions of risks which are shaped by the overall state of the economy, the firm's cash position and changes in the price level – the latter matters because all debt is denominated in nominal terms.
10. Significantly, Blinder (1987) questions even the microfoundations of macroeconomics on several grounds. The most impressive challenge put forward by Blinder seems to be that to model man as a strongly rational maximizer is not the only option open to theorists. He argues that there are many cases in which continuous optimization would be irrational; he also draws from psychologists to argue that *homo sapiens* does not behave like *homo economicus*: 'People put too much weight on what has happened to them and to their friends and too little on statistical evidence' (Blinder 1987, p. 135), questioning the very foundations of neoclassical theory. These critical remarks bring us closer to Marxian critiques of neoclassical rationality.
11. Expositions of Marxist economic theory can be found, among others, in Sweezy (1970); Marx (1977); Shaikh (1977, 1992); Fine (1979); Harvey (1982); Resnick and Wolff (1987) and Carchedi (1991).
12. Surplus labour is the quantity of human labour beyond the necessary labour which is defined as the average, socially necessary labour for the reproduction of the labourer. The necessary labour time is shaped by social and historical conditions. Thus, class as a process constitutes economic exploitation.
13. Importantly, the current debates over 'increasing' the flexibility of the labour market by changing the laws concerning minimum wages, dismissals, social security, and so forth, concern the conditions of the extraction of surplus value.
14. One mechanism that can engender cycles is innovation through accumulation (see, for example, Shaikh 1977). Marx indicated that innovations tend to increase constant capital in relation to variable capital and to lead to falling value rates of profit. A resulting generalized increase in the average productivity in an industry drives down the unit value of the commodity and can reduce the average value rate of profit, even in cases where the rate of exploitation increases. On the other hand, several Marxists (Dobb 1959; Itoh, 1980) explain crises by the effects of accumulation on the market for labour power and on its price. Accumulation results in increasing the demand for

labour power more than the supply of additional labour and thus money wages increase, eating up profits. In both cases, decreased profitability may in turn give rise to disaccumulation and crises. Other Marxists (see, for example, Sweezy 1970) explain crises by the realization problems that occur when commodities cannot be sold at a price that secures a satisfying profit for capitalists. They maintain that there is a tendency for underconsumption in capitalism because capitalists need to keep wages low and adopt labour-saving technologies. On the other hand, the regulation school (see, for example, Lipietz 1986) maintains that the exhaustion of productivity gains causes a fall in the average rate of profit and may lead to crises. Other authors (see, for example, Glyn and Sutcliffe 1972) maintain that the increased power of labour in its struggle against capital can increase wages and thus squeeze profits, leading to crises.

15. It should be noted that although historically the state was pressured by the working class and other social movements to provide goods and services for mass consumption, this indirectly also benefits the private capitalist appropriation of surplus value, by lowering the cost of reproduction for capital.
16. It actually leads to a deterioration in workers' living standards and of their ability to strive for a better life. On the other hand, it leads to an increase in after-tax profits, as firms have to pay less taxes in order to secure their conditions of existence.
17. National governments and international agreements provide and safeguard conditions for the internationalization of capital. However, this is done in a contradictory way, because national states and international organizations which arrive at these agreements are sites that include, as constituent elements, very conflicting class and other social interests.
18. Despite the importance of the internationalization of economic life and the development of international institutions and mechanisms, Marxist theory has not been adequately developed on these topics. This is especially true for European unification; we hope that contributions to this volume will help in further developing Marxist theory in this direction.
19. From an optimistic point of view, these differences among Marxists indicate that there are many options for affecting social change.
20. Nevertheless, during the 1970s, European countries resorted to policies (industrial subsidies, tax incentives, and so on) which threatened a reversal of whatever integration had been achieved (Busch 1992). Continuing economic difficulties and the perceived defeat of European multinationals by their Japanese and American rivals in research and development (R&D), as well as in the market place, are often considered the principal reasons that gave rise to the '1992' programme and to later efforts to complete the internal market (Flam 1992).
21. The main reason why fiscal autonomy would not be eliminated altogether is often claimed to be the limited mobility of the European labour force – which, however, is expected to increase substantially by the completion of the internal market.

References

Baldwin, R. (1989) 'The Growth Effects of 1992', *Economic Policy* (October), 248–81.
Barro, R.J. (1977) ' Unanticipated Money Growth and Unemployment in the United States', *American Economic Review*, 67, 101–15.
Barro, R.J. (1978) ' Unanticipated Money, Output, and Price Level in the United States', *Journal of Political Economy*, 86, 549–80.
Barro, R.J. (1993) *Macroeconomics* (New York: John Wiley).
Bean, C. (1992) 'Economic and Monetary Union in Europe', *Journal of Economic Perspectives*, 6 (Fall), 31–52.
Blinder, A. (1987) 'Keynes, Lucas, and Scientific Progress', *American Economic Review, Papers and Proceedings*, 77 (May), 130–36.
Blinder, A. (1988) 'The Fall and Rise of Keynesian Economics', *The Economic Record*, 64 (December), 278–94.
Busch, K. (1978) *The Crisis of the European Communities* (Athens: Erato) (in Greek).
Bush, K. (1992) *Europe after 1992* (Athens: Kritiki Editions) (in Greek).
Carchedi, G. (1991) *Frontiers of Political Economy* (London: Verso).
Cecchini Report (1988) *The European Challenge 1992* (Aldershot: Gower).
Commission of the European Communities (1985) *Completing the Internal Market*, White Paper from the Commission to the European Council (Luxembourg: Office for Official Publications of the European Communities).
Committee for the Study of Economic and Monetary Union (ed.) (1989) *Report of Economic and Monetary Union in the European Community* (*Delors Report*) (Brussels: Office for Official Publications of the European Communities).
Cutler, T., C. Haslam, J. Williams and K. Williams (1989) *1992 – The Struggle for Europe* (New York: Berg).
Dobb, M. (1959) 'The Falling Rate of Profit', *Science & Society*, 23 (Spring), 97–103.
Eichengreen, B. (1993) 'European Monetary Unification', *Journal of Economic Literature*, 31 (September), 1321–57.
Fine, B. and L. Harris (1979) *Rereading 'Capital'* (London: Macmillan).
Fischer, S., 'Recent Developments in Macroeconomics', *The Economic Journal*, 98 (June), 294–339.
Fitoussi, J.P. (1997) *The Forbidden Discussion: Money, Europe, Poverty* (Athens: Polis Editions) (in Greek).
Flam, H. (1992) 'Product Markets and 1992: Full Integration, Large Gains?', *Journal of Economic Perspectives*, 6 (Fall), 7–30.
Friedman, M. (1968a) 'The Role of Monetary Policy', *American Economic Review*, 58 (March), 1–17.
Friedman, M. (1968b) 'Inflation: Causes and Consequenses' in M. Friedman (ed.), *Dollars and Deficits* (Englewood Cliffs: Prentice-Hall).
Franks, J. and C. Mayer (1990) 'Takeovers', *Economic Policy* (April), 189–231.
Glyn, A. and B. Sutcliffe (1972) *British Capitalism, Workers and the Profit Squeeze* (London: Penguin).

Gordon, R. (1990) 'What Is New-Keynesian Economics?', *Journal of Economic Literature*, 27 (September), 1115–71.
Grahl, J. and P. Teague (1990) *1992 – The Big Market: The Future of the European Community* (London: Lawrence & Wishart).
Greenwald, B. and J. Stiglitz (1993) 'New and Old Keynesians', *Journal of Economic Perspectives*, 7 (Winter), 23–44.
Harvey, D. (1982) *The Limits to Capital* (Chicago: Chicago University Press).
Heilbroner, R. and W. Milberg (1995) *The Crisis of Vision in Modern Economic Thought* (Cambridge: Cambridge University Press).
Helm, D. (1993) 'The Assessment: The European Internal Market: The Next Steps', *Oxford Review of Economic Policy*, 9 (Spring), 1–14.
Henderson, J. and R. Quandt (1971) *Microeconomic Theory: A Mathematical Approach* (London: McGraw-Hill).
Itoh, M. (1980) *Value and Crisis* (London: Pluto Press).
Jacquemin, A. (1990) 'Gains and Losses from 1992 Discussion', *Economic Policy* (April), 46–9.
Krugman, P.R. (1990) *Rethinking International Trade* (Cambridge, Mass.: MIT Press).
Kydland, F. and E. Prescott (1987) 'Rules Rather Than Discretion: The Inconsistency of Optimal Plans', *Journal of Political Economy*, 87 (June), 473–92.
Laibman, D. (1992) 'Market and Plan: The Evolution of Social Structures in History and Theory', *Science & Society*, 56 (Spring), 60–91.
Lipietz, A. (1986) 'Behind the Crisis: The Exhaustion of a Regime of Accumulation. A 'Regulation School' Perspective on Some French Empirical Work', *Review of Radical Political Economics*, 18, 13–33.
Lucas, R.E. (1972a) 'Expectations and the Neutrality of Money', *Journal of Economic Theory*, 4, 103–24.
Lucas, R.E. (1972b) 'Economic Testing of the Natural Rate Hypothesis', in O. Eckstein (ed.), *The Econometrics of Price Determination* (Washington, DC: Board of Governors of the Federal Reserve System).
Marx, K. *Capital* (1977) (New York: Vintage Books).
Mankiw, N.G. (1990) 'A Quick Refresher Course in Macroeconomics', *Journal of Economic Literature*, 27 (December), 1645–60.
McCallum, B. (1989) 'New Classical Macroeconomics: A Sympathetic Account', *Scandinavian Journal of Economics*, 91, 223–52.
Mundell, R. (1961) 'A Theory of Optimum Currency Areas', *American Economic Review*, 51 (September), 657–65.
Neven, D. (1990) 'Gains and Losses from 1992', *Economic Policy* (April), 13–46.
Resnick, S. and R. Wolff (1987) *Knowledge and Class: A Marxian Critique of Political Economy* (Chicago: University of Chicago Press).
Ricketts, M., (ed.) (1988) *Neoclassical Microeconomics*, vols I and II (Aldershot: Edward Elgar).
Rowthorn, B. (1974) 'Neo-Classicism, Neo-Ricardianism and Marxism', *New Left Review*, 86 (July–August), 63–87.
Semmler, W. (1982) 'Theories of Competition and Monopoly', *Capital and Class*, 12 (Winter), 91–116.
Shaikh, A. (1977) 'An Introduction to the History of Crisis Theories' in

Union of Radical Political Economics (URPE) *US Capitalism in Crisis* (New York: URPE), 219–41.

Shaikh, A. (1992) 'The Falling Rate of Profit as the Cause of Long Waves: Theory and Empirical Results', in A. Kleinknecht, E. Mandel and I. Wallerstein (eds), *New Findings in Long-Wave Research* (New York: St Martin's Press), 174–95.

Shaked, A. and J. Sutton (1984) 'Involuntary Unemployment as a Perfect Equilibrium in a Bargaining Model', *Econometrica*, 52 (November), 1351–64.

Shapiro, C. and J. Stiglitz (1984) 'Equilibrium Unemployment as a Worker Discipline Device', *American Economic Review*, 74 (June), 433–44.

Solow, R. (1985) 'Insiders and Outsiders in Wage Determination', *Scandinavian Journal of Economics*, 87, 411–28.

Stadler, G. (1994) 'Real Business Cycles', *Journal of Economic Literature* (December), 1750–83.

Sweezy, P. (1970) *The Theory of Capitalist Development* (New York: Monthly Review Press).

Varian, H. (1984) *Microeconomic Analysis* (London: W.W. Norton).

Varian, H. (1990) *Intermediate Microeconomics* (London: W.W. Norton).

Vlachou, A. (1993) 'The Socialist Transformation of China: Debates over Class and Social Development', *Rethinking Marxism*, 6 (Winter), 8–39.

Vlachou, A. and T. Maniatis (1997) 'Paving the Road for Privatizations: The Case of the Public Power Corporation of Greece', paper presented at the Conference on 'Democracy and the Welfare State', Cultural Centre of Delphi, Greece (2–5 October).

Wolff, R. and S. Resnick (1987) *Economics: Marxian versus Neoclassical* (Baltimore: The Johns Hopkins University Press).

Part I

The Critique of the Neoliberal Economic Paradigm

2 Privatization: Theory with Lessons from the United Kingdom*

Ben Fine

INTRODUCTION

Privatization is now well established as a policy and practice throughout the world.[1] In the United Kingdom, the value of privatized assets on the British stock exchange has reached over £100 billion in 1992,[2] as much as 14 per cent of the share value of domestic companies.[3] Privatization has included state corporations previously covering electricity, gas, water, airlines, airports, cars, steel, coal and telecommunications. Nonetheless, privatization has not been as all-conquering as its media hype might suggest. The World Bank (1995) has bemoaned the limited extent of privatization in developing countries and the lack of success where it has occurred. It has even confessed that its pressure for privatization may have been premature given the absence of the necessary political and economic preconditions for privatization to be adopted and to be successful.[4]

These last reservations aside, why has privatization come so rapidly to such prominence? The first and most popular explanation is usually offered in terms of the rise of particularly aggressive right-wing laissez-faire governments, such as those linked with Thatcherism and Reaganism, together with a more general shift in the balance between market and state as Neoliberal perspectives have gained ground at the expense of Keynesian–welfarism. From a materialist perspective, however, such arguments cannot be endowed with priority. For, although the rise of Neoliberalism has undoubtedly tempered the rhythm and extent of privatization, the question remains open why it should have triumphed in the form of such policies and why they should have proven acceptable to the 'captains of industry'.[5] The political and ideological support for privatization inevitably follows and sustains its adoption. And the momentum behind privatization has remained, despite the demise of Thatcher and Reagan.

More secure grounds for explaining the emergence of privatization are to be found in the shifting conditions under which the accumulation of capital has been occurring. First, within production, the restructuring of capital has been marked by two crucial developments. On the one hand, although not new, the internationalization of production (and 'globalization' more generally) has posed challenges to state-owned companies which are confined to domestic ownership alone. Across a number of industries, joint ventures (JVs) between different firms have proved essential, with the result that state-owned companies have been viable only on the basis of participation, however fully, with private capital. On the other hand, especially in the wake of new technology and reinforcing the previous factor, traditional divisions between the various sectors of the economy have been broken down – most notably in telecommunications, office equipment and data processing, for example – so that the division between the public and the private sector has necessarily been withdrawn given that the public sector used to be confined to a number of demarcated areas of activity.[6]

Second, globalization and new technology has possibly had more impact upon the financial sector than on any others. Putting it in very loose and informal terms, the volume and range of financial services that have been made available have given rise to a wealth of 'idle capital' that makes itself busy by privatization which is in the first instance, after all, simply the financial process of transferring ownership from the public to the private sector. In down-to-earth terms, such idle capital is most noticeable in the proliferation of competing financial consultancies, desperate to gain existing privatization business and to promote more.

Third, privatization has been an important way in which the relations between capital and labour have been reorganised. In part, this reflects the advantage to be taken by capitalists from the forms of restructuring mentioned in the previous paragraphs, in conjunction with shifts in management techniques associated with new technology with the greater potential, for example, for subcontracting. In part, it also draws upon the shifting balances between capital and labour in the labour markets, as economies have experienced very high levels of unemployment and women and youth have served as a latent reserve army of unemployed. In short, privatization and so-called labour market flexibility have been intimately related to one another.[7]

In short, privatization has involved the restructuring of capital across its many dimensions. As argued elsewhere in the context of privatization but of more general relevance,[8] Neoliberalism might present itself as the withdrawal of the state in favour of the market, but it is more appropriate to view such developments in the current period of capitalism as incorporating state economic intervention rather than as its negation. What is privatized, and how, represents the state's continuing intervention within the economy, favouring certain capitals at the expense of others and mediating between capital and labour in economic, political and ideological arenas.

MAINSTREAM APPROACHES

Against this background, it is useful to begin this chapter with a review of the orthodox literature on privatization. Corresponding to the wave of privatization, there has been a wealth of theoretical and empirical research – more than 3000 articles in academic journals over the past four years, for example – and these articles are complemented by any number of books and government and consultancy reports. The academic literature has been concerned with the motives for, and the methods and consequences of privatization, together with the problems posed by post-privatization regulation. Like other developments in mainstream economic theory, the discipline found itself confronted with an empirical issue and reality which it was particularly unsuited to handle. Undeterred, the response has been characterized by two features. First, the issue of privatization has been interpreted within the existing fashions of the discipline; this has involved the new microeconomics and industrial economics around transactions costs, property rights and informational imperfections and asymmetries. Second, the literature has followed empirical developments as they have arisen in sequence with the progress of privatization itself – what to privatize, how to privatize, and how to regulate. From a position of a wide gap between its theory and material realities, the orthodox literature on privatization has been directed at a moving target as privatization has proceeded. But it is instructive in shedding light on the realities of privatization to examine how orthodox theory has evolved, even if its distance from practice remains significant.

The literature on privatization, including analytical and policy frameworks for assessing it in practice, is dominated by what has been termed a 'new synthesis' in economic thinking.[9] The analysis has evolved in the specific context of privatization in developed countries, although it is taken to be of general applicability across both developing economies and those in transition.

The new synthesis is marked by a number of general features. First, as already observed, it emerged initially, and all the key elements were put in place, prior to privatization being considered of relevance to developing countries and those in transition. As was proudly and perversely proclaimed at the time, privatization was the United Kingdom's most successful export, a boast tempered by the corresponding continuing deindustrialization of the most severe kind and disastrous performance in UK manufacturing exports. In short, privatization theory is a response, sometimes critical, to Thatcherism and is marked by its contextual origins. Second, the privatization literature followed in the wake of the privatization process as it evolved. Considerations of the economics of regulation appeared only at a later date, after the terms of the debate over the merits of public and private ownership had already been settled. Third, by the same token, the literature has only just begun to be informed by the consequences of privatization in practice, otherwise depending upon limited experience sectorally, comparatively and over time. Fourth, while, as emphasized, a response to particular economic and political circumstances, the theory of privatization has also been heavily influenced by particular fashionable developments that have been taking place in economic theory, even though these have nothing as such to do with privatization, merely serving as a convenient and fashionable illustration for the theory. For a variety of reasons, economic theory has been preoccupied with issues of asymmetric and incomplete information and the costs of transactions within a market system. Privatization proved a natural application, even though such factors are far from being its sole nor most important determinants.

Finally, irrespective of the applicability of the new synthesis to developed countries, the application of its analytical and policy framework to the radically different circumstances to be found in developing countries and economies in transition is most questionable. Indeed, it can be argued that the more pronounced changes and policy goals in such countries would have provided a sounder footing on which to formulate a theory of privatization, since the issues and consequences involved present themselves more clearly and cannot be overlooked. Anticipating what is to follow, the significance of the definition, redistribution and use of property rights emerges particularly sharply in the context of economies in transition, but they are also of importance in developing countries even if conveniently overlooked.

In short, the privatization literature suffers from the limitations of its analytical and empirical origins which, in principle, ought to have restricted its scope of application. This has not been so in practice and, partly and explicitly driven by a pro-market ideology despite its humble analytical foundations and origins, the momentum behind privatization has swept much before it. Ideally, it would be best to wipe the analytical slate clean and start again; a start is made here by a critical assessment of the key components of the new synthesis.

It can in part be seen as a reaction against the earlier tradition of 'old' public sector economics. This was itself firmly based upon the notion of market failure. Such failures fall into two types – the supposedly 'natural' or given as opposed to the 'artificial' or those created by economic agents. The first refers to conditions in production and/or consumption which lead to inefficiency in the context of a perfectly competitive, that is price-taking, economy. These might include economies of scale (natural monopoly) and externalities. In addition, the private sector might be considered to be naturally unsatisfactory if it provides an inequitable distribution of income or if it encourages or discourages consumption of goods that are considered undesirable or desirable, respectively – what are termed demerit (alcohol to be taxed, for example) or merit (education to be subsidized) goods. In this way, the economic theory of market imperfections provided the rationale for public sector intervention, for which public ownership, for example, was one extreme form relative to subsidies and taxes. In addition, having identified the role for the public sector, it was more or less presumed that the benevolent welfare state would effortlessly implement the policies necessary both to rectify inefficiency and to meet social goals. Artificial market failure, on the other hand, arises out of the uncompetitive behaviour of economic agents, especially firms. In this case, the idea is that prices will be unduly high and the market restricted, providing a role for the state to control prices.

The old public sector economics was very much a product of the Keynesian and welfarist ideology of the post-war boom. The new synthesis is a response to the collapse of that boom, and the issue that emerged in the late 1970s of public vs. private ownership. Whilst the old tradition was particularly ill suited to address the question of ownership, simply presuming that the state would do what the market would not, the new synthesis continues to be marked by emphasis on how to deal with potential market failure. Interestingly, the ways in which it has evolved can be seen as pulling in opposite directions in terms of conclusions about the relative merits of forms of public and private ownership. On the one hand, the scope of market failure has been considerably widened; it now includes issues such as how property rights are defined and utilized, informational imperfections and asymmetries and the effects of transactions costs. The recognition of these additional market failures might be expected to enhance the potential role of the state in sorting them out. On the other hand, however, the state itself is placed under closer scrutiny; it is no longer presumed that the solution to a market failure can be safely left to be remedied by benevolent intervention, partly because the state may not be benevolent – in so far as it reflects and incorporates the actions of officials and others with interests of their own – and partly because the state may have neither the knowledge nor the capacity more generally to implement what is required of it. In short, the new synthesis accepts, and even extends, the framework of market failure but also questions whether the state is able and willing to provide a corrective improvement. Complementing market failure is its *alter ego* in the form of regulatory failure. It cannot be presumed that the state will put right what the market gets wrong: it is a matter of a trade-off between the two.[10]

THE NEW SYNTHESIS OF NEW POLITICAL ECONOMY, NEW INSTITUTIONAL ECONOMICS AND NEO-AUSTRIAN ECONOMICS

The first point about the new synthesis, then, is that it supplements the old public sector economics and, in doing so, it draws upon three separate and broader types of literature.[11] One is derived from the new political economy which emphasizes the role and realm of the state as revolving around rent-seeking. In this view, the state's interventions not only distort the economy away from the conditions of beneficial perfect competition, they also encourage agents to incur the wasteful, and possibly illegal, expenditure of resources to gain such an advantage. Now, in this form, the notion of rent-seeking has a precise meaning and also a precise calculus of effects under given conditions – those of perfect competition and partial equilibrium. For it is a static theory of distortion from market-led economic efficiency, with the added wrinkle that the inefficiencies are compounded by the costs of obtaining and sustaining them. However – and this is of more general significance for other parts of the literature – the notion of rent-seeking has readily taken on a life of its own, often divorced from its origins and limited sphere of applicability. Any economic intervention by the state, in a wide variety of circumstances, has become viewed as potentially a counter-productive policy response or an invitation to rent-seeking behaviour.

The new institutional economics has also contributed to the new synthesis. Its starting point is to explain the division between market and non-market institutions, especially the internal organization of the firm as opposed to its external market relations. At its core lies the notion that market transactions are not costless and that the capacity of economic agents to uncover and incorporate all potentially relevant information is bounded. Consequently, non-market institutional forms will emerge as well as customary and collective, rather than individualistic, optimizing behaviour. Moreover, these are not, as such, evidence of inefficiency. Non-market institutions, such as the state itself but also the internal organization of large corporations, are thus inevitably the spontaneous consequence of the inadequacies of exclusive reliance upon the market alone. As in the case of rent-seeking, the new institutional economics has produced a terminology of its own, even if more technical and less focused. It is deployed widely and freely.

Central is the notion of principal–agent problems (in which there are problems monitoring those with whom one contracts because they have better knowledge than you over what they are doing, and with what effects). There are also problems of the definition and nature of property rights, and how the broader legal and other institutional environment interacts with the generation and receipt of information. Like the new political economy, however, even if the latter marches under its limited banner of rent-seeking, the new institutional economics is essentially a static theory, even if of allocation of activity within and between market and non-market institutions. This does not prevent it from being applied in a much wider range of circumstances as if this were a simple corollary. In this way, for example, increasingly in the most recent literature, the historical evolution of institutions is seen as a dynamic interaction between institutions that generate property relations, information and corresponding contracts, and vice versa.

This brings the new institutional economics into common ground with the neo-Austrian school of economics which differs from the other two influences on the new synthesis in that it is primarily concerned with the dynamics of the market economy in the context of an uncertain and changing world. In this respect, there is an antipathy to the notion of equilibrium and to the formal mathematical modelling that often characterizes the new political economy and the new institutional economics. Instead, emphasis is placed upon the greater potential for decentralized decision-making. Individual economic agents are better placed both to generate and deploy new resources and information themselves and to do the same with that generated by others. Within the neo-Austrian tradition, the market is taken to be the most appropriate institutional form in which to accommodate such creation and diffusion of innovation and change. More important, however, is the fact that the issue is raised in the neo-Austrian literature of how economic agents create and respond to a dynamic world of change and uncertainty irrespective of whether the market is favoured or not.

As a first point about the new synthesis, then, it is able to draw upon three separate, new or revitalized traditions. Each of these has itself developed in peculiar ways, from relatively narrow analytical origins. Taken together, especially in informal discourse, there is considerable licence to move seamlessly between a variety of concepts as if they were rigorously and coherently founded and integrated – which they are not. Further, there tends to be a presumption that these new analytical developments have shifted the balance in favour of the market and against the state – because of rent-seeking, the spontaneous formation of appropriate institutions and the individual economic agent best knowing and responding to change.[12] Finally, with the exception of the neo-Austrians, the focus of the old public sector economics, with its emphasis on market failure, remains central – even if supplemented by notions of regulatory failure. To a large extent, this justifies the conclusion that ownership as such does not matter as opposed to the conditions of competition and regulation governing that ownership. But, if a choice has to be made on ownership, then the new influences on the synthesis have shifted the balance in favour of the market and privatization.

MARKET FAILURE, COMPETITION AND INDUSTRIAL ECONOMICS AND POLICY

A second central point in the new synthesis is that there is a core section of the economy that is best left to the market and to be subject to the interventions of the state only in order to enhance competition, especially through easing regulations, for example, that inhibit ease of entry to a particular sector. This has been termed the quantity theory of competition[13] – the idea that a sector is more competitive if there are more competitors and that more of such competition is beneficial. However, this can be shown to be true only within orthodox neoclassical economics under the most highly restrictive assumptions such as absence of externalities, decreasing returns to scale and partial equilibrium.[14]

In addition, the quantity theory of competition involves a very narrow notion of market competition for product markets, as opposed to competition in product quality and differentiation, technological progress, access to finance, and so on. This leads to a third, more general point concerning the way in which the new synthesis has changed the understanding of what constitutes 'industrial economics'. Previously, the latter incorporated a substantial component of informal and institutional analysis as admirably summarized within the notion of structure–conduct–performance, the SCP approach. This suggested that the structure of an industrial sector, such as the degree of monopolization, would affect the way in which a corporation would conduct its business and, consequently, have an impact upon its own and more general economic performance. It allowed a whole range of factors to be brought into consideration, not least the internal organization of firms and their capacity to innovate and diversify. Now, in deference to mathematical models within industrial economics, the descriptive framework provided by SCP has been rejected for notions of equilibrium in which the anticipated effect of one's own and one's rivals' performance affects the choice of conduct and structure so that a unilinear causal relationship between the three factors is rejected. Modelling techniques have also been expanded to include game theory.

In short, irrespective of the merits of the old industrial economics, the use of the new industrial economics by the new synthesis has narrowed the range of the explanatory factors to be taken into consideration; they are confined to those that are readily amenable to formal modelling, although these models can become extremely sophisticated in terms of strategy and counter-strategy. Here, in conjunction with the previous points, the new synthesis appears to have selected the worst of all possible worlds. For, on the one hand, formal mathematical models do not sustain the simple conclusions concerning the benefits of competition. On the other, they involve the exclusion of factors which are known to be crucial to industrial performance. In this light, it is not surprising that the more informal approaches to the issues of rent-seeking, institutions and neo-Austrianism should have gained in prominence more recently, especially in the context of the economies in transition where the changes associated with privatization are so much more dramatic.

Restricting the scope of industrial economics, not surprisingly, leads to the fourth point about the new synthesis – it places a particular focus on what is the scope of industrial policy. Taking a longer view on this issue, it is apparent that the definition of industrial policy is itself highly variable both over time and between countries. This is a consequence of the capacity for almost all economic policies to affect industrial performance and for one or other of these policies to be decisive at one time or set of circumstances as opposed to another. Trade, R&D, skills, finance for industry, vertical integration, small business, provision of infrastructure, and so on have all from time to time been seen, rightly or wrongly at the time, as the appropriate focus for industrial policy. For the new synthesis, the focus is far more narrow – confined to competition, regulation (on which see later) and ownership. It follows that, just as crucial factors are neglected, so will be the corresponding policy considerations. This is true of other economic factors, especially where dynamic considerations of change are concerned, as in technological change and the generation of productivity increase and comparative advantage.

So far, the discussion has primarily been organized around the role of competition. The other side of the coin for the new synthesis is theory and policy where competitive outcomes are not appropriate as for natural monopoly, in the presence of economies of scale and scope. Here, the idea is that there is no possibility of a competitive equilibrium output so that, as best it can, a regulatory body must set prices or limit excessive profits, as well as securing quality and spread of provision to customers. A fifth point on the new synthesis, then, is that it presumes that there is a ready distinction, both conceptually and practically, between artificial and natural monopoly for which there are corresponding industrial policies

– namely, enhancing competition and regulation, respectively. It is relatively easy to show, however, that the notion of natural monopoly is not sustainable in the sense that it cannot be identified independently of the economic environment in which it operates. Consider, for example, a situation in which wages are driven down. This almost certainly reduces the scope for the economies of scale associated with natural monopoly as small-scale producers become more commercially viable. It might even be argued that driving down wages is a means of promoting the case for privatization and enhanced competition (and vice versa)! Consequently, natural monopoly cannot be defined independently of the economic conditions in which it is presumed to operate and, moreover, policy itself may change whether an industry is interpreted as a natural monopoly or not.[15]

This leads to a sixth, more general, point about the new synthesis; this is its failure to take broader social and economic conditions into account. This is evident in a number of ways. Property rights are, for example, conceived of very simply as a residual claim to income – whatever profits are left over after costs are paid go either to the state or to a private company according to ownership. Not surprisingly, this tends to lead to the conclusion that ownership as such does not matter except as a secondary issue relative to competition and regulation. But property rights in general and privatization in particular are much more complex. For privatization can involve a decisive shift in the way in which property rights are exercised. Putting it too bluntly, the public sector is to a greater or lesser extent subject to a political process which is quite distinct from the market process attached to private property. This is true even if both public and private sectors are subject to competition and regulation. It is much harder for broad-based interests to be represented politically when it comes to the private than to the public sector although, of course, there is no guarantee that political responses and processes within the public sector are always advantageous to the majority. But they do have to be taken into account and are liable to be highly variable and complex.

Two different aspects are involved in deepening the approach to the understanding of what constitutes, and what is the impact of, 'property rights'. One, the less fundamental conceptually, concerns the effect of redistributing given property rights. According to long-standing theory from the literature on transactions costs, externalities and the theory of the firm, the redistribution of property rights does not matter for efficiency as long as they are properly defined and owned. This has, however, been shown to be incorrect when there are residual property rights – those aspects of economic life which it is difficult or too costly to determine precisely within a contract. Then, who has ownership is important, not only, for example, in the power associated with the redistribution of wealth, but also for the efficiency with which that wealth is used.[16] This point is readily understandable in the context of South Africa, for example. The presence or not of racial discrimination in employment practices, for example, is very hard to pin down. It would make a difference who owned the companies and how they set about ensuring that managers dealt with the potential for racism and other issues that cannot be solely reduced to commercial or contractual conditions and for which there is considerable managerial discretion.

A more fundamental aspect in approaching the issue of property rights is to acknowledge that these might not only have an impact through being redistributed but that their very nature is not fixed but subject to change through the dependence of property rights upon economic and social factors. It has been argued, for example, that the impact of privatization is very different according to the culture and institutions through which the state operates.[17] In the United Kingdom, there is a relatively weak tradition of the state acceptably and legitimately interfering to regulate private capital in the public interest compared to France. One result is that UK regulation has been perceived to be the responsibility of the regulator, to be personalized rather than a matter of participatory accountability. As Prosser (1995, p. 512) puts it:

> Powers have been conferred personally on regulators and the assumptions seems to be that if the right people are appointed this is in itself a guarantee of legitimacy.

It follows that what is being privatized depends upon a broader set of considerations than those narrowly defined by a tranche of physical property and set of regulations. What these allow for in practice is highly contingent upon society-specific factors.

A separate way of seeing this aspect of property rights, the neglect of the socioeconomic environment, is the failure of the new synthesis to take into account the specific histories of nationalized industries, their dynamic and their broader social and economic significance. In Britain, for example, the strong popular commitment to the National Health Service is almost certainly a consequence of the tradition of free and universal provision that it embodies. There has also been a more general commitment to public service, including the ethos of public provision as opposed to pursuit of self-interest, although this is being eroded with the progress of privatization. This is because privatization has been heavily associated with an ideology, through anti-statism, of 'bureaucratic bashing'. This places the legitimacy of government into question as well as public service ethics and motivation. To be a state official is potentially to court the reputation for being superfluous, inefficient relative to the private sector and rent-seeking if not corrupt. The consequences have not been purely ideological or damaging to public service morale; the public sector has found it necessary to mimic the practices and criteria of the private sector in order to avoid or deflect such accusations and perceptions.[18] Further, irrespective of the damage done to the morale and ethos of the public sector, there is an impact on recruitment to civil service employment. Although subject to nepotism, the state has often been able to enjoy a commitment from its workforce which has allowed lower wages to be paid than in the private sector and for a benefit to accrue from the pursuit of a career as a state employee. With a shift in the ethos of public service, state employment is liable to lose such advantages, leading to inefficiencies through high turnover of staff, and the civil service seen as merely an alternative or stepping stone to more remunerative employment in the private sector. There is a danger of the private sector 'creaming' the most easily sourced and commercially viable services, leaving the state with the responsibility of providing a safety net for those hardest to serve. Poorly resourced and regarded, the ethos of public service is further undermined.[19]

History is also important in the assessment of the performance of the public sector. In Britain, for example, most of the major nationalizations arose immediately after the Second World War out of the positive experience of war-time controls, in sharp contrast to the failures of the industries under private ownership during the inter-war period[20]. In many ways, the industries' experience before privatization can be described as a period of successful restoration to commercial viability, something that had to occur in any case before the private sector would have been willing to purchase them. More generally, in assessing performance, there tends to be an inbuilt bias against the public sector, for two reasons. On the one hand, there is sample selection bias – if the private sector were not performing well, it would be eliminated and not remain to be counted.

Whilst this is considered to be a virtuous property of the market mechanism, this would discount the private sector's negative contribution for the time and to the extent it was in deficit: it is like assessing health care provision on the basis of live patients alone. On the other hand, the relative performance of the public and private sectors tends to be assessed on the basis of the criteria laid down for the private sector, more or less direct measures of commercial achievement at the expense of the equally important social measures such as employment generation and security, contribution to skills, universal provision, and so on.

In general, popular ideology to the contrary, the balance of evidence in favour of either the public or private sector is mixed and fairly balanced.[21] It is, however, difficult to make comparisons in the context of denationalization, partly because it is relatively recent,[22] limiting the capacity for before and after comparisons, and partly because it is rare that public and private sector companies operate in otherwise comparable conditions. This leads to a rather different point, re-emphasizing the need to address historical and socioeconomic factors; the differences between public and private sector performance within a country are liable to be small relative to the differences in performance of both relative to other countries. Thus, in the case of Britain, the problem is not so much the difference between public and private sector performance as the poor overall industrial performance relative to other countries. Put another way, if the productivity performance between the private and public sectors within countries were equalized, then this would make very little difference to the comparison of productivities between countries. This is not the same thing as saying that ownership as such does not matter, since the running of the state sector can form part of, and a platform for, industrial policies more generally which do affect the performance of both private and public sectors.

This leads to a seventh point about the new synthesis which incorporates many of the earlier points. Because it is essentially microeconomic and partial in its analytical scope, it takes no account of the macroeconomic environment. The theory is perceived to be generally applicable across a range of circumstance give or take a detail or two. It does not seem to matter whether unemployment is high or low, with the same applying to other targets of short- and long-run macroeconomic management – inflation, the budget deficit, balance of payments and growth in the economy and productivity.

A final point about the new synthesis is its understanding of regulation. Here, for natural monopolies, the idea is that the regulator should impose conditions on prices, quality, and so on, of the service. Whilst this is all very well in principle, there is much detail to be determined in practice and, echoing an earlier point, how the public and private sectors relate to, and attempt to manipulate, regulation is liable to be very different since each is governed by different goals and processes. Here, however, it is worth emphasizing a different aspect of regulation which follows from the other features of the new synthesis; this is that the regulator is essentially a surrogate for industrial policy, but with two special features. The first is the extremely limited powers that the regulator commands – given a focus primarily on pricing and profit at the level of the enterprise, there is usually no way of directly influencing wage differentials, employment levels, R&D, skills and training of the workforce, the promotion of economies of scope, and so on. The second feature is the limited accountability of the regulator over extended periods in terms of democratic representation. While this might be seen as a positive aspect in terms of independence from particular interests, including those of an established government, it is more fundamentally a negation of popular participation in decisions that often crucially affect the day-to-day lives of citizens dependent upon the provision of basic utilities.

LESSONS FROM THE UNITED KINGDOM

From the previous discussion, two central conclusions can be drawn. First, given the multiplicity of factors involved in any privatization, it is erroneous to seek a general theory or explanation.[23] Interestingly, exactly the same conclusion was drawn many years ago in the context of nationalized industries before privatization had been seriously contemplated.[24] Each sector of the economy in terms of its finance, markets, international position, technological prospects, political context, and so on is very different. Second, by the same token, at a systemic level, the role played by privatization will be very different from one country to another, depending upon the particular structure and dynamic of the economy irrespective of any tendencies towards 'globalization'.

These propositions are well illustrated by consideration of the British example. As argued elsewhere (Fine and Harris 1985), the

UK economy has been characterized by the three 'lows' – low productivity, low investment and low wages. This is the consequence of the particular role of finance, industry and labour. The British financial system is what is known as market-based, as opposed to the Japanese bank-based system,[25] with arm's-length relations between finance and industry and relatively limited provision of long-term industrial investment funds. British industry has been heavily based upon multinational corporations whose strategic restructuring has been concerned more with global considerations than the regeneration of British industry. Despite reputations for militancy, the British labour movement has primarily been engaged in defensive struggles to protect employment levels and advance wages and conditions of work rather than being influential in the formulation and implementation of industrial policy or economic policy more generally.

The result has been that industrial policy has long lacked coherence and commitment over the long term, since no major economic interest group has been able or willing to direct the corresponding strategies and policies. In this light, far from the privatization programme being a break with the past, it is better seen as a continuity, even a perfection, of the lack of systematic industrial policy that had gone before.

This has proved disastrous in the case of British privatization which has been accompanied by the simultaneous decline or lack of integration of industries that are mutually dependent upon one another through the linkages associated with the input–output table – coal, steel, electricity, cars and water, for example. In the case of coal, the Thatcher governments' commitment to defeat the union took overwhelming precedence over energy and industrial policy. The use of domestically produced coal within the UK electricity industry was sacrificed for reliance upon other energy sources irrespective of the direct impact on domestic employment within the coal industry itself, and quite apart from the indirect effects through the economic multiplier. In addition, coal-fired power stations have been set aside for gas-fired power stations, as the latter require less capital expenditure and incur lower risks for individual power suppliers if not for the system as a whole. These effects have had a large negative impact upon the British engineering industry; major parts of its market were suddenly spirited away without the opportunity to retool and retrain for provision of the new equipment irrespective of the rationale for its being preferred.[26]

As argued in Fine and Poletti (1992), the privatization and reorganization of the British steel industry was based upon considerable destruction of public sector basic capacity prior to privatization in order to guarantee profitability of the continuing private finished steels subsectors. McLaughlin and Maloney (1996) provide an outstanding account of the privatization of the British car industry. They demonstrate the lack of coherence and continuity in policy towards the reorganization of the major British and state-owned producer, British Leyland, with policy shifting according to the political imperatives and ideologies of the Tory government as opposed to rational industrial policy-making. Similarly, Hunt and Lynk (1995) examine the privatization of the UK water industry and conclude that it has set aside the economies of scope that exist between the provision of water supply and more general environmental services.[27]

Under privatization, both electricity and water became subject initially to distribution under 12 and 10 separate regional companies, respectively. As privatized companies, they have been able to relate to the rest of the economy quite differently than the corresponding enterprises under public ownership. Then, the companies were generally prohibited from diversifying into other sectors for fear of their competing with the private sector. In addition, the public sector was used more positively to promote the private sector – by, for example, the orders that it made for equipment which often reflected broader strategic goals. Under privatization, such restrictions on diversification no longer hold and strategic goals are different, primarily if not exclusively tuned to private profitability. Thus, for example, the first takeover bid for a UK electricity distribution company was made by a general holding company, Hanson PLC, seeking to set the electricity company's profits against its own losses in order to reduce an overall tax liability. By early 1997, 10 of the original 12 UK electricity distribution companies had been acquired, some by US utilities, others by privatized water companies.

More generally, and hardly surprisingly, the newly privatized companies have used their considerable financial muscle to speculate in the acquisition of other companies on the basis of acquiring capital gains rather than on the basis of economies of scale and scope. Inevitably, these operations involve internationalization of investment, whether inward foreign investment in public utilities or outward investment by the newly privatized companies. This makes industrial policy-making even more difficult. Interestingly, even as this chapter was being written, British Telecom merged with the US company, MCI, to form the second largest telecommunications company in the world. This may or may not be an advantageous strategic move but, more significant, it has been made without any apparent reference to UK industrial policy or broader objectives as defined by government strategy or policy.

To some extent, the differing terms and conditions under which privatized companies are now reorganizing themselves can be interpreted as a shift in the nature as well as the distribution of property rights. Nonetheless, the redistributive effects of privatization have been prominent, with a presumption amongst proponents of privatization that measures to support the disadvantaged should be pursued through other areas of policy: macroeconomics should correct unemployment, for example, and income subsidies should be used to ensure that the poor can afford public utilities rather than distorting prices by making them cheaper. As Alan Walters, a prominent economic advisor to Mrs Thatcher, reputedly argued in response to the idea that rail fares should be subsidized: 'Why do you want to favour poor people simply because they go by railway. If you regard them as poor give them money.'[28] The idea is that this will allow the poor to buy what they want and also not impair allocative efficiency by distorting price signals with a subsidy.

Of course, the unemployed and the poor might feel rather differently about whether such policies will actually be implemented. Those who favour such market-led solutions are also notorious for opposing income redistribution as providing negative incentives against the rich who would pay higher taxes, as well as discouraging the supposedly work-shy unemployed from taking up work. This is of particular significance in Britain, where the programme of privatization has been associated with a dramatic increase in income inequality. The same applies to the increasing inequality elsewhere in the world of privatization; whatever benefits privatization brings, they do not appear to filter down to the poor.[29]

For reasons that should be clear from the earlier discussion of how the theory of privatization has evolved, issues concerning industrial policy, economies of scale and scope, and the redistribution and redefinition of property rights have all arisen in the indirect form of how best to regulate the industry. Initially, regulation was seen as a more or less simple matter of devising the appropriate criteria, and hence formula, for pricing. Now, in retrospect, the process of competition is perceived to be much more complex, involving not only the market for a single output but also product composition and quality, diversification and transfer pricing across activities, access to finance, mergers and acquisitions (M & A), franchising and access to inputs, quite apart from the role of shifts in government policy and orientation and of long-term contracting. There is also the issue of what is termed 'stranded assets', those that are acquired but not necessarily falling under the purview of the regulator or the core business of the privatized company. Their presence should not simply or primarily be seen as indicative of problems in regulating privatized companies but as a lack of strategic thinking in the privatization policy itself and in industrial policy more generally.[30]

This is hardly surprising given that the imperatives to privatize often dominated consideration of the practicalities involved. The Thatcher government's plans for privatizing electricity were strongly criticized by its own parliamentary committee (Energy Select Committee, 1987/8, p. xix):

> We cannot make recommendations about policy when policy is unknown... [and] runs the risk of producing ill-considered, spatchcock legislation. Electricity is too important an industry for the country to gamble that everything will come out right.

One factor pushing the process of privatization is that it is itself a particularly profitable business for many of those concerned. The cost of arranging the sale of assets, including the commission, is usually 3 or 4 per cent of their value; but this can be a huge amount of money. It is hardly surprising that financial institutions should be keen on privatizations taking place, there has often been a close relationship between political and financial advisors. As one of these[31] commented:

> So, my first advice is to take the plunge. My second advice is, don't listen too much to too many experienced professionals. Choose advisers who will take the plunge with you and get with it. You will find as I say, that it's not perfect, but it does work.

But for whom does it work, apart from those who advise us to take the plunge? For, in order to obtain cooperation from workforces and, especially, management in valuing businesses and in keeping them in running order, their cooperation often has to be recompensed. In Britain, there has been a public scandal over the extent to which the managers of previously public corporations have been rewarded with share options and increases in salaries. More than 50 directors of previously publicly owned utilities have each made more than a million pounds more in salaries, share options and pension rights than they would have before privatization.[32]

An interesting aspect of this scandal is that the UK public were outraged both by the extent of the rewards received by the management in the newly privatized enterprises and by the absolute levels of these rewards. Not surprisingly, the rather lame but, in some sense, legitimate defence on the managers' behalf has been that their remuneration was simply being raised to a level comparable to the private sector. In effect, this suggests two different conclusions: how outrageously high but unnoticed are the levels of rewards common within the private sector brought to attention only in the context of change from public to private sector management; and how substantially and quickly can the ethos of public sector management be transformed to that of the private sector. And, of course, there is nothing that a regulator or the government can do about it.

In discussing, however suitably, the process of privatization, and the corresponding redefinition and redistribution of property rights, the literature has inevitably moved forward to the results of privatization itself for this is nothing other than the exercise of those newly formed property rights. While there has, in Britain for example, quite correctly been considerable emphasis on the excessive profits that were made out of the privatization process (with selling prices often offered too low) and the excessive profits made by privatized utilities, even leading to the imposition of an extra tax (thereby undermining or revealing the weakness of regulation), this is to some extent misleading, for it involves treating the privatized utilities as if they were simply the public utilities under private ownership. But this is not the case, as will become increasingly apparent over time as they diversify their activities in sectoral and global scope (or become the victims of others doing likewise).

Once again, it can be considered that the associated financial restructuring of the privatized corporations has been recognized only indirectly and in line with continuing analytical concerns that do not necessarily derive from privatization as such. Much has been made, for example, of the extent to which privatization has given rise to a share-ownership democracy. Although share-holding has been widened by privatization, the most important impact has been to consolidate formal ownership in the hands of institutional investors such as insurance and investment funds. However, Hayri and Yilmaz (1997) have investigated whether the prices of shares of privatized companies perform in a similar fashion to the prices of other companies. They find that they do not do so, and suggest this may reflect stock market inefficiency owing to the large number of small shareholders who act in concert on less than perfect information or motives. While an important result, from the perspective offered here, it misses the point of how the UK financial system functions as a whole. Even if the privatized stocks performed comparably to others, the overall functioning of the British financial system would remain sorely inadequate in generating and monitoring finance for investment.

Notes

* Thanks to John Sender for comments during drafting, and to participants in the COSATU Workshop for comments on a much larger study (Fine 1997a), from which this is in part drawn.

1. Throughout this chapter, 'privatization' will usually refer to denationalization, the focus of the discussion, without necessarily suggesting the lack of importance of other forms of privatization such as deregulation and the contracting out of public services.
2. See Helm and Jenkinson (1997) who come to a figure of £80 billion for July 1992, and add a further £20 billion for subsequent stock market movement.
3. See Hayri and Yilmaz (1997).
4. As Fontaine and Geronimi (1995, p. 147) report, informal talks with World Bank representatives on privatization have confirmed that there is a 'great deal of [concealed] disappointment on this issue'. For a critique of the World Bank's position, see Fine (1997b).
5. Indeed, the evidence is that the Thatcher government more or less stumbled upon the policy of denationalization in its second term of office in the mid-1980s, looking for a way to continue the populist policy of selling off public housing. See Brittan (1986) and the discussion in Fine (1990).
6. For mainstream analysis, such factors are recognized in terms of the economies of scale and scope. In these terms, privatization can be justified in terms of the erosion of natural monopolies through technical change. For a critique of the notion of natural monopolies, see Fine (1989, 1990).
7. For a critical assessment of the notion of flexibility in labour markets, see Fine (1998, Chapter 4).
8. See especially Fine and Poletti (1992).

9. The term is taken from Fine (1989, 1990) where the arguments in this section are developed in depth.
10. As Jasinski and Yarrow (1996, p. 43) conclude from their four-volume collection of articles on privatization:

   Very roughly, privatization can be viewed as a means of reducing the impacts of both monitoring failures and government failures at the risk of increasing the effects of market failures.

   For a conventional account of privatization theory, see also Vickers and Yarrow (1988). Clarke (1993) reviews the UK experience, arguing that it is far from a blueprint for other countries to follow, pro-market dogma to the contrary.
11. See Rowthorn and Chang (1995).
12. In the context of industrial policy, Chang (1994) has shown decisively that this is not so. See also Tittenbrun (1996) for an analytical and empirical critique of the various positions adopted in favour of privatization.
13. See Weeks (1981).
14. As Schmalensee (1988, p. 677) observes in his centenary survey on industrial economics for the *Economic Journal*:

   Recent theoretical research suggests that market conduct depends in complex ways on a host of factors, and the empirical literature offers few simple robust structural relations on which general policies can be confidently based. Moreover, formal models of imperfect competition rarely generate unambiguous conclusions. In such models, feasible policy options usually involve movements *towards* but not *to* perfect competition, so that welfare analysis involves second-best comparisons amongst distorted equilibria. In particular, there is no guarantee that making markets 'more competitive' will generally enhance welfare, particularly if non-price rivalry is intensified.

15. See Fine (1989, 1990).
16. See Grossman and Hart (1986).
17. See Prosser (1995).
18. For a comprehensive discussion of these issues, see Haque (1996). He argues (p. 191):

   The current ethical challenge to the public service emanates basically from an attempt of various agencies to restore their weakened legitimacy or revive their lost public confidence by adopting the values of private enterprises, although such values are relatively incompatible with mainstream public service norms. However, this incorporation of market values in the public service may lead to a further decline in its legitimacy, because there is no reason to believe that the public will have more confidence in a public service driven by market values than one based on traditional, largely democratic, values.

See also Fine and Leopold (1993, Chapter 21) where it is pointed out that public provision is increasingly been treated as an alternative form of private provision, with a corresponding language of client, customer, and so on. For a discussion of the sea-change in attitudes towards the relative merits of the state and market in the context of Latin America, see Baer (1996).
19. As Haque (1996, p. 200) observes:

> In most of the market economies, the productive, efficient, and profitable sectors are dominated by private firms, whereas the public sector is left with activities which are socially unavoidable but economically non-profit-making and unattractive, such as health care, food provision, housing, and education for the poor ... Due to this monopolization of profitable enterprises by the private sector and the imposition of economically less viable functions on the public sector, the comparison between the two becomes relatively unjust.

20. See Fine and O'Donnell (1981, 1985).
21. See Rowthorn and Chang (1992) and Chang and Singh (1993), for example. See also Haque (1996, p. 197):

> There is sufficient reason to suspect the claims of efficiency and competition made by the privatization advocates and there is need for more comprehensive studies and critical research to evaluate such claims.

For an overall assessment of the results of the UK privatization programme, see Parker and Martin (1995). See also Boussofiane, Martin and Parker (1997) and Galal et al. (1994).
22. Remarkably, in terms of its short-termism, Eckel, Eckel and Singal (1997) deduce that efficiency had improved under private ownership as airfares were lower one year later on the routes served by British Airways. Further, they suggest the same conclusions can be drawn because the share values of US competitors to British Airways fell upon its privatization, the more so for closer rivals.
23. See Parker (1994) who examines a matrix for examining changes induced by privatization with the corporations as a row vector and goals, management, labour, operational structure and nature and location of business as the column vector.
24. See Fine and O'Donnell (1981, 1985).
25. For a review of the financial systems literature, see Fine (1997c).
26. See Fine (1990) for details.
27. See also Davidson (1993).
28. As quoted in Bos (1996, p. 53).
29. See Haque (1996, p. 198):

> During the period of privatization between 1980 and 1992, the number of people in poverty in Latin America increased from 136 million to 266 million, and in Africa, the number of people in poverty has

already reached 200 million... In terms of living standards, the incidence of undernutrition increased from 22 per cent in 1979–81 to 26 per cent in 1983–85 in sub-Saharan Africa, and health services have become less affordable to the poor in countries such as Zaire, Swaziland, Lesotho, and Uganda... More recently, in many of the emerging market economies in Eastern Europe and the former Soviet republics, the standards of living have deteriorated significantly. Although these examples do not prove that privatization has caused this decline in living standards in these Third World and post-socialist countries, which might be caused by other unknown factors, they at least represent the fact that privatization does not necessarily enhance the welfare of common people.

30. These points are well illustrated by the collection edited by Helm and Jenkinson (1997), where the problems of economies of scale and scope clearly emerge in the context of price regulation. For a clear discussion of the inadequacy of the regulation of water through simplistic pricing formula, see Davidson (1993).
31. Letwin (1988, p. 61). See also Redwood (1988, p. 31), the erstwhile challenger for the Tory Party leadership and an active consultant on, as well as proponent for, privatization:

> When you are setting about your task of privatization, don't go for the two-year slog or the two million pound consultancy to work out absolutely every detail... if you are seriously interested in privatizing, there is no substitute for doing it.

32. See Conyon (1995) for a full account of directors' pay in the UK privatized industries. He finds no correlation between the extent of increases in rewards and enterprise performance.

References

Bos, D. (1996) 'Arguments on Privatization', in Yarrow and Jasinski (eds), reproduced from D. Bos, *Privatization: A Theoretical Treatment* (Oxford: Clarendon Press, 1991).
Boussofiane, A., S. Martin and D. Parker (1997) 'The Impact on Technical Efficiency of the UK Privatization Programme', *Applied Economics*, 29, 297–310.
Brittan, S. (1986) 'Privatization: A Comment on Kay and Thompson', *Economic Journal*, 96 (March), 33–8.
Butler, E. (ed.) (1988) *The Mechanics of Privatization* (London: Adam Smith Institute).
Chang, H. (1994) *The Political Economy of Industrial Policy* (London: Macmillan).
Chang, H. and A. Singh (1993) *Public Enterprises in Developing Countries and Economic Efficiency: A Critical Examination of Analytical, Empirical and Policy Issues* (Geneva: UNCTAD Review, 4).

Clarke, T. (1993) 'The Political Economy of the UK Privatization Programme: A Blueprint for Other Countries?', in Clarke and Pitelis (eds).
Clarke, T. and C. Pitelis (eds) (1993) *The Political Economy of Privatization* (London: Routledge).
Conyon, M. (1995) 'Directors' Pay in the Privatized Utilities', *British Journal of Industrial Relations*, 33, 159–71.
Cook, P. and C. Kirkpatrick (eds) (1995) *Privatization Policy and Performance: International Perspectives* (New York: Prentice-Hall 1995).
Davidson, J. (1993) *Privatization and Employment: The Case of the Water Industry* (London: Mansell).
Eckel, C., D. Eckel and V. Singal (1997) 'Privatization and Efficiency: Industry Effects of the Sale of British Airways', *Journal of Financial Economics*, 43, 275–98.
Energy Select Committee, (1987–88) *The Structure, Regulation and Economic Consequences of Electricity Supply in the Private Sector*, Third Report, HC 307 (London HMSO).
Fine, B. (1989) 'Scaling the Commanding Heights of Public Sector Economics', *Cambridge Journal of Economics*, 14 (June), 127–42.
Fine, B. (1990) *The Coal Question: Political Economy and Industrial Change from the Nineteenth Century to the Present Day* (London: Routledge).
Fine, B. (1997a) 'Privatization and the Restructuring of State Assets in South Africa: A Strategic View', paper presented to COSATU Workshop, Johannesburg (17 March).
Fine, B. (1997b) 'Apologists and Academia: A Critical Review of "Bureaucrats in Business"', mimeo, prepared for the Department of Economics, SOAS.
Fine, B. (1997c) 'Interrogating the Financial System: With an Application to South Africa', mimeo, prepared for the Department of Economics, SOAS.
Fine, B. (1998) *Labour Market Theory: A Constructive Reassessment* (London: Routledge).
Fine, B. and L. Harris (1985) *The Peculiarities of the British Economy* (London: Lawrence & Wishart).
Fine, B. and K. O'Donnell (1981) 'The Nationalised Industries', in D. Currie and R. Smith (eds), *Socialist Economic Review*, 1 (London: Merlin Press 1981).
Fine, B. and K. O'Donnell (1985) 'The Nationalised Industries', in Fine and Harris.
Fine, B. and C. Poletti (1992) 'Industrial Policy in the Light of Privatization', in Michie (ed.).
Fontaine, J.-M. and V. Geronimi (1995) 'Private Investment and Privatization in sub-Saharan Africa', in Cook and Kirkpatrick (eds).
Galal, A. *et al.* (1994) *Welfare Consequences of Selling Public Enterprises: An Empirical Analysis* (New York: Oxford University Press).
Grossman, S. and O. Hart (1986) 'The Costs and Benefits of Ownership: A Theory of Vertical and Lateral Integration', in Yarrow and Jasinski (eds), 1, reproduced from *Journal of Political Economy*, 94 (1986), 691–719.
Haque, M. (1996) 'The Public Service under the Challenge in the Age of Privatization', *Governance*, 9, 186–216.

Hayri, A. and K. Yilmaz (1997) 'Privatization and Stock Market Efficiency: The British Experience', *Scottish Journal of Political Economy*, 44, 113–33.
Helm, D. and T. Jenkinson (1997) 'The Assessment: Introducing Competition into Regulated Industries', *Oxford Review of Economic Policy*, 13, 1–14.
Hunt, L. and E. Lynk (1995) 'Privatization and Efficiency in the UK Water Industry: An Empirical Analysis', *Oxford Bulletin of Economics and Statistics*, 57, 371–87.
Jasinski, and G. Yarrow (1996) 'Privatization: An Overview of the Issues', in Yarrow and Jasinski (eds), 1.
Letwin, O. (1988) 'International Experience in the Politics of Privatization', in Walker (ed.).
McLaughlin, A. and W. Maloney (1996) 'Privatization as Industrial Policy: State Withdrawal from the British Motor Industry', *Public Administration*, 74, 435–52
Michie, J., (ed.), *The Economic Legacy, 1979–1992* (London: Academic Press).
Parker, D. (1994) 'Privatization and Business Restructuring: Change and Continuity in the Privatized Industries', *The Review of Policy Issues*, 1, 3–27.
Parker, D. and S. Martin (1995) 'The Impact of UK Privatization on Labour and Total Factor Productivity', *Scottish Journal of Political Economy*, 42, (May), 201–20.
Prosser, T. (1995) 'The State, Constitutions, and Implementing Economic Policy – Privatization and Regulation in the UK, France and the USA', *Social and Legal Studies*, 4, 507–15.
Redwood, J. (1988) 'Merchant Banks and Privatization', in Butler (ed.).
Rowthorn, B. and H. Chang (1992) 'The Political Economy of Privatization', *The Economic and Labour Relations Review*, 3, (December), 1–17.
Rowthorn, R. and H. Chang (1995) 'The Role of the State in Economic Change: Entrepreneurship and Conflict Management', in Rowthorn and Chang (eds).
Rowthorn, R. and H. Chang, (eds) (1995) *The Role of the State in Economic Change* (Oxford: Clarendon Press 1995).
Schmalensee, R. (1988) 'Industrial Economics: An Overview', *Economic Journal*, 98 (September), 643–81.
Tittenbrun, J. (1996) *Private versus Public Enterprise: In Search of the Economic Rationale for Privatization* (London: Janus).
Vickers, J. and G. Yarrow (1988) *Privatization: An Economic Analysis* (Cambridge, Mass.: MIT Press).
Walker, M., (ed.), *Privatization: Tactics and Techniques* (Vancouver: Fraser Institute).
Weeks, J. (1981) *Capital and Exploitation* (London: Edward Arnold).
World Bank (1995) *Bureaucrats in Business: The Economics and Politics of Government Ownership*, (Oxford: Oxford University Press).
Yarrow, G. and Jasinski, (eds) (1996) *Privatization: Critical Perspectives on the World Economy*, 4 vols (London: Routledge).

Discussion

Stavros Mavroudeas and Lefteris Tsoulfidis

The question concerning the extent to which government should interfere in the economy is as old as economics. Up until the great depression of the 1930s economists believed that government's role should be limited to the absolute essential functions described in general terms by Adam Smith. These functions included the provision of justice, police protection, provision of money, and so on During the great depression the emergence of Keynesianism, armed with the concept of effective demand, provided the necessary theoretical framework for extensive government intervention. The new rationale for government intervention was not confined to humanitarian reasons (such as creation of public works, provision of food and shelter for the poor, and so on), but to the necessity to enhance effective demand. Thus, the government's role expanded to include production activities as well. In recent decades (the year 1973 is considered the benchmark year), the mood has changed dramatically. Keynesianism in the late 1970s and early 1980s was in dispute and it seems that it now has merely become a chapter in the history of economic thought. Government intervention is no longer viewed as a cure for the malfunctioning of the system, but rather the cause of its current crisis. In this context, privatization is often considered as a panacea that will solve current economic problems, such as the reduction in government deficit and the national debt, the reduction of inflation because of the subsequent increase in productivity and the fall in the cost of production. The recipe is simple and easy to popularize: all it takes is a change in the form of ownership and the problems that mark the economies of most countries will sooner or later disappear.

Ben Fine's chapter critically evaluates the usual arguments that favour privatization. More specifically, by examining concrete examples from the UK economy, he shows that privatization, after all, benefits particular groups of people, by no means society at large. Fine argues that the emergence of the wave of privatizations that we have witnessed since 1980 is closely related to the shifting conditions of capital accumulation. More specifically, Fine points out three major developments: First, the restructuring of capital in the sphere of production, which has two dimensions – the globalization of production and the introduction of new technologies, which, to a great extent, rendered the distinction between public and private sector irrelevant. Second, the high rate of diffusion of the new technologies; and third, the so-called labour- market flexibility, which has clearly been exacerbated through privatization.

There is no doubt that Fine's general perspective and his appeal to the shifting conditions of capitalist accumulation are on the right track. However, he clearly, abandons any effort to develop an alternative to the orthodox economists' approach. It seems that Fine needs to explain precisely the causes of the shifting conditions of production that appeared in the period, during which even mainstream economists recognize that a slow-down in economic activity began in 1973. This slow-down is attributed by many Marxists (for example, Moseley 1990; Shaikh and Tonak 1994) to the falling rate of profit. In this analysis, the years after 1973 marked the end of the so-called 'golden age' of accumulation and the beginning of an era of crisis in profitability. The capitalist restructuring that we are now witnessing is nothing but systematic efforts to restore profitability and henceforth to re-establish the necessary conditions for accumulation. This requires – as has been repeatedly argued by many Marxists (for example, Fine and Harris 1979) – a change in the forms of extraction of (absolute and relative) surplus value and the concomitant ways of socializing production. The distinctive characteristic of this new era is the drive to increase both absolute and relative surplus value. Whereas the extraction of relative surplus-value always remains dominant, the capitalist system also increases the extraction of absolute surplus value. This is a major difference from the previous era that started after the onset of the crisis of the 1930s, during which the principal vehicle of crisis alleviation was the increase of relative surplus value. These changes are now initially located in the sphere of production, through the reorganization of the labour process on the basis of flexible work, and also through networking between firms. These dramatic changes become possible through the introduction of the new technologies, especially in the sphere of information. These new technologies are diffused quite rapidly in the rest of the economy through radical changes both in the determinants – and the forms of coverage – of the value of labour power and the forms of distribution of surplus value between the different sections of capital. Finally, they are reflected in the form of socialization of production, where the border line between the private and the public that once was clear has now become increasingly indistinguishable. At the same time the traditional (Keynesian) role of the state has been undermined.

It is within this context that an alternative critical perspective should, in our view, place the wave of privatizations. The globalization of production, as well as the abundance of idle financial capital, are derivatives of these fundamental changes. This missing link in the study of the course of capitalist accumulation is coupled with a lack of a general theory of the state and its economic activities. Advancing such a theory is extremely difficult and progress has been very slow and thus many Marxists gradually gave up the effort. Fine and Harris (1985, p. 150) for example, claim that it is impossible to derive a general theory of nationalized industries, and in the present chapter (p. 55), Fine claims that it is fruitless to seek a general theory of privatization, since each sector of the economy and each country has its own characteristics. We do not agree with such an approach and in our view it becomes increasingly necessary to give a detailed explanation of the phase change in the development of capitalism. Such an analysis would lay the groundwork for the explanation of the content of privatizations and answer the fundamental question of its cause (why is it necessary today for the capitalist system to resort to privatization?). The particular characteristics of a sector or country can be studied from within this general perspective.

One should include the role of the state as the collective capitalist in the post-war period in such a general perspective. The state planned the reconstruction of the economies and the restoration of capitalist relations; its role in the pre-war period was pretty much the same, since economies had to be reconstructed and capitalist relations reconfirmed in the face of the revolutionary threat posed by the workers' movement. At the same time, the state as a producer assumed the production of those goods that either required big capital expenditure and expensive technology, or possessed a strategic character for these economies. In the first case, private capital could not undertake these investments because of the associated low returns and risks. In the second case, it was not functional for the capitalist economies as a whole to let these activities to be organized along private lines because of concerns about the creation of monopoly situations. These goods – whether partially or fully commodified – operated either as cheap intermediate inputs in private capitalist production processes (thus supporting their profitability), or covered areas of the reproduction of labour power, thus removing the pressure of wage conflict from private capital. Finally, since the working class emerged strengthened after the war, the public sector facilitated its incorporation into the system by providing better conditions of work, security of employment, and so on. The post-war 'golden era' was based on exactly these relations, proving that state economic activity does not conflict with private capitalist success.

The crisis of the 1970s signified the end of that period. The abundance of accumulated financial capital and its search for profitable investment opportunities, coupled with the defeat of the workers' movement in the late 1980s, created both the necessary conditions and the pressure for the privatization of state economic activities. The existence of many big private capitals searching for profitable investment opportunities removed the danger of monopolization of, at least, the so-called 'strategic sectors' of the economy. The defeat of the workers' movement opened the way for the increase of the rates of exploitation of workers in public enterprises. For all these reasons, the fields previously covered by state economic activities had to be opened to private capital. The trend towards either privatization or the adoption of private economic criteria in the management of public enterprises, has the very same aim: the direct and indirect enhancement of profitability and capital accumulation.

It is imperative today to confront the neo-conservative assault on the workers' standard of living through the increase of both the length of the working day and the intensity of work without an increase in real wages – and also oppose the efforts against democratization. This confrontation will be effective when it is accompanied by a theoretical argument that shows the character and the motivation for the privatization and at the same time shows ways (new alternative institutions) that society can benefit from the dramatic increases in productivity that take place through the introduction of new technologies. There is no doubt that Ben Fine's chapter, by showing both the deficiencies of the neoclassical analysis on theoretical grounds and the distance between the officially stated purposes of privatization and what happened in reality in England, contributes to developing a credible alternative explanation of both privatization motives and effects.

References

Fine, B. and L. Harris (1979) *Rereading 'Capital'* (London: Routledge).
Fine B. and L. Harris (1985) *The Peculiarities of the British Economy* (London: Lawrence & Wishart).
Moseley F. (1990) 'The Decline of the Rate of Profit in the Post-war US Economy. Alternative Marxian Explanation', *Review of Radical Political Economics*, 2.
Shaikh, A. and A. Tonak (1994) *Measuring the Wealth of Nations: The Political Economy of National Accounts* (New York: Cambridge University Press).

3 Limiting the State versus Expanding it: A Criticism of this Debate

Richard D. Wolff

THE PROBLEM

In most ways, very little of the so-called 'Neoliberal paradigm' is new. After all, its proponents have propagated its core propositions widely for more than two centuries. These claim that economic progress will be greater (1) the more free markets (rather than other mechanisms) distribute a society's resources and products, and (2) the more productive resources and products are owned by private individuals or corporations (rather than, say, by states).

The basic theoretical support for the Neoliberal paradigm emerges from the remarkable concept of efficiency that is central to it. This concept holds that any economic act, event or institution may be interrogated as to its positive and negative consequences – usually labelled 'benefits' and 'costs'. If the latter exceed the former, the object of interrogation is declared inefficient. The implication usually drawn is that society would be better or best off if it banned, eliminated, or avoided such inefficient economic acts, events, or institutions. If benefits exceed costs, the object is efficient and hence desirable, valuable, and so on. By extension, if the issue is a comparison among two or more alternative economic acts, events, or institutions, society would be best off selecting the most efficient among them: the one with the highest ratio of benefits to costs.

From this logical foundation, the argument has developed that markets are more efficient than (and hence socially preferable to), say, state planned allocations of resources and products. Likewise, efficiency arguments underlie the socially preferable location of resource and product ownership in private vs., say, state hands. Countless cost–benefit comparisons prove, in Neoliberal reasoning, the greater efficiency for all societies of those policies that they and their followers are now executing across the globe under the slogan 'privatization'.

Questionable presumptions underlie such efficiency arguments. First, the arguments presume that it is analytically possible to link any specific act, event, or institution to a set of consequences *uniquely attributable to it*. That is, efficiency arguments must presuppose that we can know absolutely that any consequence we might measure – any particular cost or benefit – is attributable *alone* to the particular acts, events, or institutions we are investigating and comparing. If we allow the possibility that each particular cost or benefit flows from a vast number of different, interacting acts, events, or institutions – that is, from many rather than one cause – the usual efficiency arguments collapse. The presumption that we cannot attribute costs or benefits to one 'cause' – because costs and benefits are overdetermined by many causes – undermines any appeal to an efficiency calculus to support Neoliberal (or, indeed, any other) policies.

Second, efficiency arguments also presume that we can know the *entire* set of consequences that flow from any particular economic acts, events, and institutions under investigation. This is an heroic presumption indeed. The act of replacing a state-allocation system of distributing resources and products with free private markets, for example, will change virtually every aspect of the society in which this act occurs. Everything from modes of production and exchange to cultural forms, political processes and interactions with nature will adjust and react to the substitution of markets for state allocations. Moreover, the non-economic adjustments and reactions will react back upon the economic aspects of the society and vice versa. In short, the social effects of this change will endlessly ramify in overlapping, interacting ways. The contrary idea – that there is an end point of these ramifying interactions, a telos or 'equilibrium' at which the society 'comes to rest' – is simply yet another presumption necessary to make efficiency calculations; it has no other warrant or basis.

Efficiency arguments proceed by comparing the social effects of alternative ways of distributing resources and products (state allocations vs. markets, private vs. state property) in order to reach a conclusion about which is socially preferable. Such arguments presume that investigations can know *all* of these effects: direct and indirect, present and future. They likewise presume that investigations can measure all of these effects to arrive at the net balance between the costly and the beneficial effects of the two alternatives. Yet such presumptions go well beyond heroism. They cross the boundary into the fantastic. Sensing this – and responding to their enemies who pointed it out – proponents of liberalism and Neoliberalism have almost always asserted that it suffices to know and measure only the 'major' or 'most important' social effects to reach a reliable efficiency conclusion.

Such assertions beg the question. After all, how can liberals or Neoliberals be sure that the effects they designate and measure as most important are so without having compared them to *all* the other effects? If they have failed to identify and/or measure one or more effects, the possibility exists that those they missed may be more important than those they have included; that possibility undermines their efficiency claims.

The concepts and calculations of efficiency arguments have captured not only the Neoliberals but many of their theoretical and political enemies as well. Most of the latter neither reject nor question those arguments *per se*. Thus, for example, most proponents of state allocation of resources and products and of collective rather than private property have offered their own efficiency arguments. They have contested the efficiency calculations of the liberals and Neoliberals by counter-posing their own efficiency arguments. They argue that the Neoliberals wrongly count only 'private costs' without recognizing and measuring 'social costs.' Presumably, these critics of Neoliberalism also believe that they can count all or 'the most important' social costs.

The debate over Neoliberalism has thus most often been about which particular effects are to be identified and counted in tallying cost–benefit ratios. The debaters rarely challenge the logic of all such counting. The Neoliberals select and measure their subset of costs and benefits to reach their conclusion about, say, private vs. state property. The devotees of the latter, critics of Neoliberalism, select, measure and compare their subset of consequences to reach the opposite conclusion.[1] Neither side challenges the presumptions of such comparisons – namely, that a set of conditions can be traced to a single cause within the complex social totality and that all or most social effects of an economic event can be known and measured to yield efficiency conclusions.[2]

WHY DO WE HAVE THIS PROBLEM?

Most Neoliberals as well as their opponents likely understand my line of reasoning here. Many probably recognize the problems of, and sometimes worry about, the validity of the cost–benefit studies they undertake. So the question becomes: why do they nonetheless accept, teach and use efficiency arguments based on such questionable presumptions? Why, in short, do the major debates within economic policy literature display so flimsy a philosophical and methodological foundation?

An important part of the answer lies in a particular feature of modern capitalism. The history of capitalism in every country displays repeated oscillations between private and state forms. By 'private capitalism', I mean social arrangements where largely free markets allocate resources and products among their private owners. By 'state capitalism', I mean arrangements where the state significantly controls markets or directly allocates resources and products and/or where these are substantially owned by the state as well. Of course, there have been varying mixtures or degrees of both private and state capitalisms, reflecting the unique histories, cultures, and circumstances of each country.

It is appropriate to speak of 'oscillations' between forms of capitalism because the distinctively capitalist kind of class structure remains in place across both forms. By 'class structure' – as developed at length elsewhere – I refer to the organization of the production, appropriation, and distribution of surplus labour (Resnick and Wolff 1987). That is, in a capitalist class structure, the mass of productive labourers produces not only output equivalent in value to what they themselves receive as income, but also produce additional output, a surplus value. Persons other than these productive labourers instantly and automatically appropriate these surplus values and then distribute them (as interest, rents, dividends, managerial budgets, and so on) so as to reproduce this social arrangement. The productive labourers are neither the property of others, as in slave class structures, nor are they bound to the surplus appropriators by personal–religious ties of loyalty and fealty, as in feudalism. Rather they enter into formal or informal contracts for specified periods of time with those who appropriate their surplus. The latter – 'capitalists' precisely because they appropriate surplus in this way – return to the productive labourers the non-surplus portion of their output as a wage or salary.

The differences between private and state capitalism concern alternative mechanisms of resource and product distribution (that is, markets vs. state allocations) and distributions of power over objects (that is, private property vs. state property). These are *not* differences over the class structure of production: over how surplus is to be produced and, in particular, whether the producers appropriate their surplus (Wolff 1995). State capitalism is not any kind of communism. Marx was quite clear in specifying that communism entailed the workers to collectively appropriate and distribute the surpluses they produced. As shown elsewhere, capitalist class structures can (and historically have) coexisted both with markets and with state allocations of resources and products, both with private and with state ownership of property, and so on (Resnick and Wolff 1994a, 1994b).

The oscillations between private and state forms of capitalism have focused the thoughts and actions of people living in them in particular ways. Each form came to appear as the ultimate solution for problems thought to be intractable in the other. Few looked beyond these forms for solutions. Every historical form of capitalism sooner or later encountered contradictions and problems that raised questions about that form; these often evolved into rising criticisms and efforts to solve them. Minor adjustments and limited policy shifts happened first since they troubled the social order least. When these did not suffice to answer the questions or stop the criticism, voices rose to favour a more sweeping kind of change, and the existing form of capitalism itself came into dispute.

When the kind of capitalism experiencing the problems was a private capitalism, such more sweeping change entailed a transition to one or another variant of state capitalism. Likewise, when deepening troubles afflicted instead a state capitalism, the sweeping change went in the opposite direction toward private capitalism. Either way, proponents of change from one form to another insisted that such change would correct the deficiencies of the existing society. The existing form was declared to be 'inefficient' and usually also unjust, while the other form was declared to be efficient and just (or at least more efficient and more just).

Efficiency arguments lent themselves beautifully to these arguments. Advocates for a change in the existing form of capitalism appealed not to a mere partisan preference (based on ethics, philosophy, and politics) but rather to 'objective' measures of some 'absolute' efficiency standard. This suited the scientific spirit so deeply associated with all capitalisms. Liberals and then Neoliberals who argued for private and against state capitalisms couched their arguments in the efficiency framework because it allowed their partisanship for one form of capitalism to appear as support for something absolutely 'the best' regardless of any partisanship. Their opponents reasoned to the opposite conclusions in exactly the same way.

Contesting efficiency arguments contributed to stabilizing capitalism by limiting debate and action on capitalism's problems to struggles over its forms. If capitalisms' problems were formal, the appropriate solutions would likewise be formal – that is, solutions would entail oscillations between forms of capitalism rather than changes moving beyond all forms of capitalist class structures *per se*.

UNDERSTANDING CHANGE

In a remarkable and ironic twist of history, many of the proponents of change from private to state capitalism over the last century and a half understood it in different terms. Most socialists and communists spoke, of course, about going beyond capitalism, but their programmes actually favoured varying kinds of state capitalism. Some, who recognized the difference between rejecting capitalist class structures *per se* vs. rejecting merely one form of those structures, nonetheless believed that any change beyond state capitalism was an unrealizable utopian fantasy. Others declared state capitalism to be a necessary stage in the transition from capitalism to communism. The realizable, transitional stage became the prevalent definition of socialism. Socialism and state capitalism collapsed into virtual synonyms.[3]

In speeches and writings within trade unions, political parties, universities and other social movements, socialists and communists mobilized mass support for changing capitalism from a private to a state form – the latter labelled 'socialism.' Rather like their non-socialist and non-communist opponents, socialists and communists were obsessed with the twin issues of markets vs. state planning and private vs. state (or collective or social) property. They differed only in defining the conflict between private and state capitalism *as if* it were the conflict between capitalism and socialism–communism. They increasingly ignored the issue of how surplus labour was organized in capitalisms vs. how it would be organized in communism. Marx's focus on class structures as alternative modes of surplus labour's production, appropriation and distribution dropped from their thought and action.[4] This was as true of those who distanced themselves from Marxism as it was of those proud of their Marxism.

Especially when it was socialists and communists who depicted the oscillations between state and private capitalism as though they were basic class structural changes, the political consequences were profound. Among their audiences and within their organizations were people who might well have agreed that capitalism's class structures (as well as its market mechanisms and rules of property ownership) needed fundamental transformation. Those people might have formed the social basis for achieving that transformation; but that has not yet happened.

By interpreting changes between forms of capitalist class structures *as if* they were radical transitions beyond them, socialists and communists did achieve historically important blocs – in the Gramscian sense – with other proponents of state vs. private capitalism (for example, various kinds of Keynesians, democrats, radicals, and so on). This bloc responded to the great depression of the 1930s by engineering a massive, global shift from private to state capitalisms. On the other hand, achieving this bloc undermined chances for a different bloc to emerge, one built around a programme for change beyond all forms of capitalism.

Intractable problems arose within the various state capitalisms after the 1970s (just as similar problems had arisen in the various private capitalisms during the 1920s). This time it was the Neoliberals who were able to form a hegemonic bloc. It is now achieving more than the reverse change from state back to private capitalism; it is also persuading many that such a change also marks the definitive historical death of socialism and communism as alternatives to capitalism. Ironically, it uses the socialists' and communists' identifications of state capitalism with socialism to portray the current shift back to private capitalism as if it were the death of socialism and communism.

AN EXAMPLE

The great depression offers a particularly useful example for this argument. The economic collapse of the 1930s not only traumatized the societies it ravaged; it also demonstrated the awful risks and dangers inherent in the private capitalism championed by the

Neoliberal Right. Uncontrolled, unregulated – that is, 'free' – private enterprise came to define 'the economic problem'. The 'obvious solution' – increasingly practised by groping governments and most influentially theorized by Keynes – was a strategy of government supervision, regulation and interventionist management of the private enterprise economy. On one side, corporatist and fascist arrangements, largely merging the state and concentrated capitalist enterprises, comprised what we shall refer to as the 'State Capitalist Right'. This Right – dedicated to the destruction of communism and pro-communist movements – played crucial roles in the histories of Germany, Italy, Spain and other countries.

On the Left, welfare states and Keynesian economics rose triumphantly as the great depression disgraced the Liberal Right's recipes for economic success. Marxists joined Keynesians in denouncing private capitalism. Where they departed from the Keynesians was in finding state management and regulation of private capitalism an insufficient form of state intervention. Taking their cue from what had happened in the USSR after 1917, most Marxists favoured outright state ownership and management of enterprises and state-planned allocation of resources and products. In effect, this amounted to a left state capitalism where state officials replaced private individuals as owner-managers of industrial enterprises and market players and where communism was the official goal.[5] In the decades after 1929, state-managed private capitalisms or Left and Right state capitalisms displaced 'free' private capitalisms to varying degrees in many countries.

All the proponents of state capitalism – to whatever degree – couched their arguments in the framework of efficiency. The inefficiencies of private ownership and markets would be corrected by the efficiencies of state planning and state ownership. The more leftist writers expressed this idea as the dominance of socialist or communist efficiency over capitalist inefficiency. The less leftist writers made the same basic point. However, they utilized different language: certain imperfections of markets needed state regulation to achieve maximum efficiency and certain wealth and income disparities needed corrective state programmes toward the same end.[6] Private capitalism had accumulated too many social problems because of its inefficiencies; state capitalism would achieve the efficiencies that solved those problems.

The efficiency calculus served to limit agitation for change to no more than an urgent advocacy of an oscillation to state capitalism.

It also implied that the best possible economy would thereby be achieved. Hence talk of other changes – for example, changes in the organization of surplus labour – became unnecessary or irrelevant.

Liberals, of course, were hardly convinced by the barrage of critiques of private capitalism that accompanied its difficulties as the great depression deepened. But they were marginalized for the next few decades as Keynesian, socialist and Marxian theories gained adherents and attention. In the United States, FDR rode the triumphal wave, while a humiliated Liberal Right retreated. Rich financial backing remained available to it – for countless 'Freedom' foundations aimed at shaping academic and popular discourse, for politicians willing to repeat the Liberal Right truths, and so on. Classics of Liberal Right economic theory continued to be produced and widely read.[7] Yet its economics could not emerge from the margins for several decades.

What primarily enabled Neoliberalism to revive in the United States were the mounting economic problems besetting state-interventionist capitalisms. Just as the difficulties of the private form of capitalism had ushered in the great depression and the collapse of the Liberal Right, in the 1980s and 1990s the difficulties of both the state-managed forms of private capitalism and of Soviet-style state capitalisms created a new opportunity for the Liberal Right to return. While the opportunity was new, the Liberal Right that returned was not. The efficiency message was the same: since private capitalism was the most efficient, current economic problems since the great depression had all been caused by state economic interventions and would be solved by dismantling them. Reprivatization via freeing markets, returning state assets to private hands, reducing state interventions, and so on would achieve great gains in efficiency and thereby solve contemporary social problems as well.

A Neoliberal consensus emerged in which the problems of the USSR, India, the United States and, indeed, every country, were attributed to the inefficiencies flowing from what Neoliberals hated, namely state intervention and state ownership (denounced in its Western forms as welfare statism and in its Eastern forms as socialism or communism). The solution was everywhere to privatize and marketize. The oscillations from private to state capitalisms in the first half of the twentieth century were to be corrected by the reverse oscillations at the end of the second half; the same efficiency arguments that had accompanied the first oscillation ran in reverse to accompany the second.

In both historical moments, the urgent social issue was framed as which form of capitalism was the 'best'. Contending positions on these issues needed arguments that would portray their preferred solutions *as those which were absolutely 'best'*. The cost–benefit efficiency calculus provided such arguments to both sides. Caught up in the intensities of the historical tensions and oscillations between private and state capitalisms, Neoliberals and statists alike swept the questionable and problematic presumptions underlying efficiency arguments out of their minds. They thereby provided the ideological gloss that the historical moment seemed to want and require.

WHAT IS TO BE DONE?

Neoliberalism today strives to organize discussion, debate and policy action around the problems of state capitalisms in very particular ways. Neoliberalism represents its desired goal – global reaction back to private capitalism – as the only possible and effective antidote to the inefficiencies of all state capitalisms. Neoliberalism proceeds as if this latest (and, they hope, final) oscillation between forms of capitalism remains the only real policy option. More or less reluctantly, large numbers of the proponents of state capitalisms are losing their religion and switching sides. This includes formerly moderate advocates of state regulation of private capitalism and formerly strong advocates of state ownership of means of production and state planning of all distribution. So long as the reprivatized capitalisms do not encounter their own accumulating contradictions, problems and critics, the Neoliberals may postpone yet another reversal back toward state capitalism.

We may begin to displace the theoretical and practical hegemony of debate over forms of capitalism by formulating a different analysis and strategy. A first step is to attack the 'class-blindness' of the debate, its systematic ignoring of the issue of how surplus labour is produced, appropriated and distributed. Raising the class issue in this sense means to focus discussion on how the problems of *both* private and state capitalisms emerge from and depend on the capitalist class structure common to both forms. By implication, the solution to those problems lies not in oscillations between them but rather in effecting a *social discontinuity*, a break from capitalist to some other – for example, communist – class structures of producing, appropriating, and distributing surpluses.[8]

To focus the discussion in this way renders questions about private vs. state management and ownership secondary to questions about which class structures are to exist in production.[9] In any case, to raise class issues instead of or alongside issues of private vs. state opens a new front against Neoliberalism. It offers new solutions to current debates over the social problems of contemporary capitalism.

A second step entails displacing the debate's current terrain of efficiency arguments. We can expose and criticize each side's claims to have found the objectively best combination of private and state activity. We can expose the dubious presumptions necessary to make those claims. Most important, we can confront both Neoliberals and statists as sharing a common terrain. By showing that no complete or definitive cost–benefit measurement is ever possible, we can expose how the advocates of all positions are inevitably partial in calculating their measurements. The issue becomes examining and comparing the principles that govern which subset of all costs and benefits each side recognizes and measures to obtain its results.

We can shift the debate from one of spurious contests between 'best' efficiencies to one among advocates of alternative social systems who, not surprisingly, utilize different theoretical presumptions yielding different conclusions. The debate becomes a matter of stating clearly and honestly what kinds of *social organization* animate the contending parties in terms of their moral, ethical, aesthetic, political and other dimensions as well as their respective calculi of efficiencies (now plural and incommensurate rather than singular and absolute). Poles of difference become multiple (private–state, capitalist–communist, urban–rural, and so on) and not reducible to one difference as if it were the essence of all others.

We can then reposition Neoliberals within public discourse and political action as what we believe they have always been: advocates of a particular kind of capitalism. Their twentieth-century opponents would become counter-advocates of various kinds and degrees of state capitalism. We would enter the debates as advocates of a different kind of class structure – a different social organization of surplus labour – as a central component of the solution to the current system's problems. This was Marx's goal as I understand it. It remains just as appropriate as a way to respond to Neoliberalism today.

Notes

1. The form of debate between the two sides typically entails challenging (1) the other side's selection of what counts as costs and benefits, and (2) how the other side carried out its measurements.
2. It is a small irony that the most sophisticated exposure of the problematic logic of all efficiency arguments was produced by a Neoliberal, R.H. Coase (1972). He tried to make the impossibility of efficiency calculations a basis for a commitment to strict non-interference by the state in economic affairs. My intention is to move debate (over state vs. market and much else) away from the sterility of all efficiency calculations *per se* and on to altogether different terrains.
3. This is reflected in the peculiar history of 'social democracies' and 'peoples' democracies' in Europe and elsewhere. Bitter arguments among them, often couched as debates between socialists and communists, amounted to contests between lesser state capitalism (only *some* natonalization of enterprise and only *some* state regulation of markets) vs. greater state capitalism (more or full nationalization and more market regulation or full state planning). In short, the actual debates focused on the degrees of state vs. private capitalism and not, despite their language, on capitalist vs. communist kinds of class structures of production.
4. Marx's *Capital*, it is worth remembering here, has three volumes focused overwhelmingly on how capitalism distinctively organizes surplus labour; property ownership and the mechanisms of distributing productive resources and products are matters of secondary concern. Volume 1 is Marx's analysis of where and how surplus labour occurs as surplus value in capitalism (and why his precursors, who glimpsed it, did not adequately recognize and analyze it). Volumes 2 and 3 are devoted to examining how this surplus labour circulates within a capitalist economy: who divides it into portions, who obtains distributions of these portions and for what purposes, and what social consequences flow from this circulation and distribution of the surplus (Resnick and Wolff 1987).
5. The argument that the Soviet economy is best described as a state capitalism is straightforward. The point is that converting private industrial property into state property and substituting state officials for private citizens on corporate boards of directors are not sufficient conditions to establish the radical alteration in economic structure that has inspired socialists and communists for the last century. The collective of workers does not necessarily come to manage and control the disposition of its own surplus simply because the state owns and operates industrial enterprises. Indeed, if workers in state-owned and operated enterprises still produce and deliver their surpluses to others (state officials) in ways differing only slightly from the same processes within private capitalism, it makes more sense to speak of a state capitalism than a socialism or communism (Resnick and Wolff 1988, 1993, 1994a, 1994b, 1995).
6. This point has surfaced repeatedly in various arguments in which proponents of more equitable distributions of wealth and/or income seek to show how such distributions would achieve greater, not lesser,

'efficiency' (in opposition to the conservatives' notions of an 'efficiency–equity trade-off').
7. Perhaps the greatest of these was *The Road to Serfdom* written in 1943 by Friedrich A. Hayek (1962). It celebrated the great virtues of capitalism as located in its individualism and free markets. It likewise denounced the inevitable descent into totalitarianism that sprang from state economic intervention aimed at meeting people's 'needs.' Despite its millions of readers and admirers, Hayek's direct assault on Keynesianism failed to dislodge it from its hegemonic position in both academic and popular economic discourse.
8. The word 'communist' here refers strictly to a particular non-capitalist form of organizing surplus labour such that the producers collectively appropriate and collectively distribute the surpluses they produce. Marx sketched this notion of communist class structures, but never developed it in any detail. Later Marxists, drawn into the debates over alternative forms of capitalism, unfortunately tended to lose sight of Marx's surplus labour focus. Returning to Marx's original class analysis to secure the insights and changes it makes possible is a project (see references cited in fn. 5) of which this chapter is one aspect.
9. For example, collectives of workers (enterprises) organized in communist class structures could exist inside a state with members made into state officials (a kind of state communism). Alternatively, they might exist outside any official relation to the state, as communist enterprises privately owned and operated. Similarly, communist class structured enterprises could either distribute their products via market exchanges or via state allocations. Different forms of communism may coexist and struggle much as different forms of capitalism have done. In sum, property ownership and modes of distributions of resources and products are *different* matters from class structures of production.

References

Coase, R. (1972) 'The Problem of Social Cost', in R. Dorfman and N. S. Dorfman (eds), *Economics of the Environment: Selected Readings* (New York: W.W. Norton), 100–29.
Hayek, F. A. (1962) *The Road to Serfdom* (London: Routledge & Kegan Paul).
Resnick, S. and R. Wolff (1987) *Knowledge and Class: A Marxian Critique of Political Economy* (Chicago: University of Chicago Press).
Resnick, S. and R. Wolff (1988) 'Communism: Between Class and Classless' *Rethinking Marxism*, 1 (Spring), 14–48.
Resnick, S. and R. Wolff (1993) 'State Capitalism in the USSR? A Highstakes Debate.' *Rethinking Marxism* 6 (Summer), 46–68.
Resnick, S. and R. Wolff (1994a) 'Capitalisms, Socialisms, Communisms', in B. Agger, (ed.), *Current Perspectives in Social Theory*, 14, (Greenwich, Conn. and London: JAI Press), 135–50.
Resnick, S. and R. Wolff (1994b) 'Between State and Private Capitalism:

What Was Soviet "Socialism"?', *Rethinking Marxism* 7, 19–30.
Resnick, S. and R. Wolff (1995) 'Lessons from the USSR: Taking Marxian Theory the Next Step', in B. Magnus and S. Cullenberg (eds), *Whither Marxism? Global Crises in International Perspective* (New York and London: Routledge), 207–34).
Wolff, R. (1995) 'Markets Do Not a Class Structure Make', in A. Callari, S. Cullenberg and C. Biewener (eds), *Marxism in the Postmodern Age* (New York: Guilford Press), 394–401.

Discussion
Anwar M. Shaikh

I liked this chapter, and think it makes some very central points.

The first point is (essentially) that free market and managed market sides of capitalism both try to reduce very complex and fundamentally uncertain acts or institutions into a kind of very simplistic positive–negative magnitude and that that is the root of efficiency calculus. It's useful to know, (from my own background as an engineer), that the term 'efficiency', as I was taught it, was relevant inputs divided by useful outputs. The words 'relevant' and 'useful' tend to get lost in economics, because the assumption is that what is defined as relevant and useful is somehow known. Orthodox economics particularly, does this. We have to keep in mind that this is a social valuation, whether we can reduce it to a number or not, which is very crucial.

The second point is that capitalist history indicates an oscillation between less restricted and more restricted forms of capitalism, which Wolff calls private vs. state capitalism. He points out that the focus on (the debate about) whether you have private or social costs to be incorporated into the efficiency calculus displaces the tension from what is common to both of these sides, which is the idea that you continue the class basis, you continue pumping surplus labour and continue a society based on exploitation. He also makes an additional important point that the history of oscillations implies that if this pendulum swing is intrinsic to capitalism then you should expect an oscillation back towards managed capitalism, or (in a perfectly sensible way), that laissez-faire is periodically the cause of its own negation – or at least, its own restriction. I think that that is important and one can see in many parts of the world (and certainly in the United States), the reaction growing already to the idea that laissez-faire provides everything that society needs.

The third point is that Neoliberalism itself arises from the economic crisis and Wolff illustrates that by talking about both the rise of Neoliberalism in the current crisis and the ironic displacement of Neoliberalism itself by Keynesian economics in the great depression. And there, I think I would add an important point: that it is important to understand that Neoliberalism also needs to have a theoretical foundation and that it does in fact try to explain the phenomena that Keynesian economics was unable to explain. And that ability, or pseudo-ability, that attempt to address and rationalize those phenomena, was very important in conservative economics associated with Neoliberalism becoming dominant. Obviously this is not intrinsic, because Keynesian economics itself came to the fore because neoclassical economics was unable to explain how capitalism functions. So this ideological debate is also a theoretical debate of some importance.

In the last section of the chapter Wolff talks about what is to be done: attack 'class-blindness' and reject any efficiency calculus – that is, reject the idea that it's all about capitalism and talk about the other possibilities. I would make a few points here. One is that I think we need to put equal emphasis not just on class as a political and social structure, but on class as the element that structures the economic behaviour of capitalism, which means developing an economic theory based on that understanding. It is an interesting point that Marx spent a great part of his life working on, what he called his 'beloved economics', and yet what we often take from Marx is not the economics but rather the sociology, political science and philosophy. And we need, I think, to redress that balance and bring back economics into the Marxist discussion, and I think that this is a tremendous irony.

The second point is that the periodic appearance of economic crisis helps us explain this oscillation that Wolff talks about – and that is a connection that we again need to be reminded of. The great depression was not a failure of will, it was an economic collapse – and the 1970s and 1980s in my opinion, (and I have argued this for quite some time), were again a great depression – and that was the source of this oscillation. The third point is that this oscillation is not a mere repetition. I think this is implicit in Wolff's chapter, but I think we should remind ourselves that the oscillation also involves a development and a change of the system, a mutation or anyway an evolution without changing its fundamental character. And I think the last point is, as I understand it, that Wolff is not saying that the rejection of the idea of efficiency calculus is meant to be a rejection of all modes of evaluation of alternative practices and institutions. Because if that was the case, then obviously we would not be able to make any judgement about how to proceed. In addition, the emphasis on the efficiency calculus, I think, is just on that particular mode of evaluation of what are admittedly complex and fundamentally uncertain phenomena. Political practice, and scientific practice, in so far as it is different from political practice and human life itself, is based on evaluations of outcomes. We cannot exist without doing that, and so whether or not we do it perfectly, we do it. And the best thing we can try to do is to try to improve how we do it and confront our mistakes, theorizing with the empirical and historical evidence and learn from our mistakes. And I take that to be one of the themes of the chapter – and I hope a correct reading.

4 Explaining Inflation and Unemployment: An Alternative to Neoliberal Economic Theory

Anwar M. Shaikh

INTRODUCTION

For much of the post-war period, the problems of inflation and unemployment have been central to economic and political agendas. And in this domain Neoliberal economics has come to dominate both modern macroeconomic theory and policy.

Capitalism has undergone a world-wide economic crisis in the last two decades. Its response has been a series of attacks on labour and its supporting institutions, widespread business failures and bankruptcies, a dizzying spiral of concentration and centralization and an urgent drive to make available new markets and new resource areas to the unchecked power of the dominant world capitals (Shaikh 1987). Neoliberal economic *policy* arose out of the need to support and coordinate these characteristic responses of the capitalist class.

But Neoliberal economic *theory* came to the fore because Keynesian theory was unable to provide an adequate explanation for the 'stagflation' deriving from the economic crisis. This is a particular irony, given that Keynesian economic theory itself rose to power 30 years earlier because the neoclassical economic theory which underpins neoliberal economics was itself unable to explain the huge and persistent unemployment of the last great depression.

Modern heterodox macroeconomics finds itself caught in this conflict, because by the 1970s much of it had come to be subsumed under Keynesian concerns. Thus both radical and postkeynesian economics typically begin from some version of Keynesian or Kaleckian effective demand theory: a static equilibrium framework in which markup pricing insulates prices from demand, thereby shifting the adjustment process onto output and employment – at least until the vicinity of full employment. Within this framework, the obstacle to full employment with stable prices is generally political, not economic, rooted in the welter of conflicting interests arising out of the tri-cornered tug-of-war between capital, labour and the nation-state. The marxian wing of this tradition differs only in its somewhat greater emphasis on monopoly power and on the potential problems associated with 'full employment' (Kalecki 1968).

Neoclassical economic theory has no such problem, for it assumes that the capitalist system delivers full employment automatically and efficiently. In its basic form, inflation arises when an increase in the money supply stimulates aggregate demand in the face of a full-employment-constrained aggregate supply. More recent versions incorporating concepts such as the natural rate of unemployment are merely refinements of this basic argument. Here too, as in Keynesian–Kaleckian theory, inflation is expected to arise in the vicinity of full employment.

In contrast to these familiar perspectives, I would like to present a classical marxian explanation of inflation and its relationship (or lack thereof) to unemployment. Broadly speaking, a classical marxian framework considers economic growth to be the normal state of a capitalist economy, driven by the ceaseless attempts of each individual capital to constantly (self-) expand. Since each capital operates individually, without any direct regard for its place in the overall social division of labour, the interaction of these individual units produces an intrinsically turbulent process: the imagined division of labour created by the expectations of individual capitals is constantly confronted by an actual division of labour created by their own mutual actions, and the discrepancies react back on both expectations and actions, creating fresh discrepancies, and so on. This inherently turbulent process is precisely what neoclassical economics tries to cover up through its recourse to perfect competition and general equilibrium. But in fact, disequilibrium is always the existing condition, and it is precisely through offsetting phases of overshooting and undershooting that the inner tendencies are realized. From this point of view, balance conditions of various sort (demand–supply, output–capacity, sectoral growth, and so on) represent the inner forces which impose a hidden order on the outer disorder: order-in-and-through-disorder, an old concept in Marx which has finally been given legitimacy via non-linear dynamics.

In my own work, I have tried to show that this approach can be formalized so as to provide an *integrated* dynamic non-equilibrium framework for the analysis of endogenous growth, endogenous money and endogenous cycles (Shaikh 1989, 1991, 1992). Building upon Goodwin's classic work (Goodwin 1967), such a framework can be extended to incorporate an endogenous theory of persistent unemployment rooted in competition itself. This is what Marx calls a 'reserve army of labour', which we might today call an 'intrinsic rate of unemployment' to distinguish it from the pernicious Neoliberal idea of a 'natural rate of unemployment'. The former concept is rooted in the notion that the system is behaving perfectly well when it creates and maintains a pool of involuntarily unemployed people at the disposal of capital; the latter claims that it is imperfections in the system which give rise to voluntary employment – that is, to abstentions from work (Friedman 1968).

In the present chapter, I would like to address the other great problem: the question of inflation and its links, if any, to unemployment. I will trace the treatment of these issues in orthodox theories, as they arose historically in the face of challenges from historical events. Then I will outline an alternate approach to the question of inflation, and illustrate it with data for an average of the main OECD countries, and for the United States in particular.

UNEMPLOYMENT AND INFLATION IN THEORY AND HISTORY

Modern macroeconomics has its origins in the turmoil of the great depression of the 1930s. While the prevailing economic theory continued to insist that capitalism was intrinsically efficient, self-regulating, and automatically able to offer employment to all who desired it, economic reality told a different story. Widespread business failures, massive unemployment, generalized social misery – these were the social and historical facts of the day. It is in this context that Keynes' *General Theory* (Keynes 1936, 1964) stepped forward to provide an explanation for persistent unemployment, as well as a prescription for its cure. The familiar income–expenditure model derived from this approach was to dominate both macroeconomic theory and policy for a third of a century in most of the advanced capitalist world. It was systematic, quantifiable, flexible in its application and easily adapted to fiscal policy. The model is driven by exogenous components of aggregate demand, under the assumption that there are unemployed resources, most notably labour. A rise in the exogenous demand component stimulates output and employment, the resulting higher incomes then stimulate consumption and hence further increases in aggregate demand (but by a lesser amount than in the preceding round), and so on, until the original impulse has eventually produced a multiplied effect on output and employment.

Within such a framework, fiscal policy appeared to be a powerful tool for regulating the level of employment, since a government deficit was thought to give rise to a multiplied increase in production and employment. Keynesians tended to believe that unemployment was a normal feature of an unregulated capitalist economy; but with the judicious use of fiscal deficits, the government could pump up the level of employment and achieve something resembling full employment. This became a fundamental premise of post-war social policy (Artis 1992, p. 139).

Later modifications somewhat softened the analysis of the powers of budget deficits, but did not reverse the basic thrust of the argument. It was recognized that a government deficit might raise interest rates, and insofar as these inhibited investment demand, this might offset some of the original expansionary impact of the deficit. The idea also grew that a reduction of unemployment owing to an expansion of aggregate demand might also lead to higher money wages and hence induce inflation. The notion of a Phillips curve trade-off between inflation and money wages (Phillips 1958), which was rapidly recast as a trade-off between inflation and unemployment, became a standard part of the arsenal. Fleming (1962) and Mundell (1963) extended the analysis to the relation between output and employment and the balance of trade ('external balance'). The resulting complexity of the analysis, with its multiplicity of potential 'targets' (desired levels of employment, inflation, interest rates, foreign trade balances, and so on), implied that economic policy was a task for the sophisticated. But it was clear that these complications were extensions of the basic theory, not a challenge to it.

Central to all of these developments was the notion that inflation would arise only when the economy was in the *vicinity of full employment*. But this confidently held conception had begun to break down by the late 1960s. By then, inflation had not only become a practical problem of some importance, it had also become a serious *theoretical* problem: whereas the Phillips curve predicted that inflation would be accompanied by a fall in unemployment (which would stimulate a rise in money wages and hence prices), this actual new round of inflation was attended by a *rise* in unemployment. This new pattern seemed to contradict the very notion of a tradeoff between the two.

One attempt to get around the difficulty was to suppose that expectations played a significant role in the wage–price spiral. Thus was born the concept of an expectation-augmented Phillips curve (Phelps 1967; Friedman 1968), along with a particular 'natural rate' of unemployment (NAIRU) which would keep inflation in check. Conflict models of inflation as well as the infamous NAIRU have their root in this same ground (Godley and Cripps 1983; Rowthorn 1984).

But these ideas proved to be of ambiguous benefit to the Keynesian paradigm: not only did they undermine the basic thrust of Keynesian social policy, they also provided the basis for the New Classical (NC) macroeconomics which was to eventually supplant Keynesianism itself (Artis 1992, pp. 140–2). For instance, the idea of a natural rate of unemployment has its roots in the automatic full employment paradigm of neoclassical economics – the very thing that Keynesians were trying to overthrow. In the neoclassical vision, it is assumed that when all markets are in equilibrium, all workers will be able to achieve their desired level of employment at some labour market-clearing wage. But if information is not quite perfect, and if there are impediments in the labour market, there will always be some frictional level, some 'natural' level, of unemployment even in general equilibrium (Mathews 1992, p. 247). Such a natural rate is *voluntary*, since it arises out the decisions of individuals not to work in the face of existing costs of job search and existing unemployment benefits, welfare benefits, and so on. Thus, contrary to Keynesian views, the mere existence of unemployment, even rising unemployment, did not prove that it was involuntary. Not surprisingly, Neoliberal economists have been quick to proclaim that existing unemployment was in fact all voluntary (Bennett 1995).

Secondly, it was claimed that the actual level of inflation depended not only on the level of unemployment but also on inflation expectations. A higher level of inflation expectations could give rise to a higher level of actual inflation at any given level of unemployment. Since inflation expectations were assumed to change slowly (exhibit persistence), it followed that it might be necessary to tolerate (perhaps even induce) an unemployment rate higher than the 'natural' rate for long enough to lower inflation expectations.

As these fell, they would lower the actual rate of inflation consistent with any level of 'unnatural unemployment' (unemployment in excess of the natural rate), thus permitting excess unemployment to be also reduced somewhat – until finally the economy would glide into a state of long-run equilibrium in which actual inflation and expected inflation would be zero, and unemployment would be at the natural rate (the lowest sustainable rate).

Keynesian economics might have accommodated the idea that 'wringing out' inflation could be costly. But the notion that any observed rate of unemployment was essentially voluntary was far afield from the original Keynesian conceptions. In any case, it was reality which once again dealt the decisive blow to Keynesian economics. Country after country in the capitalist world floundered in the 1970s and 1980s, exhibiting inflation, unemployment, slow growth and a rise in poverty and social misery – in spite of record budget deficits. These dismal patterns fuelled the growing sense that the Keynesian theory of fiscal policy, however much it had been modified, was simply inadequate in this new epoch.

CONVENTIONAL THEORY VS. THE EMPIRICAL PATTERNS OF INFLATION AND UNEMPLOYMENT

We have seen that neoclassical and Keynesian theories differ on their explanation of inflation and unemployment. But it is important to note that they nonetheless share one a critical notion: namely, that there is an *empirical trade-off between inflation and unemployment*.

But is such a claim empirically supportable? Three points can be made here. First, as shown in Figure 4.1, between the first and second halves of the post-war period, the historical rise in average unemployment levels in OECD countries is directly associated with a corresponding fall in average output growth rates. I have tried elsewhere to show that this can be explained by the fact that a fall in the rate of profit gradually undermines the foundation for growth and hence produces the jump in unemployment rates (Shaikh 1987).

Second, as Figure 4.2 shows, there is *no general historical trade-off between unemployment and inflation*. As one can see, the patterns for the OECD countries as a whole indicate that while such a trade-off appeared to exist for the more recent period from 1975–91, the very opposite pattern holds for the early period from 1964–74 (comprehensive data is not available for unemployment before 1964).

Figure 4.1 OECD growth and unemployment, 1964–91

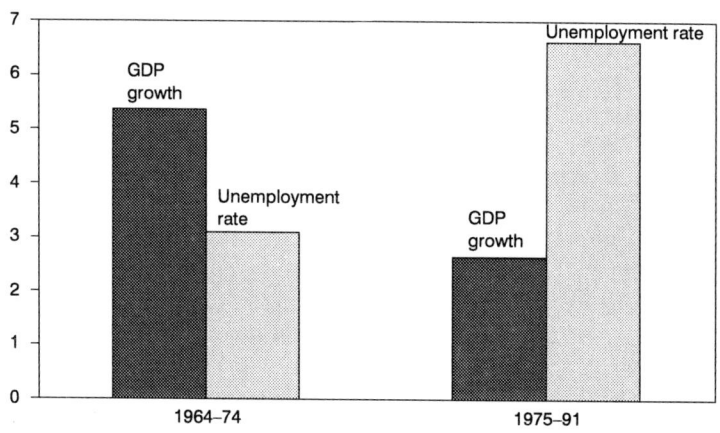

Source: *OECD Main Economic Indicators.*

Figure 4.2 OECD inflation vs. unemployment: 1965–91

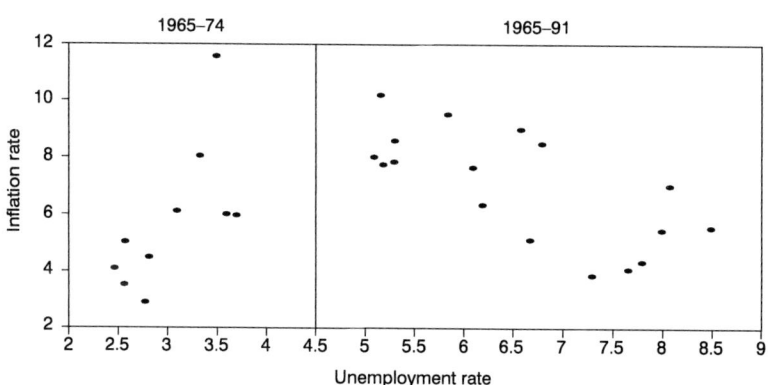

Source: *OECD Main Economic Indicators.*

Indeed, this earlier pattern seems to have reasserted itself in recent times, as unemployment has fallen in countries like the United States with no discernible resurgence of inflation – much to the dismay of proponents of the natural rate hypothesis. By 1995 for instance, the US unemployment rate had fallen to 5.4 per cent, at a time when leading proponents such as Martin Feldstein and Robert Gordon had pegged the natural rate of unemployment – the trigger point of inflationary pressure – to be 6.0 per cent or even 6.5 per cent. Yet by 1997, with the unemployment rate still lower, there is still no evidence of renewed inflation (accelerating or otherwise). Gordon, at least, has responded by successively lowering his estimate of the natural rate as the actual rate fell below it (Bennett 1995).

There is, however, an interesting clue in the empirical relation between inflation and economic growth depicted in Figure 4.3. In the first period from 1965 to 1974 (Figure 4.3a), even if one excludes the 1974 OPEC oil price jump in the upper left quadrant, there appears to be little relation between inflation and growth. If anything, it would suggest that lower growth is associated with *lower* inflation. But in the succeeding period from 1975 to 1991 (Figure 4.3b), lower growth is associated with *higher* inflation. As in the previous case, this behaviour is puzzling from the point of view of conventional theories. We will see that it need not be so in a classical–marxian theory of inflation.

RECONCILING THE EMPIRICAL EVIDENCE: AN ALTERNATIVE APPROACH TO INFLATION

The facts presented above are quite consistent with an alternative approach to inflation and unemployment derived from the classical and marxian traditions. There are three elements to this approach.

The first has to do with the question of short-run equilibrium. Both Keynesian and neoclassical economics tend to analyze actual output and the price level as if they were equilibrium levels associated with the short-run equality of demand and supply. From this point of view, the business cycle is a fluctuation in the short-run equilibrium output itself (Kalecki 1968). But I have argued consistently that the *process* of equalization of aggregate demand and supply is what gives rise to the observed three–five year business (growth) cycle: what we nowadays call 'the' business cycle is the fluctuation in actual (disequilibrium) output as demand and supply

Figure 4.3 OECD inflation vs. growth

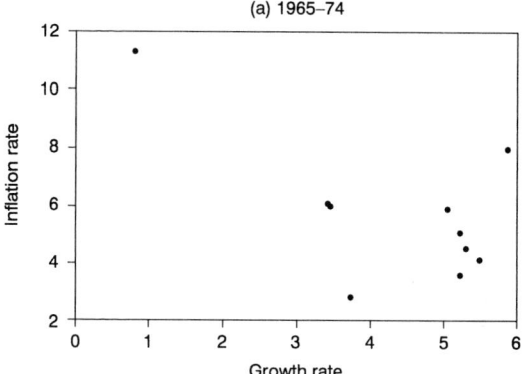

Source: *OECD Main Economic Indicators*.

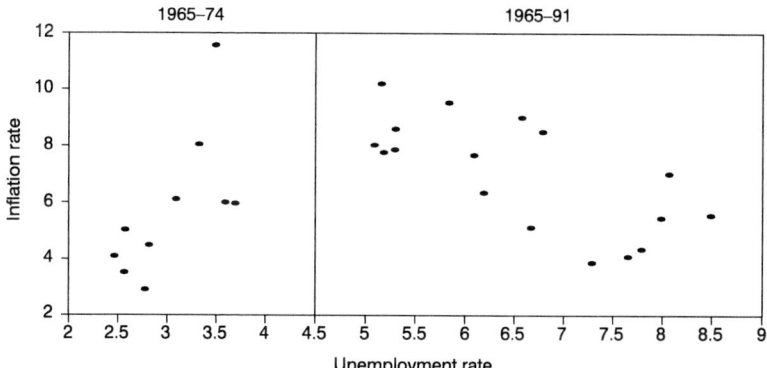

Source: *OECD Main Economic Indicators*.

chase each other around an endogeneously generated growth path. This means that up and down phases of the cycle are associated with phases of positive and negative excess demand, respectively (Shaikh 1989, 1991, 1992).

The second element has to do with money and credit. Deficit spending by any unit – that is, its spending in excess of its current income – can be financed only by running down its assets (borrowing from stocks) and by borrowing from others (Earley, Parsons *et al.* 1976). For the economy as a whole, this boils down to the creation of new loans by private banks and new high-powered money by the central bank. Since neither new credit nor new high-powered money is created to satisfy the demand for money as a liquid asset, this can easily give rise to persistent episodes of aggregate excess demand fuelled by an endogenously generated excess supply of money (Moore 1989, p. 483). Aggregate deficit spending by governments, by the private sector (including households), combined with foreign inflows of purchasing power, can therefore result in persistent pressure on various markets, particularly the commodity market. In an ongoing project, we are developing measures of aggregate excess demand and of the finance behind it, and attempting to demonstrate their relation to growth and inflation in the US economy.

The third element involves the implication of persistent excess demand. Excess demand, which is the excess of a generally growing demand over a growing supply, accelerates the growth in supply. The limits to this process then arise from the limits to the growth in supply. Both neoclassical and Keynesian traditions assume that the availability of *labour* provides the general limit to commodity supply. Therefore they both anticipate that excess demand will stimulate inflation only after practical full employment has been attained. They differ, of course, on what practical 'full employment' means, and whether or not it is the normal state of capitalism, but they share the notion of a trade-off between unemployment and inflation. The trouble with this, as we have seen, is that it requires considerable contortions on their part to explain persistent periods of both rising inflation and rising unemployment.

Neither marxian theory nor capitalist history gives us any reason to suppose that output is limited by the supply of labour. Indeed, within the classical tradition there is a separate *intrinsic* limit to growth. In effect, *even when labour is freely available at the going real wage*, the maximum sustainable rate of capital accumulation within an economy is given by the normal-capacity rate of profit.

Marx was the first to demonstrate that sustained accumulation requires balanced growth, and it is clear from his schemes of expanded reproduction that the maximum sustainable growth rate occurs when all surplus value is reinvested – that is when the rate of growth equals the rate of profit (Marx 1981). One can arrive at a similar result along a Harrodian warranted (that is normal-capacity utilization) path with a (Kaldorian) classical savings function, since there the investment-savings equality $I = S = sc \cdot P$ implies that the warranted rate of accumulation of capital

$$gk^w = I/K = sc \cdot (P/K) = sc \cdot r$$

where sc = the savings propensity of capitalists, P = aggregate (normal capacity) profits, K = the stock of capital, and $r = P/K$ = the normal-capacity rate of profit.

It follows from this that the maximum warranted growth rate occurs when all profits are saved ($sc = 1$). Finally, the celebrated articles by von Neumann and Leontief demonstrate the existence of this same limit in multisectoral models (von Neumann 1945–6; Leontief 1953).[1]

I will call the maximum sustainable growth rate the 'throughput limit' of the economy. Now, suppose that in some period there exists persistent excess demand, along with unemployed labour. Then the excess demand will stimulate (accelerate) the rate of growth of output and of capital and reduce the unemployment rate – as long as the growth rate is not constrained by the throughput limit. *But if for any reason the gap between the actual growth rate and the throughput limit narrows*, there will less and less room for output growth and consequently more and more pressure on prices. The ratio of the actual accumulation rate to the throughput limit (the normal-capacity rate of profit r), which I will call the 'throughput coefficient', is therefore an index of inflationary pressure. Note that the throughput coefficient is simply the ratio of investment to normal-capacity profits, since the capital stock appears in the denominator of both the rate of accumulation (I/K) and the rate of profit (P/K).

The process described above need not come about through a rising growth rate. If the normal-capacity rate of profit were falling, as it has done for most of the post-war period in the United States, then one would expect growth rates of capital (which depend on expected profitability of investment), also to fall. But if the accumulation rate fell more slowly than the profit rate, the throughput coefficient (which is the ratio of the former to the latter) would *rise*. In this way, it becomes possible to understand how *falling profitability can induce both rising unemployment through slowed growth*, and also *increased inflationary pressure via a rise in the throughput coefficient*. I would argue that this precisely why most advanced economies experienced both stagnation and inflation in the 1970s and 1980s – something neoclassicals and Keynesians have had great difficulty in explaining.

To test the relationship between the throughput coefficient and inflation, one needs data on aggregate profits, capital stocks and capacity utilization. In what follows I will use data for the United States alone, because I have consistent series on the necessary variables.[2] It should be noted that the United States is a large part of the OECD as a whole. Figure 4.4 shows that both the US normal-capacity corporate profit rate and the corresponding rate of accumulation (growth rate of capital) fell sharply from the mid-1960s to the early 1980s. Such a fall explains the rise in unemployment rates over this period.

It is in Figure 4.5, which compares the US inflation rate with its throughput coefficient, that we find that the same movements also explain inflation over the period. The key empirical expectation is that the rate of inflation will tend to rise as the economy's accumulation rate approaches its throughput limit – that is, as the throughput coefficient rises. We can put this proposition to a crude empirical test by directly comparing the two. Figure 4.5 depicts the US rate of inflation (in terms of the GDP deflator), and the throughput coefficient defined here as corporate investment in plant and structures relative to total normal-capacity corporate profits. Normal-capacity profits are defined in a similar manner to normal-capacity (potential) output, by dividing actual profits by the level of capacity utilization, the latter being based upon a measure developed in Shaikh (1987).

It is quite striking how closely the inflation rate in the United States mirrors the movements of the throughput coefficient. Looking at Figures 4.4 and 4.5, we see that from 1947 to 1962 the profit rate is high and both the profit rate and the accumulation rate are stable. Therefore in this period the throughput coefficient is low and stable, and so is the inflation rate (and the unemployment rate). Then follows a brief Vietnam War induced profit boom from 1963 to 1965, in which the profit rate rises but the accumulation rate rises even more, so that the throughput coefficient rises substantially

Figure 4.4 US profit rate and accumulation rate (corporate sector, real rates), 1947–95

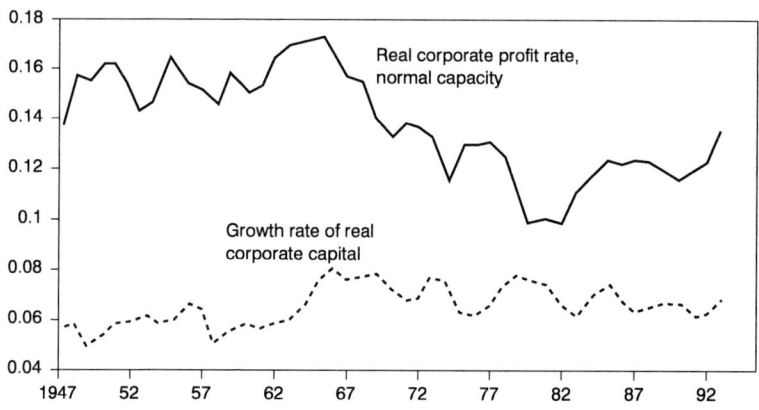

Figure 4.5 US inflation rate vs. throughout coefficient, 1947–95

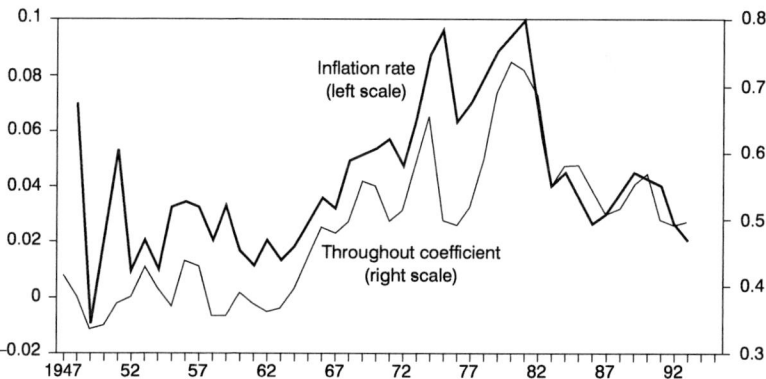

– taking the inflation rate with it. From 1966 to 1982, however, the normal-capacity profit rate declines, and the the rate of accumulation follows suit. But the latter declines less rapidly, so that the throughput coefficient continues to rise, and hence so does the inflation rate. It is only in the last period, from 1983 to 1995, that a rising corporate profit rate manages to outstrip the accumulation rate, thereby sharply reducing the throughput coefficient. And it is precisely in this period that we find that the inflation rate falls just as sharply. On the whole, the throughput coefficient performs extremely well as an indicator of inflationary pressure in the US economy.

SUMMARY AND CONCLUSIONS

Both Keynesian and neoclassical theories expect that inflation will arise only in the vicinity of full employment. They differ among themselves on whether capitalism is normally in a state of full employment. But they share the critical notion that the expansion of supply is limited by the availability of labour, so that the pressure on prices increases as the system approaches full employment. This presumed trade-off between inflation and unemployment has been a central concern of both theory and policy over the post-war period.

But within marxian economics, no such presumption need exist. The concept of an endogenously generated and maintained pool of (involuntarily) unemployed workers is central to this tradition. This implies that the growth in labour supply will not generally provide the limit to the growth of output. And historical evidence certainly bears out the notion that inflation is not necessarily, or even usually, associated with (effective) full employment.

So how does one explain the fact that rising inflation was associated with rising unemployment in the 1970s–1980s, and that falling inflation is associated with unemployment remaining unchanged (in many OECD countries) or even falling (in the United States), in more recent times? I argue that the relevant limit to the growth of the system lies in its normal-capacity rate of profit, because that constitutes the maximum rate of accumulation (growth rate of capital) of the system. The ratio of the actual growth rate of accumulation to the normal profit rate, which I call the throughput coefficient, can therefore be viewed as strain guage for inflationary pressure.

The differential dynamics of the two variables involved provide the key to explaining inflation and its various links to unemployment. The data for the US economy over the postwar period bear this out by showing a strong connection between the throughput coefficient and the inflation rate (Figure 4.5).

Lastly, it is worth mentioning that although labour appears as the basic limit to production in a static framework, as in most accounts of Keynesian and Kaleckian theory, the notion of an intrinsic growth limit is perfectly compatible with dynamic versions of the very same theories. Harrod obviously comes to mind here. There need be no contradiction, therefore, between the ideas set forth here and those of the Keynesian and Kaleckian traditions. Indeed, the throughput coefficient, which is a kind of utilization rate of growth potential, frees us from the contortions involved in trying construct some mechanical trade-off between inflation and unemployment.

Notes

1. The aggregate Harrodian-type relation makes it clear that the same limit would exist even if over time the rate of profit were to change due to technical change and class struggle. Pasinetti, however, argues that in a disaggregated multisectoral model with ongoing technical change and changing demand proportions, the technology-based maximum rate of balanced growth derived by Leontief and von Neumann (1953; 1945–6) is no longer relevant (Pasinetti 1981, pp. 118–23). But while this may be strictly true, in the sense that ongoing differential rates of technical change and demand growth might modify the exact definition of the maximum sustainable growth rate (the throughput rate), it seems equally clear that they cannot abolish the limit itself.
2. Data for Figures 4.4 and 4.5 are from Citibase. Real investment = residential + non-residential investment, in 1987$. Real profits = total domestic corporate profits with IVA and Capital Consumption Adjustment, deflated by the implicit price deflator for investment. Normal capacity profits = real profits divided by capacity utilization. The measure for capacity utilization is derived from Federal Reserve Board survey data on capacity additions and expansion, as explained in Shaikh (1987, Appendix B). It was updated by regressing it on the published Federal Reserve Board series for manufacturing capacity utilization.

References

Artis, M. (1992) 'Macroeconomic Theory', in J. Maloney (ed.), *What's New in Economics?* (Manchester: Manchester University Press), 135–67.

Bennett, A. (1995) 'Inflation Calculus, Business and Academia Clash over a Concept: "Natural" Jobless Rate', *Wall Street Journal* (January 24), A1, A8.

Earley, J.S., R.J. Parsons, *et al.* (1976) 'Money, Credit, and Expenditure: A Sources and Uses of Funds Approach', *The Bulletin*, Center for the Study of Financial Institutions, New York University Graduate School of Business Administration.

Fleming, J.M. (1962) 'Domestic Financial Policies under Fixed and under Floating Exchange Rates'. *IMF Staff Papers*, 9 (November), 209–22.

Friedman, M. (1968) 'The Role of Monetary Policy', *American Economic Review*, 58 (March), 1–17.

Godley, W. and F. Cripps (1983) *Macroeconomics* (New York: Oxford University Press).

Goodwin, R.M. (1967) 'A Growth Cycle', in C.H. Feinstein (ed.), *Socialism, Capitalism and Economic Growth* (London: Cambridge University Press).

Kalecki, M. (1968) *Theory of Economic Dynamics* (New York: Monthly Review Press).

Keynes, J.M. (1936, 1964) *The General Theory of Employment, Interest, and Money* (New York: Harcourt, Brace & World).

Leontief, W. (1953) 'Dynamic Analysis', in W. Leontief *et al.*, *Studies in the Structure of the American Economy* (New York: Oxford University Press).

Marx, K. (1981) *Capital*, Vol. II (New York: Vintage).

Mathews, K. (1992) 'Macroeconomic Policy', in J. Maloney (ed.), *What's New in Economics?* (Manchester: Manchester University Press), 238–84.

Moore, B. (1989) 'On the Endogeneity of Money once more', *Journal of Post-Keynesian Economics*, 11 (Spring), 479–87.

Mundell, R.A. (1963) 'Capital Mobility and Stabilization Policy under Fixed and Flexible Exchange Rates', *Canadian Journal of Economics and Political Science*, 29 (November), 475–88.

Pasinetti, L.L. (1981) *Structural Change and Economic Growth: A Theoretical Essay on the Dynamics of the Wealth of Nations* (Cambridge: Cambridge University Press).

Phelps, E.S. (1967) 'Phillips Curves, Expectations of Inflation and Optimal Unemployment over Time', *Economica*, 34.

Phillips, A.W. (1958) 'The Relation between Unemployment and the Rate of Change in Money Wage Rates in the United Kingdom, 1861–1957', *Economica* (November), 283–99.

Rowthorn, B. (1984) *Capitalism, Conflict and Inflation. Essays in Political Economy* (London: Lawrence & Wishart).

Shaikh, A. (1987) 'The Current Economic Crisis: Causes and Implications', in R. Cherry *et al.* (eds), *The Imperiled Economy* (New York: URPE).

Shaikh, A. (1989) 'Accumulation, Finance, and Effective Demand in Marx, Keynes, and Kalecki', in W. Semmler (ed.), *Financial Dynamics and Business Cycles: New Perspectives* (Armonk: M.E. Sharpe).

Shaikh, A. (1991) 'Wandering around the Warranted Path', in E.J. Nell and W. Semmler (eds), *Nicholas Kaldor and Mainstream Economics* (New York: St. Martin's Press).

Shaikh, A. (1992) 'A Dynamic Approach to the Theory of Effective Demand', in D. Papadimitriou (ed.), *Profits, Deficits, and Instability* (London: Macmillan).

von Neumann, J. (1945–6) 'A Model of General Equilibrium', *Review of Economic Studies,* Vol. 13, 1–9.

Discussion

Thanassis Maniatis and Nikos Petralias

CLASSICAL MARXIAN ECONOMICS

Anwar Shaikh's chapter comes from the classical marxian perspective, a theoretical tradition that is based on Marx's economic analysis. As is well known, the distinguishing feature of the latter is that it concentrates on and emphasizes the inherently antagonistic, anarchic and crisis-prone nature of the capitalist economy. In a similar way classical marxian economics[1] regards the following points as fundamental: (1) the validity of the labour theory of value (and the concept of exploitation as defined by Marx) – namely the argument that prices can be derived theoretically and empirically from labour values; (2) the notion of competition as warfare between capitals, as opposed to the belief in the unlimited power of monopolies that are able to escape the laws of competition in the current era; (3) the endogenous character of growth and technical change in capitalism which gives rise to persistent unemployment; and (4) as a combined result of the previous tendencies, the necessity of the occurrence of economic crisis due to a falling rate of profit. Thus, according to this theoretical school, the structural characteristics of the typical capitalist economy do not allow the development of policy proposals directed at the state that would promote some common national interest which would be beneficial for capital, labour and the 'national economy'. Partly as a result of this feature, classical marxian economics usually remains analytically at a relatively high level of abstraction. This is therefore a welcome contribution, since it tries to deal with an issue (inflation and unemployment), that is not usually addressed by this theoretical tradition.

UNEMPLOYMENT AND INFLATION

It is well known that the Phillips curve implies the existence of a trade-off between unemployment and inflation. Those two variables are expected to move in an opposite direction on theoretical and empirical grounds. This implies that inflation will arise only when the economy is close enough to the point of full employment. Furthermore, since the actual inflation rate may also depend on inflationary expectations, it is usually necessary (unless expectations are perfectly rational), for the economy to go through a serious recession ('sacrificing' output), or to suffer an adverse supply shock, in order for inflationary expectations to come down. Shaikh attempts to break this causal link between (low) unemployment and inflation.

Shaikh presents three general empirical observations for the OECD economies during the post-war period. First, higher unemployment is associated with lower growth rates, which can be attributed to the fall in the rate of profit. Secondly, there is no general historical trade-off between unemployment and inflation. During the 1965–74 period this relationship was positive while in 1975–91 it was negative. Thirdly, at least for the 1975–91 period, lower growth has been associated with higher inflation.

Those empirical facts that neoclassical and Keynesian theories had problems coping with can be explained by a classical marxian theory of inflation. Since in marxian theory the 'reserve army of labour' is present even in periods of high growth, supply is not inhibited by the availability of labour, as in neoclassical and Keynesian traditions. Thus, the crucial point is that in marxian theory it is not the availability of labour, but the normal rate of profit that is the limit to supply. The maximum sustainable growth rate, which Shaikh calls the 'throughput limit', is r_n and the 'throughput coefficient' is defined as

$$tc = \frac{g}{r_n} = \frac{\frac{I}{K}}{\frac{P_n}{K}} = \frac{I}{P_n}$$

where g is the actual rate of capital accumulation. This expression can be used as an index of inflationary pressure as the fraction increases and especially when it assumes values close to one. Since the throughput coefficient can increase when both g and r are rising, but also when both are falling at different rates, we can have a situation where

$$r \downarrow \rightarrow g \downarrow \rightarrow U \uparrow$$

where U = unemployment, and at the same time if the decrease in g is smaller than the decrease in r, tc increases, resulting in an increase in the inflation rate. Shaikh argues that this is what actually happened with the stagflationary experience of the 1970s and the 1980s. Furthermore, in Figure 4.5 (p. 101) it is shown that the throughput coefficient performs extremely well as a predictor of inflationary pressure in the post-war US economy.

THE 'THROUGHPUT COEFFICIENT' AND INFLATION RATES IN THE GREEK ECONOMY

How well does this theory perform in the case of the post-war Greek economy?

We should note first that as we can observe in Table D4.1 and Figures D4.1 and D4.2, the three empirical findings reported above for the OECD as a whole, characterize the Greek economy as well.

Table D4.1 Output, unemployment and inflation in the Greek economy, 1960–94

Year	Unemployment rate	inflation rate	GDP growth rate
1960–73	4.6	4.5	7.7
1974–9	1.9	15.5	3.7
1980–9	6.6	18.1	1.8
1990–4	8.5	15.6	0.7

Source: OECD (1996).

First, higher unemployment is associated not with (falling) inflation but with lower growth (owing to a falling rate of profit for most of the post-war period). Secondly unemployment and inflation have been rising together after 1980; there is no historical trade-off between the two. Third, lower growth has been associated with higher inflation after the high growth period of 1960–73. It should be added that the fall in inflation after 1994 has been associated with a moderate increase in growth and not so much with a further increase in unemployment, which has remained more or less stable.

In order to test the ability of the measure proposed by Shaikh to explain inflationary movements, we construct the 'throughput

Figure D4.1 GDP growth and unemployment, 1960–94

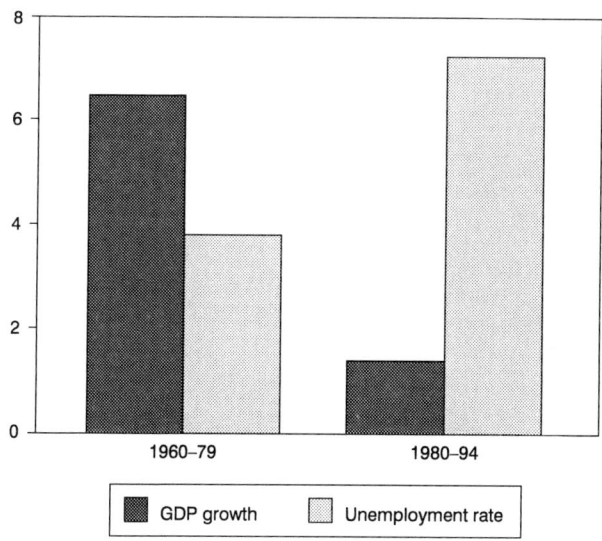

Figure D4.2 GDP growth, unemployment and inflation, 1960–94

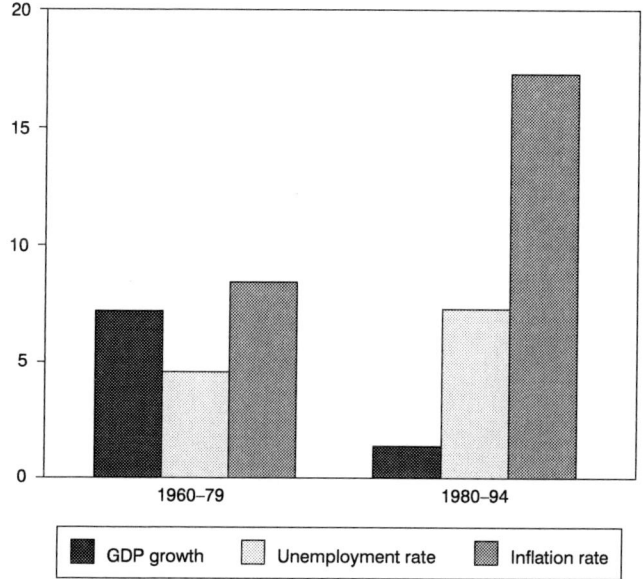

Figure D4.3 Greek inflation rate and throughput coefficient, 1959–94

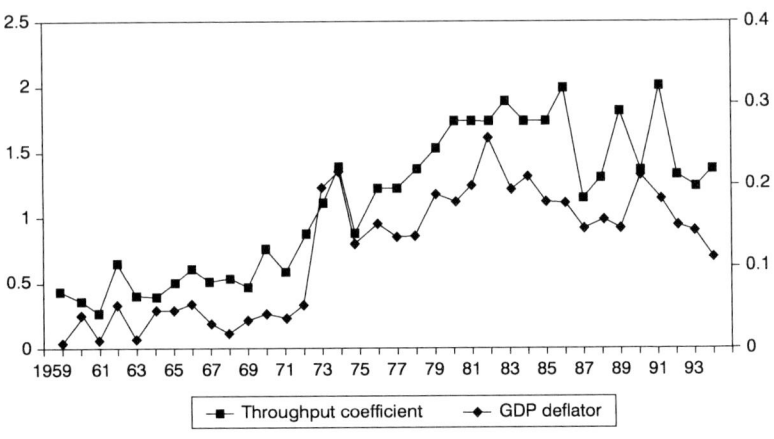

Figure D4.4 Greek inflation rate and throughput coefficient[a], 1959–94

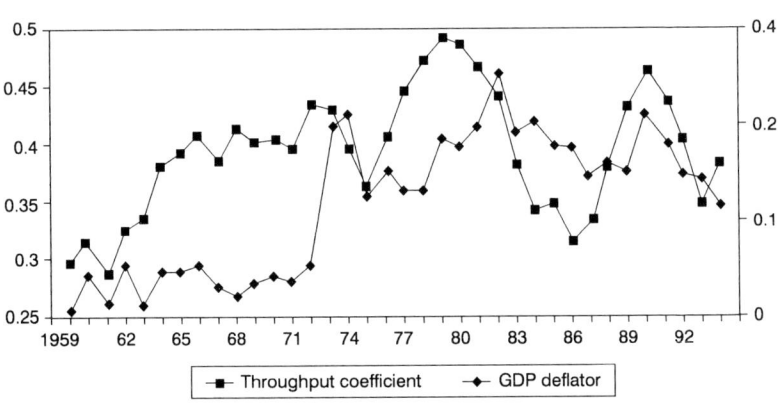

Source: OECD Main Economic Indicators.

Note:
[a] private net investment (excluding dwellings)

coefficient' for the Greek economy which, as noted above, can be approximated by the ratio of investment to normal profits.[2] We use two different measures for the numerator of the actual rate of accumulation, namely investment. The first is the difference in the non-agricultural, non-dwellings capital stock from that of the previous year (including public infrastructural investment); and the second is net investment of the private sector excluding dwellings. Since the first measure includes public investment, a significant share of total investment – especially in the early post-war period, it reflects more accurately the pressure on available resources (savings). Figure D4.3 is based on the first measure of investment while Figure D4.4 is based on the second.

As Figures D4.3 and D4.4 indicate, the behaviour of the throughput coefficient in relation to the inflation rate is very similar to that observed for the US economy in Shaikh's chapter, despite some data deficiencies[3] in the Greek case. Those deficiencies may account for the fact that, whereas the US throughput coefficient predicts accurately even the very short-term (year-to-year) movements of the inflation rate, the Greek measure performs satisfactorily as an index of inflationary movements over longer periods of time (approximately three–five years).

In summary, it could be argued that this is a very fruitful approach in the direction of explaining inflationary patterns, based on a non-neoclassical theoretical framework. This means that it is not 'high' employment and/or wages, subjective expectations of any kind or unexplained supply shocks that determine inflation; instead it is the approach of the real growth limit, as defined by the productive capabilities of the system (and not the availability of labour) that fuels inflation.

Notes

1. See Shaikh (1994) for a presentation of the analytical structure of classical marxian economics.
2. The measure of the mass of profits used is total after-tax profits and they are derived from Maniatis, Tsaliki and Tsoulfidis (1998).
3. There are no reliable and consistent measures of capacity utilization for the Greek economy. The measure of profits used in the calculation of the throughput coefficient is thus actual profits instead of normal profits.

References

Maniatis, T., P. Tsaliki and L. Tsoulfidis (1998) *Issues of Political Economy: The Case of Greece* (Athens: Sakis Karageorgas Foundation) (in Greek).

OECD (1996) *Historical Statistics, 1960–1994* (Paris: OECD).

Shaikh, A. (1994) 'The Analytical Structure of Classical Marxian Economics', paper presented at the 1994 ASSA Conference (Boston).

5 Revisioning Socialism: The Cherry Esplanade Conjecture*

David Laibman

SETTING THE STAGE

The monumental transition of 1989–91, in which authoritarian regimes based in revolutionary working-class movements lost state power in large parts of the world, has given rise to a new interest in reexamining the idea of socialism itself. It has given us the opportunity to pose fundamental questions in a fresh manner, and to rework the challenge to capitalism based in the Marxist tradition (which remains, I think, the only coherent alternative to free market conservatism and neoliberalism).

With few exceptions, however, this renaissance has not drawn upon the actual experiences of socialist construction in the twentieth century. These experiences – especially that of the Soviet Union from the mid-1930s to its demise – gave rise to an enormous body of theory and evidence concerning different forms of state property, the relation of socialist structures to markets and money, concepts and methods of planning, the organization of popular participation in management, the special characteristics of incentives and prices in socialist conditions, and much more. Much of the left in the Western capitalist countries knows little of all this, having bought into the wholesale rejection of the Soviet 'model' (and having unconsciously absorbed not a small dose of anticommunist ideology in the process).

The post-Soviet literature on socialism partakes of two broad conceptions: (1) a revived 'market socialism', in which the instrumentality of 'the market' is associated with public ownership of enterprises (for example, Roemer 1994; Roosevelt and Belkin 1994; Schweickart, 1996; Wright 1996); (2) communitarian and/or neo-anarchist positions, which stress cooperation among production and consumption sites, non-authoritarian (and non-hierarchical) planning and (in some cases) a return to the imagery of the original pithy formulations found in Marx's works (Devine 1988; Albert and Hahnel 1991; Ollman 1996).

In recent publications, I have attempted to chart a different course, one that acknowledges and builds on the positive as well as the negative elements in the Soviet and East European experience (Laibman 1992, 1995). The model emerging from these studies projects a system of 'comprehensive planning', with a critical core of central planning; an iterative procedure linking central plans to continuous planning at the micro, or decentral, level; systematic democratic controls at *both* levels; and complementary but subsidiary forms of market relations, whose social content is progressively transformed as the democratically planned core of the society matures and develops.

I have also tried to pose some basic questions concerning the foundation conceptions and goals of socialism. In particular, I suggest that the *problem of democracy* in the socialist context is the need to coordinate and effectuate the diverse wills of highly educated and individuated citizens, in the performance of labour and allocation of goods. This requires what (for want of a better term) I call 'consensualization': coordination of conscious activities based on a shared, mutually created and accepted understanding of the main lines of social and economic activity. Consensualization is brought about in socialism through the planning process, which involves constant and systematic participation of the members of society – in a word, economic democracy. Consensualization, in fact, emerges as the *primary* role of planning; the physical coordination of production and distribution, commonly regarded as its main objective, occupies a secondary position.[1] Democratic planning, then, is the practical embodiment of the mastery of people over things, of the de-alienating control by workers over the means of production, of the conscious and cooperative social existence posited, but not operationalized, in the classical formulations of Marxism (for example, Marx 1933; Engels 1966). I now think that this conception, while suggestive, is still too closely linked to older ways of thinking – especially to the 'plan vs. market' dichotomy. In this chapter, I want to offer some tentative approaches toward reconceptualization.

The initiating premise is to reconsider the relation between the 'utopian' and 'scientific' dimensions in socialist thought, by allowing

– in the present context of disarray and revisioning on the left – full play for creative speculation and bold conjecture. This sort of activity, far from lapsing into *idealist* utopianism, has a material base in all of the experiences of the past century; if according to the materialist premise ideas derive ultimately from social experience, conjecture necessarily draws upon that reality for its raw material. What may appear as arbitrary speculation must emerge from real history and can, if fruitful, be integrated into a truly imaginative science of human emancipation. In this interpretation, the advance from utopia to science in socialism (see Engels 1966; Maler 1998), does not replace the utopian dimension; rather, it incorporates it. What we need now, above all, is bold thinking about the core elements in the socialist vision.

The main current in the market socialism discussion has come from the camp of 'Analytical Marxism,' where there is a pronounced tendency to confuse rigour with precision in thought. Thus, Roemer (1994) asks: 'what do socialists want?' The answers, in the collection edited by Wright (1996), range from 'equality' to 'democracy'. The underlying paradigm is thoroughly instrumental. It is a matter of constrained optimization: we determine what we 'want' (our objective function), and then seek means, in the form of ingenious institutional arrangements, to achieve our goals (to the extent possible). There is something of the same instrumental constriction of vision also in the common way of posing the problem of socialism in broader circles: 'Is it feasible?' 'Is it desirable?'

Suppose we say, instead, that socialism is the embodiment in theory and practice of the most fundamental and non-arbitrary moral commitment possible: affirmation of the overriding value of human life and potential. Socialism, then, is about creating the best possible conditions for human development, along two dimensions: the effective (quality of action upon the external environment), and the experiential (the way life impacts upon consciousness). The two dimensions, in fact, define the space of human growth: the objective advance in mastery and understanding of the world, embodied in what is usually narrowly called 'productivity'; and subjective progress in the way people experience their life activity. This latter may involve (an incomplete list): creativity; fulfilment in work and personal relations; 'rational understanding' of social and technological processes (in Karl Mannheim's sense of grasping the inner forces at work; compare 'functional understanding'); connectedness to other people, and sharing with others (including the exquisite satisfaction of teaching and guiding the young); personal growth. Against this canvas – which I think is absolutely central to a thoroughgoing socialist revisioning – the problematic of 'desires' for and 'feasibility' of equality and/or democracy seems narrow indeed. Before using this perspective to frame a quest for ingredients in a renewed socialist vision, I make one observation about the quality of the first-wave socialist societies of recent experience. The notorious H.L. Mencken uttered his famous wisecrack: 'The trouble with socialism is: not enough free evenings.' This hurt – just as did the comment by (far less notorious!) Nancy Folbre (in Z Magazine) on the Albert–Hahnel horizontal planning conception: 'Like one long University of Massachusetts student government meeting.' Socialists know this from experience. In 1994, in Havana, I heard a paper delivered by a Cuban economist, entitled 'The Objective Insufficiency of Cuban Economic Relations'. This was in part a retelling of the several rectification campaigns that have been launched in Cuba in recent decades. There is nothing wrong with rectification, of course, but one must eventually wonder why such massive political effort must be devoted to getting socialism (back) on track: why some sort of *self-rectification* – an internal corrective mechanism – does not develop. Cuban socialism appears to be like a *guagua* (a small bus, in Cuban Spanish) without a steering wheel. It goes forward, but inevitably veers to the side of the road into a ditch; the passengers must then get off the bus and physically heave it back onto the road, so that the next stretch of the journey can commence. The general question is: what is there in the nature of socialism that appears to require both continuing and periodically massive political interventions for its functioning? After all, it is all of that political work that eats into poor Mencken's free evenings.[2]

INGREDIENTS

To frame the inquiry, I start with some concepts from the theory of capitalist crisis, focusing on one site within capitalism: the workplace.

In attempting to theorize one aspect of crisis at this site (Laibman 1997, Chapter 11), I distinguish between incentive and control as two problems faced by capitalists at the point of production. These are the positive and negative aspects, respectively, of the need to reproduce and maintain capitalist domination. They are both affected by the degree to which creative and managerial functions are devolved to lower and broader layers of the workforce. I propose to measure this quality (imprecisely, but possibly rigorously) by a variable called the *devolution ratio*.

The devolution ratio has an upper limit, above or at which capitalist control over the work process as such is threatened; this is the *control ceiling*. There is, correspondingly, a lower limit, at or below which incentive is compromised (here is a link to the efficiency wage theory of present-day labour economics); this is the *incentive floor*. The ceiling and the floor together define the space within which the strategic choice of a position of the devolution ratio can be made by capitalists.

I further hypothesize that the ceiling falls as the real wage rate rises, and that the floor rises as the real wage rate rises. Upward pressure on the real wage rate, then, pushes the capitalist workplace in the direction of an increasingly severe contradiction: the space for the choice of a devolution ratio progressively narrows, until a (theoretical) point is reached at which a unique position of that ratio forces an encounter with ceiling and floor simultaneously. This defines a critical, historically high, level of the real wage rate that calls the antagonistic relations of the capitalist workplace into question. The historical materialist insight at work here is the link between levels of productive development on the one hand, and possible and necessary forms of social organization on the other. Within one broad range of levels, the capitalist forms of incentive and control – involving the social irresponsibility of markets in labour power, fear of unemployment and destitution and the reification and mystification of the power accruing to property ownership – are efficacious for productive development. At the upper end of that range, however, we discover, in the form of a critical high level of the real wage, a secular crisis of those forms, suggesting a need for their transcendence.

Now let us presuppose that transcendence. We have an inherited general level of productivity, or efficiency, X, achieved by means of antagonistic capitalist incentive and control systems, now requiring replacement. The 'devolution' concept is now no longer appropriate. Indeed, the distinction between incentive and control itself withers away, as control is vested in workers and their organizations themselves: this is the world-historic reversal of the subsumption of labour to means of production that defines the onset of the socialist era.[3] The twin features of incentive and control merge into the single concept of *motivation*. Motivation is governed by the power of workers over their own lives, their rational understanding, the effectiveness and democracy of their forms of organization and their autonomy – in the crucial double sense of absence of determination from outside *and* presence of inner capacities to act. It therefore appears as the central feature of the labour process reflecting the subjective dimension defined above. We may give this dimension the label Q, from *q*uality of socialist work–life experience.[4] (The objective dimension is captured in X, which must be a *broad* measure of productivity, including effects on living communities, the environment, and so on.)

The relation between the two dimensions – subjective and objective, inner and outer – will be the focus of our ingredients list. There will evidently be two principles of determination, each running in one of the possible directions, from Q to X, and from X to Q.

The π curve

This is the $Q => X$ link. Reflecting the motivation qualities of the capitalist precursor period, represented by the vertical intercept of the π curve in Figure 5.1, increasing levels of Q are associated with *decreasing* levels of X; hence, the inverse shape of the curve. At this stage, this is to say, we posit, with hard-headed realism, the existence of an inverse trade-off between two broad socialist goals: increasing productivity (X) and increasing workers' fulfilment–democracy–equality–autonomy (in short, and hereafter, Q). 'Productivist' goals and strategies therefore involve some sacrifice of social objectives, and we are deep into the Leninist problematic: one can hear strains of 'catching up and overtaking', the need for 'one-man management', and so on, in the background of this conception.[5]

The fact that the curve slopes downward from its X intercept suggests a socialism taking over from *developed* capitalism; no consideration is given here to the motivation effects of productivity levels that are low in comparison not only to the same country's recent past but also to the even higher levels of advanced capitalist countries elsewhere.

The classic issue of material and moral incentives, and the cross-cutting distinction between individual and collective incentives, is embedded here. A materialist approach to this problem begins by acknowledging that material and individual incentives *exist* objectively; it is then not a matter of a policy choice between the two

Figure 5.1 The π curve

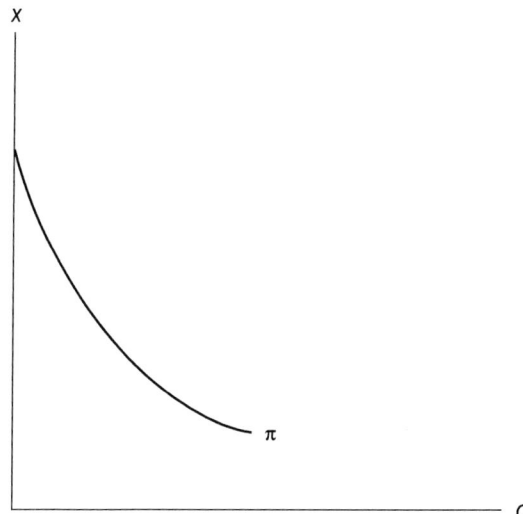

terms — material vs. moral, individual vs. collective — but of finding ways to combine and unite them that open up the widest possibilities for advance in socialist consciousness. The π curve slopes downward, not necessarily only because an increase in Q leads to deterioration of discipline and effort; it may slope downward also because of the difficulty of finding a structure of incentives, rewards and evaluations that is simultaneously Q- and X-increasing.

The δ curve

To capture the opposite relation, with X in the position of independent variable, $X \Rightarrow Q$, we observe that, in socialist conditions, the level of productivity is the essential basis of the working-class standard of living. (The wage share represents a subsidiary division of that standard between individual and collective forms of consumption, and between present and future.) A higher X, therefore, means a greater amount of resources available to enhance the quality of life in the broadest sense, including education, job enrichment, cultural opportunities, and so forth. Within any given period, the relation is positive, as drawn in Figure 5.2. This determination from X to Q is not (to put it mildly!) automatic: the use of higher levels

Figure 5.2 The δ curve

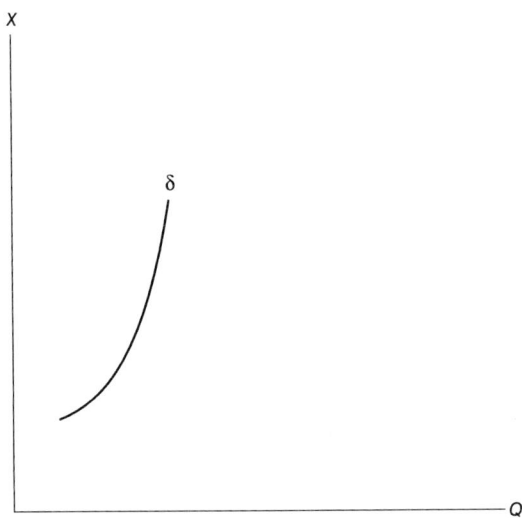

of productivity to improve the quality of work–life is a major area of struggle and political concern. Improvement is certainly not *guaranteed* by a simple rise in the material standard of living.

To the extent that the possible higher levels of Q afforded by higher levels of X are actually brought into existence, the δ curve determines a set of possible combinations of X and Q within a given, fairly short, period. To capture the fact that the use of higher levels of productivity to increase Q is a matter of intense and problematic social development, and presumably limited in any given short period, the curve is drawn rising at an increasing rate – that is, showing rapidly diminishing returns to increases in X.

The two curves, π and δ, are brought together in Figure 5.3. The point *a* represents a combination of levels of productivity and autonomy satisfying both relations at once, and therefore consistent both with the achieved degree of motivation (as defined above), and the available resources that can be devoted to sustaining a given quality of working-class life. Given the causal links between Q and X associated with both curves, we can trace a path of development, invoking the classic 'cobweb' theorem, showing progressive convergence to *a* over time. Convergence is assured by the sharp diminishing returns determining the steepness of δ.[6]

Figure 5.3 Early socialist equilibrium

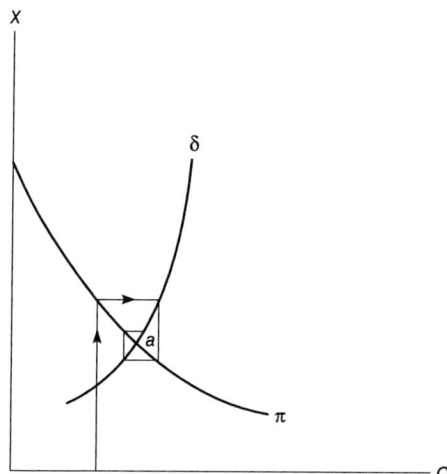

The point *a* thus represents a given level of possibility for a socialist society. The productivity level is below the intercept level inherited from the capitalist precursor. The static position at *a* thus serves as the basis for the endless litany of allegations in pro-capitalist journalism and scholarship – which undoubtedly has a strong anecdotal base – concerning the 'inefficiency' of socialism. The π curve, in fact, is a version of the famed efficiency–equity trade-off, which is a staple of the neoclassical (and Neoliberal) ideological diet, but which has, in fact, a very slim basis in theory (however one reads the empirical evidence). It shows clearly that to achieve specifically socialist goals (that is, to increase Q), a price will have to be paid in terms of falling productivity, which may indeed endanger the entire enterprise.

One further hypothesis rounds out our list of ingredients. The π curve may be thought of as essentially stable over time (barring an assumption of increasing ecological pressure, according to which it could shift downward!). By contrast, the δ curve is subject to advances in consciousness, which make it possible to achieve higher levels of Q at *given* levels of X. In fact, successful socialist education and political work should make it possible to develop higher qualities of job enrichment, participation, continuing education, and so on, at any established degree of productive development. This would amount to shifting the δ curve to the right, and presumably would require high levels of political mobilization. The result, in the environment framed by the curves as currently drawn, would be a higher quality of work life (and social life in general), at a cost of *lower* levels of productivity. And, as indicated, this would require political mobilization of a high order. Indeed, the pull of those higher levels of productivity originally inherited from capitalism may be such that political mobilization and appeals to moral incentives are required just to hold Q at the achieved level. Figure 5.3 therefore illustrates the characterization of socialism as (relatively) inefficient, and excessively political (the 'no-free-evenings' syndrome).

THE CONJECTURE

In one of those prescient passages for which they are justly famous, Marx and Engels wrote:

> in the beginning this ['increas(ing) the total of productive forces' after raising 'the proletariat to the position of ruling class'] cannot be effected except by means of despotic inroads on the rights of property and on the conditions of bourgeois production; by means of measures, therefore, *which appear economically insufficient and untenable* but which, in the course of the movement, *outstrip themselves*, necessitate further inroads upon the old social order, and are unavoidable as a means of entirely revolutionizing the mode of production. (Marx and Engels 1971, 111, emphasis added)

This passage anticipates, I think, the further explorations of the shape of the π curve, to which I give the name 'The Cherry Esplanade Conjecture'.[7]

The 'economically insufficient and untenable' measures are, of course, the massive political efforts required to shift the δ curve to the right, and thus move *down* along the π curve (see Figure 5.4). The conjecture is that production eventually comes to depend on a motivation structure of a new type, so that productivity gains increasingly *depend* on higher levels of Q. *The curve therefore becomes flatter, eventually bottoms out* (at point *b*), *and then rises*, reflecting the new dependence of productivity increase on an advanced quality of work and social life.

Figure 5.4 The Cherry Esplanade Conjecture

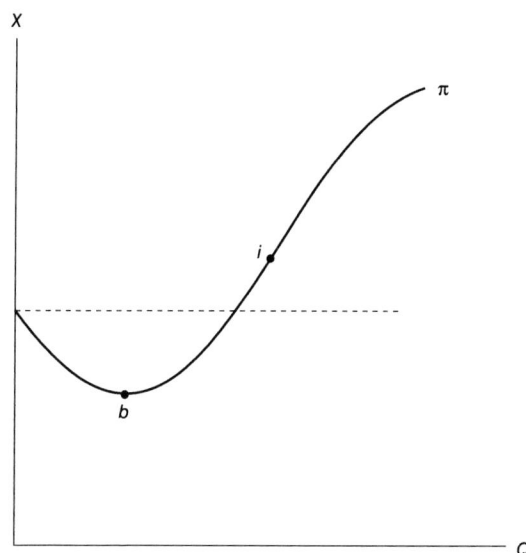

The point of inflexion, i, reflects the eventual onset of diminishing returns to this new relation between Q and X, as does the flattening out of the curve at the right end. Notice how productivity increases eventually 'outstrip themselves': having fallen below inherited levels originally, productivity now can rise far above those levels (the dashed horizontal line in Figure 5.4).

The conjectured shape of π represents, of course, a central historical materialist postulate. There is a moment at which all prior growth in the productive forces has brought humanity to a crucial position: further growth is not possible under the pre-existing antagonistic systems of incentive, control, coercion and domination (or is possible only in a cramped and distorted form, and associated with ever-present crisis). The rise in Q beyond existing historical levels signals a shift to new, more principled forms of motivation and consciousness, which – and this is the crucial postulate – are indispensable for the *further* development of the productive forces. Production has come to require levels of democracy, equality, autonomy, intellectual functioning and moral and social responsibility such that new qualities of creativity and principle must necessarily be vested in each individual worker, and in the various collective structures in which she participates, if production is to

Figure 5.5 Stages of socialist development

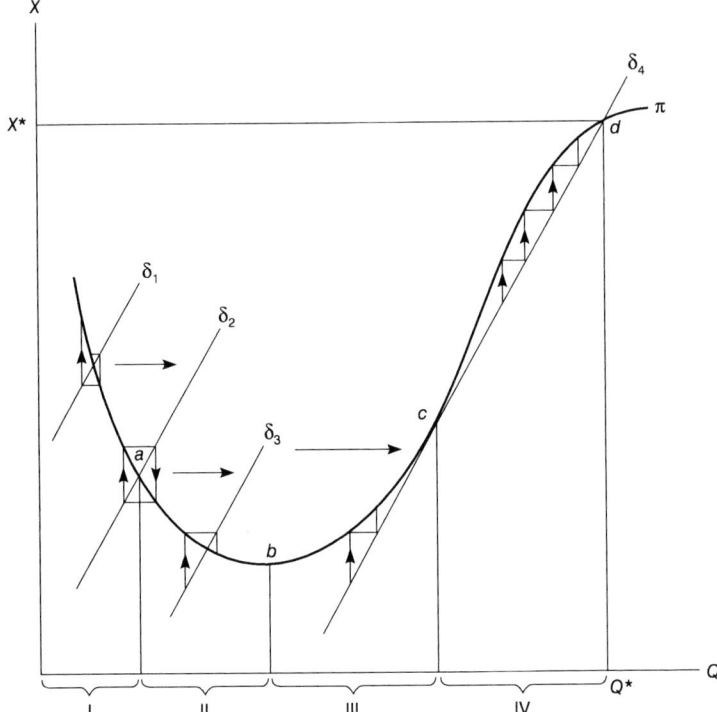

be both efficient and dynamic. (It need hardly be mentioned that even to pose this transition, the private accumulation and exploitation characteristic of capitalism, as well as the authoritarian and bureaucratic distortions of many recent socialist experiences, must have been long transcended.)

To grasp the implications of this new, fully formed π curve, refer to Figure 5.5. A series of δ curves is drawn; these are linearized, for simplicity.

We begin toward the left, in the downward-sloping region of π, with δ curves δ_1, δ_2, and δ_3. This of course is 'primitive' or 'early' socialism: the falling π curve is the familiar inverse trade-off between socially progressive measures and productivity, akin to the inevitable constraint portrayed by the Neoliberal naysayers as a fundamental Law of Nature. The three situations depicted differ, however, in their stability properties. The curve δ_2 is drawn for a case in which deviations of Q and X from a result in a stable limit cycle, as shown. In the even 'earlier' situation represented by δ_1, at which the motivation structure is very preliminary and any attempt to improve the autonomy and power of the workforce results in a drastic fall in productivity, the cycle around the consistent point is unstable; political effort is therefore needed to stabilize the central process, as well as to shift the δ curve to the right. By contrast, the cyclical process around π and δ_3, representing a more developed stage of early socialism, is stable and damped. Point a, therefore, qualifies as a strategic marker between stages I and II, as identified along the horizontal axis: having progressed beyond a, the socialist structure is stable, and attention can be focused on the further shift in δ.[8]

Point b is clearly highly significant; it signals the end of the inverse trade-off, so inexorable and eternal in the minds of the paleoliberals, and the beginning of a crucial new historical stage, in which further advances in Q are not only consistent with productivity increase, but necessary for such increase. Point b therefore marks the terminus of stage II and the onset of stage III. Between b and c, however, the dynamic stability property holds at any point. Convergence to c from below is illustrated in Figure 5.5. In the interval between b and c, each point is similarly stable, with convergence from above or below (not drawn in Figure 5.5) instead of the cobweb pattern associated with the falling region of π. But, crucially, in stage III experience gradually establishes consciousness of a positive relation between work–life quality and productivity, greatly easing the task of shifting δ to the right.

The final turning point, defining the upper limit of stage III and the onset of stage IV, is reached when $\delta = \delta_4$, at point c. As the support lines indicate, that point is stable from below, but *unstable from above*, and this is a momentous instability! The *spontaneous* movement – after one final political push, to displace Q upward – is *away* from c in the direction of d, a point of singularly high (and outstripping) levels of both autonomy and productivity, Q^* and X^*. Point c is therefore a crucial watershed in socialist evolution: it signals the onset of the possibility of self-sustaining development in both the objective and subjective dimensions of human welfare, *without the massive political mobilization effort that was required before.* At point c, we may say, the *guagua* acquires its steering wheel; the spontaneously emerging micro-activity of workers now serves as its own guarantee of stability and progress, without continuous political intervention (which, as noted, is a limitation of early socialism, even when the intervention in question is highly democratic). A foundation is laid in working-class experience that validates principled behaviour as also self-interested behaviour; put another way, space is opened for autonomous, even spontaneous, activity of individuals (and, of course, of teams and collectives as well) that is not atomizing, alienating, or polarizing.[9]

Point d represents a high and self-sustaining level of both productivity and work–life quality.[10] It also marks levels of these social goods that are clearly unattainable by capitalism. With measured political activity, either or both curves (π and δ_4) might be shifted so as to move d further upward and/or to the right. This is not necessary, however, and the construction suggests that socialist evolution may arrive at a high but stable terminus. Progress, of course, continues in a qualitative sense; it is not a matter of stasis, only of an end to *systematic* expansion in productivity; perhaps even in absolute levels of output, if population stabilizes. The implications for ecological constraints are clear: the entire construction could well come to grief if a horizontal barrier representing an upper limit to productivity expansion were drawn in! Prospects for 'solar communism', however, seem eminently reasonable in a conception that does not require unending advance in productivity applied in production (as distinct from continuously expanding knowledge and widening of the range of human possibilities) (see Lovejoy 1996; Schwartzman 1996).

The Cherry Esplanade Conjecture is, at this stage, just that: an unproved hypothesis. Future work might well focus on research concerning the underlying determinants of the shape of the π curve, both in theory and with regard to data from all known experiences of socialist construction – and, indeed, of struggle for transforming social relations within capitalism. The crucial issue, of course, is the existence and location of the turning point b. It is quite likely that the curve is path-dependent – that is, that the position of b may depend, at least in part, on the course of the struggle to attain it. But *if b* exists – or if some such point can be created through socialist mobilization and development – then there also exist powerful forces in today's world that do *not* want us to find it!

This section may be concluded with a final comment on the stadial (stage-theoretic) properties of the conjecture. The model discovers four stages in post-capitalist evolution (not the usual two or three). The stages are defined analytically: that is, their beginning and end points (a, b, c, and d) are not mere postulates of convenience, or arbitrary readings of clusters of empirical events. (This is quite a different matter from the question whether we know, or even can know, precisely where they are located.) Point a is defined by the stable limit cycle; b by the bottoming-out of the π curve; c by the tangency of π and δ; and d by the intersection of the *same* δ curve (δ_4) and π, representing the high-level equilibrium of mature socialism evolving toward full communism. Theories that posit stages of development (regimes of accumulation/modes of regulation; social structures of accumulation) without a basis in theory usually lose the insight afforded by periodization: the nature of the immanent tendency for transition from one stage to another and consequently the directionality of the process as a whole.

WIDER PERSPECTIVES

What, if anything, does the Cherry Esplanade Conjecture tell us about the wider issues in the contemporary socialism debate?

Its central implication is that there is no reason why mature socialism should not provide us with *more* free evenings than capitalism does! In their (implicit) preoccupation with stages I and II, socialists have tacitly accepted an insidious premise of Neoliberal thinking: the idea that 'capitalism' promotes the private, non-political existence of individuals in civil society, while socialism entails constant public–political interference, bureaucratism, and so on. We often say, or imply, that the political life is a *good* and rewarding life; we speak of 'politics in command', and so forth.[11] 'The Cherry Esplanade Conjecture', however, suggests that the highly political character of socialism may be a characteristic of its early stages of development, but not of its later ones.

One of the great silences in the Soviet economic reforms, beginning in the 1960s, concerned the question of horizontal ties among enterprises. Through all of the metamorphoses of the system of planning and management, this possibility was never seriously investigated – a sign of the dead weight of the authoritarian legacy. Enterprises were legally entitled to initiate most plan details, including desired contracts with suppliers and customers; these, however, had to be approved through a vertical process of communication, never directly with the principals concerned.

I have suggested (Laibman 1992) that horizontal ties among state enterprises, taking place in conditions of overall price and financial planning, with full disclosure and visibility and subject to qualitative evaluation for the purpose of assigning bonuses for plan fulfilment, would represent a new, higher form of a socialist market or commodity relation. I now wonder whether this process can be better characterized as a *convergence* of market and plan, in the context of the high levels of socialist consciousness and functioning represented by stages III and IV in the conjecture model. In a sense, *both* market *and* plan are transcended, in a regime with a large amount of individual autonomy and creativity. Along with the communitarian or traditional critics of 'market socialism', one must, I think, reject the 'market socialist' notion of socialism as equality in private property ownership (enforced by means of vouchers, or a related gimmick) plus regulation by means of *atomistic* markets, *given the levels of social consciousness and motivation inherited from capitalism*. But in the advanced stages under consideration here, the centrifugal and polarizing aspects of such market relations are absent; autonomous horizontal activity cannot generate unprincipled, self-interested behaviour, manipulation, accumulation, and so on. Socialist autonomy is not 'market' behaviour in any sense consistent with capitalist horizons. It is also not 'planned' activity, in the sense that prior confirmation from higher bodies is necessary.[12] I envision, as an inherent component of a modern socialism, a system of ongoing cybernetic macrocoordination (see Cockshott and Cottrell 1997), perhaps better called 'programming' than 'planning'. High levels of participation, visibility at all levels and a critical political culture are vital in this programming–planning system, if it is to serve as the means of consensualization – especially concerning the price and income constraints (income differentials) within which individuals make production and consumption decisions. But whatever it is called, in stages III and IV it embodies autonomous but principled activity, and it transcends the conventional plan–market dichotomy; this dichotomy, even when stripped of its binary oppositional simplicity, appears increasingly inadequate to convey the complexity of the process of social interaction and growth being described.

This chapter, as its title makes clear, is a conjecture; 'for purposes of discussion', as a footnote on the first page of non-sanctioned articles in Soviet journals used to say. It does not try to address many monumental problems for socialism, especially those involving bureaucratic organization and power. My hope is that it will help steer the global conversation about alternatives to Neoliberal capitalism into more fruitful channels – at least concerning some aspects of this massive and vital subject. I believe the tools are available now to begin to envision a socialism that is both technically sophisticated and 'inspirational'; that transcends narrow conceptions of 'plan' and 'market' as economic institutions; and that goes beyond both the nihilism and eclecticism of the 'market socialist' schemes, and the naiveté of cooperativistic conceptions that rely on semantic imagery and slogans of democracy and participation, but do not wrestle with the hard questions of individuation, autonomy and the motivational and organizational complexities of modern social life.

Notes

* Thanks we owed to several people – Andrew Kliman, Dimitris Milonakis, Bertell Ollman, Anwar Shaikh and Rick Wolff in particular – for comments on an earlier draft of this chapter.
1. The relevant contrast is with *valorization* in capitalism. The primary function of spontaneous market relations in capitalist societies is thus to establish and reproduce alienation, reification and, therefore, exploitation. Coordination of production and distribution, the centrepiece of mainstream conceptions of the role of 'the market', is secondary in importance.
2. It is also fraught with danger: intense politicization brings cadres of activists to the fore, and these cadres can consolidate into an elite with interests opposed to the majority – especially in the early socialist atmosphere struggling to escape from the authoritarian, unprincipled and 'power-hungry' political culture inherited from capitalism.
3. It will be apparent that I am using 'socialism' as the general term for the form(s) of society transcending and replacing capitalism. In this use it should be distinguished both from a transitional phase, in which the question of class power is not yet settled, and from the higher stage of communism. Some features of the latter will emerge in the discussion of the Cherry Esplanade Conjecture, below.
4. There should, of course, be no association between this usage and the limited (and occasionally cynical) concept of 'quality of work life' circles (QWL) promoted in some capitalist countries – at least at the time when the Soviet Union was still in existence.
5. The assumption of a protracted period of *conflict* between the twin goals of raising X and raising Q is quite deliberate, and represents a rejection of the idea that the solidarizing conditions of revolutionary struggle against capitalist power and the elemental cooperation formed within modern productive forces are by themselves sufficient to generate sustainable advanced levels of worker motivation and consciousness.

While some might wish to postulate a π curve that rises immediately from its X intercept, I believe it is better, from the standpoint of a long-term viable socialist strategy, to err on the side of prudence and caution.

6. It is important to understand the logic behind this movement. Since determination runs from Q to X along the π curve, movement from any point is toward that curve in a vertical direction. Once there, the achieved level of X then determines Q, along the δ curve; movement toward δ takes place in a horizontal direction. Vertical to π and horizontal to δ: this formula will generate the dynamics of all of the various situations examined below. Of course, if the two movements take place simultaneously, the convergence is more rapid and less 'angular'. For full discussion of the mathematics of cobweb type adjustment in economic models, see Allen (1966).

7. So named because it was conceived by the author while sitting on a bench at the Cherry Esplanade, a particularly beautiful setting of cherry trees within the Brooklyn Botanic Garden in New York City.

8. A caution may be in order concerning the use made of stability analysis in this exercise. Cobweb stability depends on the relative slopes of the π and δ curves, and bears no relation to either the 'Walrasian' or the 'Marshallian' formulation, according to which, respectively, changes in X are inversely related to $Q(\delta) - Q(\pi)$, and changes in Q are directly related to $X(\pi) - X(\delta)$. When π is negatively sloped and π is positively sloped, both the Walrasian and the Marshallian measures suggest stability; in other cases (see p. 125 in the main text), they yield opposite conclusions, and a choice must be made based on the presumed realism of one or other behavioural assumption. I find the 'Marshallian' view, according to which Q responds to a divergence between possible and necessary X, to be superior to the alternative, especially since Q is much more the outcome of policy than is X. But the cobweb movement is decisive for dynamic stability, in any case.

9. The movement up to the onset of stage IV has been described in this chapter in terms of the political effort to shift the δ curve to the right. Is it possible, instead, that the π curve shifts upward, reflecting the gradual rise in productivity (at every hypothetical level of Q)? The answer is 'yes', and a little experimentation will show that an upward-shifting π curve against a given δ curve will eventually produce the same 'explosion': a point like c in Figure 5.5 (p. 124). While the stages of socialist development can therefore be depicted with either form of movement (or both), I continue to think that most emphasis should be placed on the political project of shifting δ, again erring on the side of prudence and caution.

    It might be noted that even if one adopts the 'optimistic' standpoint of a π curve rising monotonically from its X intercept (see n. 5 above), a period of political effort to shift δ to the right toward point c will still be necessary.

10. This is clear in terms of dynamic (cobweb) stability. It is also supported by the 'Marshallian' view (see n. 8 above), in which Q adjusts to divergences of necessary and possible X, but not by the 'Walrasian'

view, with X adjusting to divergences of Q. As I have indicated, the Marshallian story seems superior to the Walrasian one for this model.
11. This writer lived a very political life in the 1960s, as part of the US student movement, anti-Vietnam War movement and civil rights movement; like many others, I burned out of this intense activity after a few years. In (formerly) existing socialist societies, those who did not burn out became the core of Party activists; what often emerged was not a meritocracy, but rather an 'activocracy', much more benign than the bureaucracies beholden to a capitalist ruling class in capitalist societies, but a seriously alienating presence nevertheless. I believe the left has to rethink the way it advocates democracy (not, of course, its commitment to democracy as such). People resist 'participating in all aspects of managing their lives'; they often would rather leave at least some of that to others, as anyone who has tried to recruit volunteers to serve on a housing cooperative board or community school board can attest.
12. A major advantage of modern computer-assisted production (design, manufacture) is the ability to combine detailed specification and creativity at the micro-level with overall coordination and balance, without necessarily pre-envisioning and sanctioning each particular set of microactivities.

References

Albert, M. and R. Hahnel (1991) *The Political Economy of Participatory Economics* (Princeton: Princeton University Press).
Allen, R. G. D. (1996) *Mathematical Economics*, 2nd edn (London: Macmillan).
Cockshott, W. P. and A. F. Cottrell (1997) 'Value, Markets and Socialism', *Science & Society*, 61 (Fall), 330–57.
Devine, P. (1988) *Democracy and Economic Planning: The Political Economy of a Self-Governing Society*, (Boulder: Westview Press).
Engels, F. (1966) *Herr Eugen Dühring's Revolution in Science (Anti-Dühring)* (New York: International Publishers).
Laibman, D. (1992) 'Market and Plan: The Evolution of Socialist Social Structures in History and Theory', *Science & Society*, 56 (Spring), 60–91.
Laibman, D. (1995) 'An Argument for Comprehensive Socialism.' *Socialism and Democracy*, 9 (Fall–Winter), 83–93.
Laibman, D. (1997) *Capitalist Macrodynamics: A Systematic Introduction* (London: Macmillan).
Lovejoy, D. (1996) 'Limits to Growth?', *Science & Society*, 60 (Fall), 266–78.
Maler, H. (1998) 'An Apochryphal Testament: Socialism, Utopian and Scientific', in J. Kircz and M. Löwy, (eds), 'Friedrich Engels: A Critical Centenary Appreciation', Special issue, *Science & Society*, 62 (Spring).
Marx, K. (1933) *The Critique of the Gotha Programme* (New York: International Publishers).
Marx, K. and F. Engels (1971), *The Communist Manifesto*, in D. Struik (ed.), *Birth of the Communist Manifesto* (New York: International Publishers).

Ollman, B. (1996) 'Market Mystification in Capitalist and Market Socialist Societies', paper presented to American Political Science Association, San Francisco, 29 August–1 September.
Roemer, J. E. (1994) *A Future for Socialism* (London: Verso; and Cambridge, Mass.: Harvard University Press).
Roosevelt, F. and D. Belkin (eds) (1994) *Why Market Socialism? Essays from Dissent* (Armonk: M. E. Sharpe).
Schwartzman, D. (1996) 'Solar Communism', *Science & Society*, 60 (Fall), 307–31.
Schweickart, D. (1996) *Against Capitalism* (Boulder: Westview Press).
Wright, E. O. (ed.) (1996) *Equal Shares: Making Market Socialism Work*, J. E. Roemer and Contributors (London and New York: Verso).

Discussion
Richard D. Wolff

These brief comments intend to stimulate discussion by distinguishing my points of agreement and disagreement with Laibman's chapter. First of all, I think it is important to applaud his determination to learn from the concrete experiments and experiences, the successes and the failures, of Eastern European socialisms (rather than the current fad of dismissing them wholesale). If we fail to learn from their mistakes, the future efforts to move beyond capitalism will probably reproduce those mistakes. Likewise, the chapter's demotion of the plan–market dichotomy to a secondary significance suggests – although it does not develop – a profound critique of those discourses that insist on placing that dichotomy at the core of all differentiations of capitalism from socialism. Lastly, Laibman rightly rejects the presumption that some necessary inverse relation exists between worker productivity and worker autonomy. Laibman's effort to reverse that presumption – to show that greater worker autonomy can yield greater productivity – is a theoretical step in the right direction.

My disagreements with Laibman's chapter all refer to those theoretical gaps or weaknesses which, if corrected, could much improve the thrust of his argument. The first of these is perhaps the most fundamental. If, as he says, many of the practices of socialist economies need now to be interrogated and critically transcended, those practices must surely include how the very terms 'socialism' and 'capitalism' were defined. Strategies, policies, and tactics depended significantly upon those basic definitions; yet Laibman proceeds as if everyone agrees as to what differentiates capitalism, socialism and communism. But that is plainly not the case. To offer one illustrative example, we may recall that no less an authority than Lenin wrote and said repeatedly in the early years of the USSR that its class structure was 'state capitalism' which he hoped would function as a transitional situation toward socialism and communism. Depending on how one defines 'capitalism', 'socialism' and 'communism', the alternative conclusions one can reach are: (1) the transition was never achieved and the USSR remained always an evolving state capitalism, (2) a partial transition was achieved to something distinctive called 'socialism' that is neither capitalist nor communist, or (3) communism was achieved. All three positions (as well as mixtures and variations of them) have been advanced and attacked over the years.[1] Laibman – like any other writer – cannot legitimately proceed as if the definitions of capitalism, socialism, and communism were resolved, settled, or universally agreed matters. Indeed, Laibman also uses a host of other basic terms as if the actual history of Eastern European socialisms did not warrant asking and answering basic questions about them as well (and also acknowledging the different definitions of them that have always been contested inside and outside Marxism). A brief list of such terms would include: productivity, democracy, autonomy, socialist consciousness, incentive, market and exploitation, among others. Let me conclude this criticism by posing a hypothetical question: if the actual experiences of Eastern European socialisms lead us to inquire critically about the productivity–autonomy trade-off presumed by so many friends and foes of those socialisms, would it not lead us to question all such terms as well? After all, they were all linked in general, hegemonic discourses that are surely part of what must be rethought in the aftermath of what happened to those socialisms. Yet Laibman seems not to recognize or address this problem, even in a preliminary way.

One term remarkably absent from Laibman's argument is class. Yet the particular class structure in which production is organized must surely influence both workers' productivity and their notions of, and efforts to achieve, autonomy. Moreover one would expect especially a Marxist theorist to pay attention to how class affects such important phenomena as labour productivity and autonomy and thereby to demonstrate the importance of class. Of course, to have offered a specifically class analysis would once again have confronted Laibman with the problem that definitions of class – like those of other key terms in the social-analytical discourses of the twentieth century – are contested terrain. To undertake a Marxist class analysis, he would have had to distinguish the property definitions of classes (in terms of who owns what), the power definitions (in terms of who rules whom) and the surplus labour definitions (who produces, appropriates and distributes surplus labour, and in what manner). The different definitions would yield different conclusions on the possible relationships between productivity and autonomy: the analysis you get depends in no small part on the definitions and conceptions you use.

Finally, a one-sidedness haunts Laibman's arguments. He seems to see the issue in starkly either/or terms: either autonomy undermines productivity or else it does not. The more dialectically nuanced perspective – which might better serve Laibman's argument – would hold that greater (or, for that matter, lesser) worker autonomy both enhances and also undermines productivity, a contradictory relationship. In other words, it is always a matter of balancing the positive and negative impacts on productivity of any degree of worker autonomy. Indeed, capitalist corporations have long understood and experimented with various enlargements of worker autonomy, self-management, and so on in the hope of establishing them in ways that would, on balance, raise rather than lower productivity. Sometimes workers have responded as hoped; under other circumstances, workers responded to new autonomy in ways useful to them but not by raising productivity. The point is that autonomy enhances productivity in some ways and undermines it in others. That is always the case; only the balance between the two contradictory effects varies depending on the social context. A successful policy would then be one that acknowledges and accommodates the contradictory effects while seeking to tilt the balance between them in the desired direction by focusing on the social context of the contradictory relation. It is never a matter of a level of autonomy either enhancing or undermining productivity; it is always a contradictory matter of both effects happening at the same time. Armed with such a nuanced approach, Laibman might have been drawn into considering what social conditions (and especially class conditions) might have been put in place in the Eastern European socialisms to make more autonomy yield higher productivity.

In summary, Laibman's chapter joins other studies which seek to rethink many of the basic assumptions, presumptions and 'givens' of the hegemonic discourses surrounding the Eastern European socialisms in the light of their collapse. The autonomy–productivity relationship is a fine place to start, but treating that relationship needs to be placed in the context of a far more systematic and basic rethinking of basic terms than is evident in this chapter. My disagreement thus focuses on Laibman's not engaging the rethinkings already under-way nor performing them himself. I think, had he done so, his argument would have been richer and more persuasive.

Note

1. See, for example, the discussion of some of these contesting definitions among those concerned with the USSR in Resnick and Wolff (1993).

Reference

Resnick, S. and R. Wolff (1993) 'State Capitalism in the USSR? A High-stakes Debate', *Rethinking Marxism*, 6 (Summer), 46–68.

Discussion
Dimitris Milonakis

David Laibman's contribution is to be welcomed since it represents an attempt to put some socialist fundamentals back on the agenda at a time when much of the current thinking on the left has been infiltrated by Neoliberal ideology. This is evident, for example, in the proposals of the market socialist school which has dominated the debate on alternative economic systems. Saying a few words about the market socialist model is instructive not only because of its popularity but also because its apparent inconsistencies and contradictions will lead us directly to David Laibman's proposals. So what does this model involve?

The premises on which this model is built lie in the belief that central planning is necessarily inefficient as well as having been discredited by the Soviet experience. The basic question, according to John Roemer, one of the protagonists of this camp, is whether we can create an ecomomy that is about as efficient as capitalism, yet has qualitatively better distributional properties (Roemer 1994).

The answer John Roemer himself and other market socialists give to this question is that the alternative model must keep the properties of the market system that, according to them, make it efficient (that is, atomistic competition, profit maximization, and so on) and get rid of the property that brings about unequal distribution (that is, private property). Because, the argument goes, the two are not necessarily connected. In other words, we can have efficient competition whithout private property because market institutions are far more significant in generating efficiency than are property relations. In this proposal, the attempt to find a third way between Western-type capitalism and the command-administrative system which would combine efficiency with equity, is obvious.

If we adopt Berliner's (1993) taxonomy of economic systems, then these can be divided according to two basic rules: (1) the type of property ownership (public or private), and (2) the type of economic mechanism (planning or markets). In this taxonomy, Western capitalism, classical socialism and market socialism represent three different ways of combining these two rules. Thus Western capitalism combines private ownership with the free reign of markets, classical socialism combines public (state) ownership with economic planning while market socialism occupies a middle position, combining some form of non-private or public ownership rule with market competition. In effect what market socialists propose is a sort of capitalism without capitalists, a view that Marx rebutted more than a century ago.

The strength of market socialist models and their main source of appeal lies in their insistence on dealing in a straightforward manner with hard questions and giving concrete answers wherever possible, as well as applying the latest developments of the neoclassical theoretical apparatus. Some of the questions they deal with include the problem of the 'soft budget constraint', first developed by Janos Kornai (1986), the question of the forms of ownership (favouring either worker ownership or public ownership or some other form of non-private ownership), the problem of incentive compatibility between the principal–owner and the agent–manager or director, the problem of monitoring and disciplining of managers, the problem of capital markets, and so on.

However, it is not at all certain that the system they propose can actually achieve its proclaimed goals. For one thing market socialists conceive socialism as a kind of egalitarianism rather than as an economic system based on specific property relations. In fact, as John Gray (1995) puts it:

> Roemer's market socialism is based on egalitarian liberalism as advocated by John Rawls and other liberal moral philosophers, which involves an individualist and legalist preoccupation with justice and rights.

For another, market socialism is a purely academic model not associated with any social or political movement.

Apart from this, market socialist models in fact reproduce most of the evils associated with modern western type capitalism. Thus, for example, as Dobb (1935a, 1935b) has argued, autonomous decision making, a basic property of market socialist models, creates imperfections of knowledge with the resulting uncertainty bringing about instability and economic fluctuations (see also Adaman and Devine 1997).

The asymmetric information associated with these models can

also cause markets not to clear – as, for example, with the labour market thus causing unemployment. Then there are the alienating and commodity fetishism properties of commodity production and free markets which are not tackled by these models.

But perhaps the most fundamental criticism that has been levelled against market socialism is that it is self-defeating as far as its socialist goals are concerned (Adaman and Devine 1997). The model requires the full autonomy of enterprises which are coordinated by market forces. The incentive mechanism of market forces, however, that is competitive success or failure, itself generates inequality. Hence the model defeats the very purpose of its construction – that is to combine efficiency with equity. This self-defeating property of market socialist models is even more apparent in the model proposed by Brus and Laski (1989) who seek to combine 'state ownership with full autonomy of firms and true entrepreneurship' through the functioning of real capital markets along with real product and labour markets. However, as Adaman and Devine (1997) put it:

> the conditions that have to be met to achieve this effectively replicating capitalism are such as to render the retention of formal state ownership artificial and redundant.

One final property of market socialist models that seems to contradict socialist goals is the assumption that people are selfish and narrowly self-interested. Indeed one of the main points of Laibman's chapter is that such an assumption must be rejected; the behaviour of individuals is instead seen as being shaped by social institutions.

As against these recent attempts by the market socialist camp to redefine the socialist project, Laibman's chapter represents an attempt to put traditional socialist goals back on the agenda. Thus socialism, rather than being some form of egalitarianism is, according to him, about creating the best possible conditions for human growth and development, the latter incorporating not only the objective advances of our mastery over nature as encapsulated in the concept of productivity, but also subjective elements such as creativity, work fulfilment, connectedness to other people, and so on. In this direction the basic task of socialist economic theory is to find ways of combining these two apparently contradictory goals of socialism – increasing productivity on the one hand and enhancing workers' fulfilment, democracy, equality and autonomy on the other. At the beginning, there appears to be a trade-off between these two socialist goals as is depicted in Laibman's δ curve. In other words 'productivist goals and strategies involve some sacrifice in social objectives' (p. 118). This is a version of the efficiency–equity trade-off tackled also by the market socialist tradition, only that now both efficiency and equity are much more broadly defined.

Later on, however, through successful socialist education and political work, a point is reached (point b on the δ curve) after which the trade-off ceases to exist and productivity increases become a positive function of the quality of work lives. Once this point is reached a new era begins, where both socialist goals can be achieved at the same time.

There are three crucial properties of this system that differentiate it from other existing frameworks: first, a *planning or programming system* is considered to be an inherent component of socialism, but this would take the form of what Laibman calls 'cybernetic macrocoordination' (p. 128). Second, *direct political work and socialist education* especially in the formative stages of socialist construction is considered essential until, third, a *new motivational structure* is established which involves a combination of material and moral incentives taking either an individual or a collective form.

The main problem with Laibman's thesis is that it represents no more than an hypothesis (a conjecture, as he calls it), without any theoretical backing. Moreover, this is done at a general and abstract level and as such it begs some important questions, some of which Laibman himself poses at the beginning of his chapter.

The first question is about the relation of this system to the realities of present-day capitalism. The link Laibman identifies between the secular crisis of capitalism and the establishment of socialism is somewhat schematic and formalistic as well as being neo-Ricardian in character. Second, and related to this, is that no connection is identified between this societal transformation and any social or political movement.

Third, Laibman's chapter works at the level of long-term socialist goals and ideals. In order for this utopia to be transformed into a science of the socialist system, these socialist ideals have to be vested in concrete social forms and institutions. The lack of such a discussion in Laibman's chapter begs further questions. This is more apparent, for example, in his discussion of motivation, a very basic element in any discussion of alternative economic systems. He writes (p. 118), for example, that

Motivation is governed by the power of workers over their own lives, their rational understanding, the effectiveness and democracy of their forms of organization and their autonomy.

But the question is exactly what *are* the forms of organization that will bring about such a huge transformation in the incentive structure? And how is workers' autonomy to be achieved within such organizations?

As far as the emergence of a new motivational structure is concerned, this indeed represents a basic requirement of any socialist economic system. Laibman talks, correctly in my view, about the need to combine material with moral incentives. However, nowhere in his chapter does he take up this point. On the contrary, he focuses exclusively on moral incentives. The problem with this is the heavy reliance on excessive political work and socialist education during the first period of socialist construction, in order to enhance socialist consciousness and provoke shifts in the a curve. The question, however, is how does one guarantee that this excessive politicization of the economic sphere does not degenerate into the overcentralized and bureaucratic type of state experienced in the former socialist countries? Because if this happens the whole process will get locked in, thus making it impossible to reach the higher stage (that is go beyond point b on the δ curve). This is indeed what happened in the former socialist countries.

Last, one cannot possibly disagree with Laibman's plea for an optimal combination or even the transcendance of the plan–market dilemma. This problem has indeed been on the socialist agenda ever since the first debates of the early 1920s. In fact, this optimal combination has been the target of most reforms in the former socialist countries that came to be known as 'central planning with a regulated market'. Again, however, these experiments failed. Why did they fail? And what are the social institutions and economic mechanisms that can guarantee such a transcendance?

The list of questions seem endless, as indeed are the problems facing socialists. Laibman himself is well aware of this (p. 128) when he writes that:

> this chapter... is a conjecture [and] does not ... address many monumental problems for socialism, especially those involving bureaucratic organization and power.

What his chapter does do, however, is to redress the balance in favour of true socialist goals. Given the current state of the debate and the ideological surrender of the market socialist trend to the free market ideology, one should certainly hope that Laibman succeeds in his proclaimed aim of 'steer[ing] the global conversation into more fruitful channels [for]... a socialism that is both... sophisticated and inspirational' (p. 129). The best way of achieving this, in my view, is if future research is directed towards providing a rigorous theoretical backing of Laibman's path-breaking proposals as well as giving concrete theoretical answers as to the specific social forms and institutions that will make Laibman's socialist project workable.

References

Adaman, F. and P. Devine (1997) 'On the Economic Theory of Socialism', *New Left Review*, 221 (January–February), 4–80.

Bardham, P. and J. Roemer (eds) (1997) *Market Socialism: the Current Debate* (Oxford: Oxford University Press).

Berliner, J. (1993) 'Innovation, the Soviet Union and Market Socialism', in Bardham and Roemer (eds).

Brus, W. and K. Laski (1989) *From Marx to the Market* (Oxford: Clarendon Press).

Dobb, M. (1935a) 'Review', *Economic Journal*.

Dobb, M. (1935b) 'Economic Theory and Socialist Economy: A Reply', *Review of Economic Studies*, 144–51.

Gray, J. (1995) 'Harnessing the Market', *New Left Review*, 210 (March–April), 147–52.

Kornai, J. (1986) 'The Soft Budget Constraint' *Kyklos*, 39, 1, 3–30.

Laibman, D. (1998) 'Revisioning Socialsim: "The Cherry Esplanade Conjecture"', chapter 5 in this volume.

Roemer, J. (1994) *A Future for Socialism* (London: Verso; and Cambridge, Mass.: Harvard University Press).

Part II

European Monetary and Economic Union

6 The Single Currency: Prospects and Problems
Georgios Katiphoris

INTRODUCTION

This chapter aims at attempting an exercise in unashamedly old-fashioned political economy. I stress the 'old-fashioned' in order to disabuse the reader of expectations of any flights of fancy into the realm of 'New Political Economy', a discipline which, for me, would be too arcane to contemplate. My version of old-fashioned political economy when confronted with the title 'the Single Currency, Problems and Prospects' asks, with Pavlovian spontaneity 'problems for whom and prospects for whom'. Let us begin with the answer to the first part of this question.

THE CRITERIA AND THEIR FULFILMENT

The answer has undergone a certain historical evolution over the last few years. Originally, it was the very attempt at creating a European Monetary Union (EMU) which appeared to be problematic. The Treaty of Maastricht (Article 109,j,3) stipulated that the earliest date for taking the decision and fixing the date for the start of EMU could be 31 December 1996, subject to a majority of states having satisfied the criteria for nominal convergence by the said date. As this did not occur, the Commission's and the European Parliament's optimism notwithstanding, we may conclude that, in the first round, it was the EMU initiative and its chief proponents who became overwhelmed by problems inherent to the very nature of the process. But this was not the end of the story, nor was it intended to be. A second deadline – this one both compulsory and free of any reference to necessary majorities – followed fast upon the heels of the first one. And lo and behold, given a modicum of compulsion, virtually all member states, which in 1997 seemed to be finding themselves light-years away from EMU, suddenly started falling over themselves, one after another, to fulfil the criteria. Whether that was the consequence of a gradual accumulation of momentum reaching a critical point – quantity turning into quality as the old Dialectician would say – or whether the prospect of being left out in the cold concentrated the minds of Finance Ministers to the task at hand (and what this teaches us about human nature in general, or the nature of Finance Ministers in particular, I leave as an exercise to the reader). The fact of the matter is that fulfilment of the criteria of nominal convergence was transformed from being a problem for the proponents of EMU into a problem of member states, with most of them proceeding with alacrity, although with unequal degrees of success, to solve it.

Let us, now use certain data to assess the degree of success of each candidate member states.

From the vantage point of 15 months before the fateful date (September 1997), the state of play with regard to fulfilment is currently as follows:

- *Inflation*
  Criterion (September 1997, provisional data): 2.6 – with average of best three 1.1. All countries of the European North satisfy this criterion with ease. Of the countries of the South, Greece is excluded, while Spain, Italy and Portugal are on the margin and may go either way. We are, it appears, in the presence of a North–South split which may prove – and in my own (minority) opinion will prove – crucial for the May 1998 decision.
- *Long-term interest rates*
  Criterion: 6.4 per cent. This rules out Greece, Spain, Ireland, Italy, Portugal, Sweden and the United Kingdom. The last two are, of course irrelevant, since they have chosen to opt out of the Single Currency for the time being.
- *Public finance criteria*
  Here, failures become considerably more serious. The public deficit criterion was in 1996 satisfied by five of the 15 candidates (Denmark, Ireland, Luxembourg, the Netherlands and Finland). As for the debt criterion, strictly speaking, this is satisfied only by four candidates, one of them irrelevant, the United Kingdom, the other three being France, Luxembourg and Finland. (Germany just misses by the narrowest of margins, 60.7 but has the disadvantage that the amount of its debt is increasing.

Finally the exchange rate criterion (two-year adherence to the ERM without devaluation) was satisfied in September 1997 by 12 member states (the United Kingdom, Sweden and Greece excepted).

THE PROBLEM AND THE SOLUTION

This brief survey of the state of play, which places in relief the main problem of the member states points at the same time to its solution. The problem is simply that, if we take all the criteria equally seriously, and adopt a rigid attitude to their interpretation, there is no chance of producing a meaningful set of member states as a nucleus of the single currency. The public debt criterion simply excludes everybody, with the exceptions mentioned, and of those exceptions France has to be excluded because of its excessive deficit. This leaves us with Luxembourg and Finland fully satisfying all five criteria, a rather unconvincing duo for the task of giving an auspicious start to the single currency. To attempt to discuss or even summarize all the contortioned arguments by which single currency advocates have tried to wriggle out of the impasse and squeeze a meaningful set of countries – inevitably including France and Germany – out of the imbroglio of a rigid application of the rules would be a waste of time. Given a rigid interpretation, there is no legally respectable way out. Given a flexible interpretation, which admittedly comes closer to the spirit of the EMU enterprise, there is enough room in the escape clauses for even a moderately competent jurist to drive a coach and horses through the relevant articles of the Treaty. Ultimately, the burden of selection falls on the political judgement of the Council, subject to endorsement or annulment by the financial markets.

This approach is not as arbitrary as it might at first sight appear. The key to breaking the formalistic logjam lies in the realization that, in the preparation of EMU not all criteria are of equivalent importance. The old target–instrument duality turns out to be crucial in this respect. The convergence criteria can be separated into targets and instruments. The convergence of the level of inflation – both current and expected – as proxied by the long-term rate of interest, is the target which has to be respected, because upon it depends the relative stability of the EMU currencies. It has always been the intention of the architects of EMU that the Single Currency arrive not as an arbitrary impost but as the crowning act of a natural evolution of the relevant economies. They have reasoned as follows: a set of different currencies may be treated as a single currency if the exchange rate among the members of the set does not vary significantly. Barring the case of deliberate competitive devaluation, which among close associates should be ruled out, the only reason for exchange rate misalignments is different rates of current and/or expected inflation. It follows that if convergence to a single inflation rate can be achieved, no changes in exchange rate need to occur and the relevant set of currencies can be treated as a single currency. The formal introduction of a single currency following upon such developments would then simply be the formal and official endorsement of a real economic development and, as such, it could go through without any upheaval. This is what gives the inflation rate its special role among the rest of the criteria, the role of a target.

The same cannot be said about the fiscal criteria. These need have no direct impact on the exchange rate, they impact upon it via the rate of inflation. Therefore, their status is that of instruments which may be discarded if the effect they are aimed at has already been achieved either by different means, or by an application of the force of instruments milder than foreseen in the original set-up of the Treaty.

Regarding the single currency, what has taken place is that the inflation target has been achieved at a range of values of the instruments less stringent than the ones provided for in the Treaty. This should not blind us to the fact that our main aim, the inflation target, has been achieved, thus clearing the way to the single currency irrespective of the very partial fulfilment of the public finance criteria. This, I suggest, is the logic behind the trend of turning half a blind eye on the public finance figures, and allowing the Council to exercise political judgement in the selection of the original members.

SUSTAINABILITY, OR THE NUMBER OF THE ORIGINAL MEMBERS

It is consistent with the above logic that the original members of the single currency can be widely defined and encompass all member states that have reached hailing distance of the fulfilment of the fiscal criteria. This may indeed turn out to be the case apart from two further, but quite substantive, hurdles.

The first is the hurdle of sustainability. It is not enough for monetary stability – a low convergent rate of inflation – to have been achieved momentarily, by dint of an outburst of extraordinary effort over a short period of time. Evidence also has to be present of the permanence of the change; and what better evidence than long-term interest rates which, we have just seen, would tend to disqualify all South European member states. It might be argued that this objection is illogical, since in the prospect of a common single currency no possibility of differential expected rates of inflation, expressing themselves through long-term interest differentials, can exist. Monetary fragility, however, may then assume different forms – that is, the tendency of a government to overborrow, risking default. Introduction of a single currency would not eliminate this kind of risk; it might even make it worse if sustainability of monetary stability has not taken root in the real costs, prices behaviour and the whole ethos of the economy.

The second hurdle concerns the need for a prior two-year membership of ERM without devaluation of the central parity on the initiative of the member state in question. This rule, at the time of writing, affects only states which have expressed their unwillingness to proceed with EMU anyway. It might be possible to by-pass it by interpreting Article 109j of the Treaty and Article 3 of Protocol 6 as requiring not formal membership of the ERM but simply adherence to its rules. If the United Kingdom decided to adhere to the single currency it is very doubtful whether the strict rule would be insisted on by its partners. Until the United Kingdom (and Sweden) decide to join, this question remains academic. Sustainability, however, is not. At the moment the prevailing opinion tends to accept that sustainability has either been achieved or that, in any case, it will not be made into an issue barring entrance to certain countries. If so the forecast would be that all member states which desire to become also EMU members will be admitted, all 12, that is to say, πλην των Λακεδαιμονίων. My own opinion, which I freely admit to be in the minority right now, maintains that the sustainability divide between North and South in Europe will assert itself in the original selection of EMU members, principally out of regard to the international credibility of the euro during its early days. Southern member states will not have to wait long outside, however. Their economic policy will be taken in hand by the

Commission, using reinforced, rigorously supervised convergence programmes and they will be made ready to become admitted into membership in a couple of years time, at the moment of introduction of the actual euro banknote. The Lacaedemonians will, I am afraid, have to wait considerably longer before they are judged mature for membership. The problem created here is that the loyalty of outsiders, or 'pre-ins', to the whole common project might collapse and they might start seeking their salvation in competitive devaluations against the euro. Coming from Italy and Spain such a threat cannot be treated lightly, especially by France who already had a taste of this medicine during the 1993 European currency upheavals, which favoured devaluing countries (the United Kingdom, Italy) to the detriment of the exports of stable currency economies (France, Belgium).

PROBLEMS OF TRANSITION

We can identify three periods of transition in the process towards constructing a full single currency:

(1) The first is between the selection of the early members and the irrevocable fixing of the parities, set to take place on 1 January 1999.
(2) The second is between the irrevocable fixing of the parities and the actual introduction of the Euro banknotes, at the latest on 1 January 2002. 'At the latest' is important; it establishes a qualitative difference between the first and second periods, insofar as the second can be shortened by subsequent decision of the members while the first, admittedly a much briefer one, cannot.
(3) The third is between 1 January 2002 and the actual replacement of the national banknotes, coins and electronic money by the euro. Again, this third period, foreseen to last six months, can be shortened and will probably be shortened. It presents various quite formidable problems in its own right, but their nature is technical rather than economic. In what follows, I will deal with the periods (1) and (2) only.

The reason why there has to be a first period of transition lies in the requirement of the Treaty that at least six months before 1 January 1999 be allowed to the European Central Bank (ECB), in order to organize itself and be ready to assume the direction of monetary policy as soon as the parities are fixed. Since the Bank cannot be organized before the membership of its ruling bodies can be established and that cannot be established before the original EMU members are known, we end up with the inevitability of selecting the original membership of the euro some considerable time before the official beginning of the new currency. Various dangers which might scupper the whole project lurk in this period of suspended animation of the euro. I will identify four:

(1) The markets may try to second-guess the Council and one another at what the final conversion rates will be on 1 January, thus letting loose an orgy of speculation which might unsettle monetary conditions to the point of making the very introduction of the single currency impossible.
(2) The markets may take the line that even the fundamental decision to proceed, as demonstrated by the selection of the original members, is not in fact irrevocable, particularly if early members are selected widely. In that case, markets might decide to test the strength of particular currencies which they consider weak, as they did in 1992–3. Needless to say, the single currency project will find it very hard to survive the collapse of the exchange rate of a pre-selected currency during the run-up to the fixing of the parities.
(3) The selection of the early members will also indicate which ones are not deemed yet capable of assuming the burdens of membership. These outsiders, or 'pre-ins', will thus become legitimate targets of speculative attacks which might end up involving some of the insiders as well.
(4) The EMU members-designate, having secured their selection but not having to yet abide by the Stability Pact (the latter's entry into force depending on the parallel introduction of the single currency) cast discipline to the four winds for a while, in an effort to extract some last-minute comparative advantage over their competitors.

The obvious antidote to all this is to create conditions of stability and certainty in the markets, so that the markets themselves are enlisted in support of the new currency, not against it. To this effect it has already been decided in the latest EcoFin in Luxembourg that, simultaneously with the designation of the first wave of members, bilateral conversion rates between the participating currencies will also be determined and announced. Although no formal decision has been taken, the bilateral conversion rates of the euro will be patterned upon the existing ERM central rates which adequately reflect the alignment of real costs per unit of output – except in the cases of Greece and Portugal, in both of which costs are very much out of line with those of the rest of the Community. Markets are therefore already being given a signal regarding the conversion rates and they can be expected to exercise their arbitrage in the direction desired by the authorities so that, by the end of the year, actual exchange rates of the insiders will reflect the conversion rates that will be sanctioned officially.

More than that cannot be achieved, under existing legislation. In particular, parities cannot be irrevocably fixed simultaneously with the selection of the original members both because that would require a revision of the Treaty and because the monetary authority responsible for the administration of the new currency, (the ECB), will not assume its duties until 1 January 1999. The solution decided upon is less than perfect and final also from the point of view of limiting itself to the bilateral rates and leaving undetermined the conversion rates between the participant currencies and the euro itself. It will not be possible to fix such rates before the official starting date, for the following reasons: the Treaty stipulates that at the commencement date 1 ECU, the common currency actually in existence, will be equivalent to 1 Euro. But differently from the euro, which is a currency in its own right, the ECU is a basket of currencies and that basket contains both prospective members of the euro and also currencies, like the British pound, which we know will not be members. By definition, no bilateral conversion rates between such currencies and the ECU can be fixed, therefore no ECU conversion rates are possible between future euro members and the ECU. Further, by the equivalence of the euro with the ECU, no multilateral conversion rates can be fixed with the euro either.

Do the markets have to respect the bilateral conversion rates which will be announced? Not necessarily, but assuming the first group of countries to be convincingly stable, the markets will be well advised to take note. It is a fact that, under existing legislation, the definitive conversion rates cannot be different from the exchange rates prevailing in the markets on the last day before EMU. But this apparent market sovereignty is, in the present case, illusory because, given the certainty of the advent of the single currency, central banks acquire the capacity of unlimited intervention in foreign exchange markets, even to the point of totally eliminating a currency under speculative attack. The markets cannot face up to such pressure and will, therefore, be motivated to cooperate, especially if the original set of members and the conversion rates are realistic, as there is no reason why they should not be. It follows that the first transition problem can be considered as solved.

The second transition problem regards the period between the irrevocable fixing of the parities and the introduction of the banknotes. The nature of EMU will still not be that of an actual new currency but of a reinforced fixed exchange rate regime, of which we have already seen various types. The euro will exist only as accounting money for the transactions among commercial banks and themselves and the ECB. It will also be used as unit of account for the issuing of new government debt and the quick conversion of public debt outstanding to the new currency. It will obviously also be the accounting unit of the ECB. As for private companies, they will be free to convert to the euro immediately but they will not be compelled to do so. In day-to-day transactions national currencies will continue to exist and be treated as local subdivisions of the euro. The situation is complicated by the fact that, although national currencies will be formally treated as mere subdivisions of the euro they will not be legal tender in one another's territory.

These arrangements allow sufficient reality to persist in the continuing existence of the national currencies even after 1 January 2002 as to have encouraged some economists with classical predilections in their thinking with regard to money to suggest that ever-hopeful speculators might attempt to place one-way bets against the euro by buying deutsche marks for the weaker currencies of the group and sit on them and wait for EMU to collapse. If it does, they will gain large sums from the revaluation of the mark in relation to the weaker currencies, if it does not they risk to lose nothing, because the mark, as a subdivision of the euro, of course, will keep its value constant. There is no fool-proof answer to that problem, apart from the capacity of the Central Banks, as subdivisions of the ECB, to create unlimited amounts of one currency, while withdrawing another, thus leaving the total monetary mass in the Union unchanged. Apart from atavistic syndromes there is no reason why they should not be prepared to do so. This possibility should be sufficient to throw cold water on the heads of even the most enthusiastic of speculators.

In conclusion, the two transition periods between the selection of the early members and the actual introduction of the euro banknotes will be characterized by a gradual but progressive hardening of the European fixed exchange regime. In theory, such hardening could be frustrated by adverse market developments but markets are subject to the disciplining power of Central Banks which, in this case, can be increasingly effective. Moreover, it is not clear what the markets would gain by seeking to move against a new monetary development, assuming it is sound, as it is likely to be. All this does not amount to saying that a shorter period and a more decisive transition would not have been better. Undoubtedly they would have been, but we should consider ourselves lucky to have achieved reasonable progress in the construction of the euro in the face of the suspicion, hesitation and fear such a monumental change is likely to arouse, and should not grumble too much about the time it takes.

PROSPECTS, GOOD AND BAD

I now pass to a quick overview of the prospects of EMU. Inevitably, such an exercise, pertaining as it does to futurology, can only be highly subjective. I will not even attempt to do full justice to the topic, limiting myself to addressing up what appear to me two or three of the main trends. The first area I would focus upon is the one where predictions can be more certain. It regards the re-establishment of an independent monetary policy on the part of the European nations. As long as the European currencies remained divided they were easy victims of interest and exchange rate speculation, as a result of which some were victimized compared to others while none of them could confront, on equal terms, the one major international currency, the dollar. The establishment of a single currency certainly does not do away with the different relative sensitivity of the various economies of Europe to events on the international arena. Even under a single currency, the trade of the United Kingdom will be more vulnerable to changes in the value of the dollar than that of continental Europe. However, the additional element of intra-European speculation, detonated by extra-European events, which ultimately rendered monetary policy inside Europe inoperative, will no longer be there. This is a clear gain from EMU.

Things look different in the area of fiscal policy. While monetary policy will be subject to one single authority, the ECB, enjoined to watch over price stability before anything else, no similar institutional apparatus exists in the case of fiscal policy. An attempt to fill the gap has been made in Amsterdam by means of the Stability Pact. Opinions on this are bound to vary greatly, depending on the commentators' fundamental positions on basic questions of economic policy. I happen to be one of those who believe that the Maastricht criteria have been unjustifiably deflationary and that their consecration and perpetuation through the Stability Pact, in a period of prolonged and persistent unemployment, verges on the insane. I lay no store by the heavily touted causal sequence which claims to establish links between 'stability' (that is, deflationary disinflation), heavy-handed wage discipline, investor confidence, low interest rates and an uptake in productive investment. The link between low interest rates and a rise in investment has never, so far as I know (I freely admit that my reading on this is a bit rusty) been established empirically. As for investor confidence, unaccompanied by other contributing factors, that tends to be translated principally to portfolio, at best, or speculative, at worst, investment which contributes either negatively or not at all to the growth and welfare of nations. It certainly contributes a lot to the welfare of financiers who, being rather more articulate than immigrant unskilled workers, have created all this ballyhoo of propaganda extolling the virtues of globalization, while the practice of their art has coincided with increasing misery and polarization of society.

Holding such views on the theory of economic policy I might seem a natural opponent of the single currency, but I am not. I consider EMU a step forward in the fortunes of Europe so enormously positive, in the long run, that I would not wish it sacrificed to the wrong-headedness or the special pleading of those interests that dominate the European political scene at the present moment. I would oppose their restrictive policies as best as I could but I would preserve the piece of gold that comes along with all the neoclassical, monetarist, Reaganomic or whatever else you like to call it dross; I would preserve the unifying force of the single currency.

Nowhere is such force likely to demonstrate itself better than in the area of international economics. A currency like the euro, with the full weight of the commerce of that whole of the European continent behind it, cannot fail but become one of the main reserve currencies in the world. Europe will then have the capability of running an expansionary policy without coming up against the foreign balance constraint which has so often plagued European nations. Of course, achieving reserve currency status will not automatically render European policy expansionary; under wrong-headed ideas like those that prompted Churchill take Britain back to the gold standard in the early 1920s, it might well have the opposite effect. The European construction encompasses the possibility of a valid expansionary policy for the benefit of working people; it does not entail any certainty of such a policy. So, if I may conclude by returning to my earlier political economy question 'problems for whom and prospects for whom' I could answer the following: construction of EMU has so far thrown the burden of the resolution of the problems of the European economy onto the backs of the weaker European nations and, inside each nation, onto the backs of Europe's working people. However, the strengthening of the competitive position of Europe world-wide as well as its greater internal cohesion as a result of the single currency are both advances of historical importance which can be used, under a proper change of orientation and mechanisms of economic policy, into instruments for raising the standards of living of the vast majority of the people in Europe.

References

Akerlof, A., G.W. Dickens and G. Perry (1996) 'The Microeconomics of Low Inflation', *Brookings Papers on Economic Activity*, 1, 1–75.

Alesina, A. and R. Perotti (1995) 'The Political Economy of Budget Process', *IMF Staff Papers*, 42, 1–31.

Alesina, A. and R. Perotti (1996) 'Fiscal Discipline and the Budget Process', *American Economic Review, Papers and Proceedings*, 86, 401–7.

Alogoskoufis, G. and R. Portes (1992) 'European Monetary Union and International Currencies in a Tripolar World', in M.B. Canzoneri, V. Grilli and P. Masson (eds), *Establishing a Central Bank Issues in Europe and Lessons from the US* (Cambridge: Cambridge University Press).

Ball, L., N.G. Mankiw and D. Romer (1998) 'The New Keynesian Economics and the Output–Inflation Trade-off', *Brooking Papers on Economic Activity*, 1, 1–65.

Barro, R.J. (1996) 'Determinants of Economic Growth: A Cross-Country Empirical Study', NBER Working Paper, 5698.

Bayoumi, T. and B. Eichengreen (1993) 'Shocking Aspects of European Monetary Unification', in F. Torres and F. Giavazzi (eds), *Adjustment and Growth in the European Monetary Union* (Cambridge:Cambridge University Press for the CEPR).

Bayoumi, T. and B. Eichengreen (1995) 'Restraining Yourself: The

Implications of Fiscal Rules for Economic Stabilization', *IMF Staff Papers*, 42, 32–48.

Bayoumi, T. and E. Prasad (1996) 'Currency Unions, Economic Fluctuations and Adjustment: Some New Empirical Evidence', IMF Working Paper, 81.

Bean, C.R. (1994) 'European Unemployment: A Survey', *Journal of Economic Literature*, 32, 573–619.

Briault, C. (1995) 'The Costs of Inflation', Bank of England Quarterly Bulletin, 35, 34–5.

Buiter, W.H. (1995) 'Macroeconomic Policy During a Transition to Monetary Union', CEPR Discussion Paper, 1222.

Buti, M., D. Franco and H. Ongena (1997) 'Budgetary Policies in Severe Recessions – Lessons from the Post-war Period for the Stability Pact', *Economic Papers* 121 (Brussels: European Commission, Directorate-General for Economic and Financial Affairs).

Eichengreen, B. (1996) 'Saving Europe's Automatic Stabilizers', *National Institute Economic Review*, 159, 92–8.

Eichengreen, B. and J. von Haagen (1995) 'Fiscal Policy and Monetary Union: Federalism, Fiscal Restrictions and the No-Bailout-Rule', CEPR Discussion Paper, 1247.

European Commission (1990) 'One Market, One Money', *European Economy*, 44 (Brussels: Directorate-General for Economic and Financial Affairs).

European Monetary Institute (1997) 'The Single Monetary Policy in Stage Three: Elements of the Monetary Policy Strategy of the ESCB' (Frankfurt: EMI) (February).

Feldstein, M. (1996) 'The Costs and Benefits of Going from Low Inflation to Price Stability', NBER Working Paper, 5469.

Giavazzi, F. and M. Pagano (1990) 'Can Severe Fiscal Adjustment Be Expansionary?', *NBER Macroeconomics Annual* (Cambridge, Mass.: MIT Press).

Gordon, R.J. (1996) 'Macroeconomic Policy in the Presence of Structural Maladjustment', in *OECD Proceedings, Macroeconomic Policies and Structural Reform* (Paris: OECD).

Gros, D. and N. Thygesen (1992) *European Monetary Integration* (New York: St. Martin's Press).

Hahm, S.D., M.S. Kamlet and D.C. Mowery (1995) 'Influences on Deficit Spending in Industrialized Countries', *Journal of Public Policy*, 15, 183–97.

Kenen, P.B. (1995) *Economic and Monetary Union in Europe: Moving Beyond Maastricht* (Cambridge: Cambridge University Press).

Krugman, P.R. (1991) *Geography and Trade* (Cambridge, Mass.: MIT Press).

Krugman, P.R. (1993) 'Lessons of Massachusetts for EMU', in F. Torres and F. Giavazzi (eds), *Adjustment and Growth in the European Monetary Union* (Cambridge: Cambridge University Press for the CEPR).

Lamfalussy, A. (1989) 'Macro-coordination of Fiscal Policies in an Economic and Monetary Union', in Committee for the Study of Economic and Monetary Union (ed.), *Report on Economic and Monetary Union in the European Community (Delors Report)* (Brussels: Office for Official Publications of the European Communities).

Lucas, R.E. (1973) 'Some International Evidence on Output–Inflation Tradeoffs', *American Economic Review*, 63, 526–34.

Mishkin, F.S. and A. Posen (1997) 'Inflation Targeting: Lessons from Four Countries', *Federal Reserve Bank of New York Economic Policy Review* (August).

Peters, T. (1995) 'EMU, Wage Policy and Unemployment', paper presented at the journées de l' ASFE, Europe-Kollege Hamburg (June).

Pissarides, C.A. (1996) 'The Need for Labour Market Flexibility in European Economic and Monetary Union', London School of Economics, mimeo.

Vinals, J. and J. Jimeno (1992) 'Monetary Union and European Unemployment', CEPR Discussion Paper, 1485.

Wyplosz, C. (1991) 'Monetary Union and Fiscal Policy Discipline', Chapter 8 in Commission of the European Communities (ed.), 'The Economics of EMU', *European Economy*, Special Edition, 1 (Brussels: Directorate-General for Economic and Financial Affairs).

7 Financial Governance and Democratic Consolidation: The Dual Challenge of the EU

Louka T. Katseli

INTRODUCTION

Only a couple of years before the turn of this century, Europe is facing the task of building an effective Economic and Monetary Union (EMU) without destabilizing financial markets and/or deconsolidating democratic processes. At a time of increased capital volatility, of high unemployment and of social exclusion, the strengthening of financial governance and the consolidation of democracy emerge as two of the most important challenges for the Union.

The central argument of this chapter can be simply summarized: Growth and employment performance as well as the rise of what is perceived to be a 'democratic deficit' in present-day Europe are intimately tied to the process of European economic integration – that is, to the means and ways by which European institutions have evolved and have distributed competences between them. If this is in fact the case then the joint pursuits of growth and employment, of financial stability and of social cohesion presuppose the rebalancing of power and the reorganization of competencies across national and community institutions.

The first section of this chapter analyses the dynamics of European integration in an attempt to substantiate the argument that low growth and unemployment in the 1990s are not transitional phenomena or cyclical variations in economic activity but economic outcomes which are structurally related to the process of European integration and the policy agenda that shaped it.

The second section evaluates the European integration process from an economic and political perspective, attributing the 'policy deficit' that has emerged to the prevalent distribution of competencies across national and community institutions.

Finally, the third section attempts to highlight three areas of potential conflict within the Union which would require for their resolution either extensive institutional reform at the European level or a reorganization of competencies across different regulatory areas.

THE DYNAMICS OF EUROPEAN INTEGRATION

One of the striking features of the European economy in the 1980s and 1990s is the persistence of high and rising unemployment rates in most member states, especially in comparison with the United States and Japan. From an average unemployment rate of 2.2 per cent in the 1970s, the average European unemployment rate in the 1980s and 1990s has risen to 9.0 and 10.4 per cent, respectively, exceeding the corresponding rates of the United States and Japan by more than four percentage points (Table 7.1). The rise in European unemployment has taken place in the context of a low-growth environment, intensifying the debate among policy-makers and economists as to whether or not unemployment is the outcome of an aggregate demand deficit in Europe or of persistent rigidities in European labour markets.[1] It is only recently that political scientists and political economists have started linking specific policy outcomes to systematic policy biases inherent in the process of institutional formation (Held 1987; Katseli 1989a, 1989b, 1997b; Tsinisizelis and Chryssochoou 1997, 1998; Tsinisizelis, Yfantis and Chryssochoou 1999).

According to this argument, there exist multiple links between the ways in which the transfer of competencies from national governments to European institutions has evolved over time and the policy biases or outcomes that are the by-product of this process.

The transfer of economic competencies started to be discussed in Europe and the United States in the early 1960s, as a response to the dollar supremacy and the need to enhance international liquidity by strengthening the European monetary base.

As early as 1960, in his pioneering work on *Gold and the Dollar Crisis*, Triffin (1960) spoke of the need for a European Reserve Union and a common currency to contribute to international liquidity and to minimize risks from the use of the dollar as the only reserve currency. The aim at that time was

Table 7.1 Unemployment rates (u) and GDP (annual percentage change) at 1990 market prices, 1961–97

	1961–70		1971–80		1981–90		1991–7	
	u	GDP	u	GDP	u	GDP	u	GDP
EUR 15	2.2	4.8	4.0	3.0	9.0	2.4	10.4	1.6
United States	4.7	3.8	6.4	2.7	7.1	2.7	6.2	2.3
Japan	1.2	10.5	1.8	4.5	2.5	4.0	2.8	1.7

Source: European Community, *European Economy* (1988, 1997), Tables 3 and 10.

to turn the EEC into one of the three economic blocs in the world, the other two being the dollar and the sterling areas. (Tsoukalis 1977, p. 53)

Around the same time, the Commission's Action Programme for the Second Stage (European Economic Community 1962) placed great emphasis on economic planning at the Community level and on the need for a common monetary policy. It considered fixed exchange rates as the very essence of monetary union and envisaged the creation of a European reserve currency arguing that 'this would facilitate international monetary cooperation and the reform of the present system' (EEC 1962, pp. 63 ff).

The competencies transferred in the 1960s and 1970s pertained exclusively to economics or 'issues of welfare' that were carefully delineated from foreign policy or defence, which were considered highly political and controversial matters. For the proponents of what came to be known as the 'neo-functionalist' school of thought, the supranational institution was seen as an honest broker, which would take an active pro-European stance, striking package deals across different areas, mobilizing an increasing number of experts and relying on a number of technocrats and committees for policy making and conflict resolution (Tsoukalis, 1977, pp. 22 ff). It would thus turn itself into a vehicle for deepening European integration as its activities would have spillover effects to other more highly political issues. The same view was held by the proponents of the 'power politics school': entrusting 'welfare issues' – which were considered separable from political issues – to European agencies and politicized beauraucrats would create its own momentum and would facilitate European integration.

The collapse of the Bretton Woods system in the early 1970s provided a new impetus for European integration as the high private costs of exchange rate fluctuations and the ensuing strains on the domestic and international banking systems created incentives for the institution of collective arrangements that would hedge foreign exchange risks and enforce stable rules of financial regulation.

Under the assumption that economics and politics were discontinuous, important economic decisions, such as the management of exchange rates, was thus removed from the domestic policy agenda and assigned to technocratic intergovernmental committees including the Board of Governors of Central Banks and the Monetary Committee of the Union. This was facilitated by the highly technical nature of exchange rate management and the fact that monetary policy was never under tight parliamentary control at the national level.

The fundamental assumption of 'policy separability' was not seriously challenged, as long as Community competencies focused, at least till the mid-1980s, essentially on monetary and exchange rate coordination.

This was facilitated by the fact that this was a period of great turbulence in exchange rate markets and of increasing deregulation of financial systems. Between 1980 and 1992, the daily average foreign exchange trading increased from $80 billion to $880 billion and the rates of foreign exchange trading to world trade increased from 10/1 to 50/1 (Table 7.2).

As regulatory barriers were removed and exchange rate volatility increased, the maturity of net global foreign exchange transactions was drastically reduced. By 1992, more than 80 per cent of currency exchanges had a maturity of less than seven days (Table 7.3). The increasing volatility of private short-term financial flows provided incentives for the creation of new financial instruments to hedge risk and for the development of exchange rate management arrangements at the regional and supranational levels.

The early Europeanization of financial and monetary policy, through the operation of the European Exchange Rate Mechanism (ERM), had important institutional and policy implications. Financial and monetary authorities were already by the late 1970s able to reap strategic, early-entry advantages over economic policy decision-making at the Community level. The creation of a system of decision-making, whereby the interests of financial capital and monetary authorities were overrepresented, shaped perceptions

Table 7.2 Growth of financial activity, 1980–2000

Year	FX Trading[a] (daily average) (billion)	Ratio of FX/trading[a] to world trade	Stock of all traded to financial assets[b] (billion)
1980	80	10:1	5000
1992	880	50:1	35 000
1995	1260	70:1	
2000			83 000

Sources: [a] Bank for International Settlements, Survey of Foreign Exchange Activity in April 1992 (Basle, 1993).
[b] Mc Kinsey Global Institute, as quoted by Eatwell (1997).

Table 7.3 Maturity of net global foreign exchange transactions, April 1992 and April 1995 (percentages)

	Spot[b]		Forward[c]	
	$X \leq 2$[a]	$2 < X \leq 7$	$7 < X \leq 365$	$365 < X$
1992	47.3	33.9	18.2	0.6
1995	43.5	38.1	17.5	0.8

Notes: [a] X = Number of days' activity.
[b] Single outright currency exchanges with cash settlements within two business days; excludes the spot leg of swaps
[c] Swaps, outright forwards traded on exchanges or 'customarized' and currency options at their notional value; cross-currency swaps of interest and amortization instalments not included.

Source: Eatwell (1997), p. 4.

regarding the causes of economic problems and the choice of desired policy instruments, in a way that was consistent with these groups' preferences over targets and instruments (Katseli 1989a, p. 49 and 1989b, p. 4).

The influence exercised by financial capital interests and by monetary authorities over supranational and European institutions, for example, produced a shift in policy perceptions regarding capital market liberalization, its effects and the merits for global financial regulation. In the early 1930s, Keynes argued passionately in his *General Theory* that 'finance should be primarily national' (Keynes 1936, p. 236); today, there is a widely held perception that capital market liberalization at the global level enhances economic efficiency, despite academic arguments to the contrary that challenge the underlying assumptions of efficient global markets (Eatwell 1997). Furthermore, at least till the mid-1980s, the rise of unemployment in Europe, was attributed to limited labour market flexibility, to real wage rigidities and to an unfriendly business environment, identified in both academic and non-academic circles with 'Eurosclerosis'. This view was espoused by most monetary authorities, even in the face of lagging demand and rising unemployment. Since labour markets and real wages were considered to be rigid, there was no room for either unilateral or coordinated expansion. Macroeconomic inactivism was espoused even after real unit labour costs declined substantially in all major European countries.

The pursuit of appropriate adjustment policies was similarly perceived to be the responsibility of national authorities, which were responsible for increasing labour market flexibility and for pruning the public sector deficits that were threatening the consolidation of convergence towards monetary stability (European Community 1986, p. 30).

The deflationary policy stance adopted by European intergovernmental institutions which were entrusted with coordinating exchange rate policy and with safeguarding monetary stability, was challenged in the 1980s by European enterprises and by industrial capital. Squeezed in domestic markets as a result of falling profitability and declining world market shares, European enterprises and industrial capital interests with the active assistance of the Commission, initiated and supported actively the creation of the Internal Market. In so doing, they sought to reap strategic trade advantages *vis-à-vis* American and Japanese transnationals in world markets, through the reduction of transaction costs, the exploitation of economies of scale and scope, the rationalization of industrial structures and the harmonization of national tax and procurement policies. Greater cost effectiveness and the facilitation of the relocation of production became principle objectives of policy (European Community 1986).

The initiation of the Internal Market Project signalled a further important step in European integration. Intergovernmental institutions were now called upon to extend their competencies beyond the coordination of monetary and exchange rate policy and to oversee the elimination of all trade impediments, including subsidies and taxes, the abolition of capital controls, the harmonization of procurement policies and the introduction of an active competition policy. European institutions thus extended, in a very short period of time, their effective sphere of competencies over large areas of trade, industrial, credit, interest and tax rate policies without any prior institutional restructuring or revision of traditional modes of decision-making.

Both the European Court of Justice (ECJ) and the Commission became actively involved in the process of enacting legislation and undertaking initiatives that broadened EC jurisdiction extensively. Their extension of competencies, however, was not complemented by a comprehensive set of positive harmonizing measures at the European level, but limited itself to assaults on existing national regulatory structures and the initiation of cumbersome legislative procedures.

The ECJ thus focused its activities on breaking down barriers to the single market erected by the legislatures of member states. Using the conduit of the Article 177 reference procedures, the Court proceeded to strike down national measures which were thought to be incompatible with the aims of the Treaty. Any national measure which was deemed to have a protectionist or discriminatory effect could come under the Court's scrutiny, unless justified by the Treaty or one of the judge-made justifications. Many aspects of the market structure and functions of member states fulfilled these criteria, even though they were initially thought to be relatively innocuous: the laws forbidding Sunday trading in the United Kingdom, for example, were a case in point.

The Commission, on the other hand, found itself confronted with the task of reaching concensus on a growing number of subjects. Its activist pro-European stance often ran counter to the politics or interests of individual member states, which were represented at the Council of Ministers. At least 15 different types of legislative procedures were enacted, each requiring the participation of different institutional arrangements and voting patterns.

Thus, while the competence of European institutions steadily expanded, their ability to pass positively harmonizing legislation did not increase correspondingly.

EVALUATING THE EFFECTS OF THE INTEGRATION PROCESS

The exigencies of integration, as manifested by the collective action of the ECJ and the Commission, in the absence of positive harmonization measures, spurred a 'deregulatory race to the bottom', while it introduced a systemic deflationary bias in Community policy. In 1979, in the case of the celebrated *Cassis de Dijon Case*, the German government spoke of a European 'deregulatory race', warning that all member states were being forced to the lowest common regulatory denominator lest traders moving across borders would face double burdens.

The same can, in fact, be said about the exercise of macro-policy. Lest any member state became tempted to impose an inflation tax in order to reduce its debt or to gain a competitive advantage through a devaluation, member states became increasingly deprived of national policy instruments to manage aggregate demand and to meet internal and external imbalances. National governments of member states engaged in 'streamlining competition' to make their policies compatible with Community imperatives and to gain the necessary credibility required to attract foreign capital or to avert destabilizing capital outflows. The speed of adjustment and of convergence was, thus, elevated into a policy target and governments started to be compensated accordingly.[2]

There is no doubt that the negative harmonization measures which evolved over the 1980s and 1990s facilitated the creation of a single internal market, contributed to the reduction of costs within the Community and reduced the risk of exchange rate destabilization. On the other hand, they led to macroeconomic inactivity at both national and European levels, even in the face of stagnant demand and of widening inequalities in income distribution. This was exacerbated by the absence of counter-balancing positive measures at the Community level, such as the expansion of the Community's budget, the adequate financing of European investment projects, a coordinated expansionary monetary policy or the introduction of a unified tax and transfer system. As a result, the deregulatory and deflationary races gained momentum, producing a policy vacuum and systemic negative real output, employment and distributional effects.

Both the Maastricht Treaty (1992) and the Stability Pact, signed in Amsterdam in 1997, proceeded to institutionalize these processes (Katseli 1997a). More specifically, the obligation assumed at Maastricht, to reduce inflation to the lowest rate prevalent in the Community, to preserve the ratio of budget deficits to GNP under the 3 per cent limit and to maintain the exchange rate practically fixed for two years prior to entry into EMU, has effectively tied government hands *vis-à-vis* the exercise of macroeconomic policy and has eliminated the use of important economic policy instruments from the national policy agenda. In the context of present-day European economic institutions, where monetary authorities and financial capital interests are overrepresented, these decisions amount to the institutionalization of contractionary policies throughout the Union and the introduction of a systemic deflationary bias in Community policies.

This bias has become even more pronounced after the endorsement of the Stability Pact at Amsterdam, when the fear of excessive budget deficits prompted decision-makers to restrict even further the competence of national governments in the conduct of fiscal policy, to introduce penalties and even to allow a pro-cyclical policy stance to maintain 'the sanctity' of the 3 per cent target.[3]

The absence of positive harmonizing measures have not only had negative real output effects but have also contributed to financial fragility. On the one hand, the deregulation and liberalization of domestic financial systems and of international capital markets have prompted domestic enterprises to raise capital in international markets, where costs are often lower; in so doing they assumed additional exchange rate risks. On the other hand, the growth of short-term financial transactions, many of which are speculative in nature, has increased financial volatility and uncertainty.

The liberalization of capital markets has not in fact succeeded in improving the allocation of capital within the Community from capital-rich to capital-poor countries.

Foreign direct investment (FDI) has instead become increasingly concentrated in the more developed countries of the Union (Table 7.4), attracted either by the availability of human capital infrastructure and of business services or by the thicker markets and the more competitive home bases.

In the light of increased financial instability, the introduction of a common currency, the euro, is the logical sequence in market participants' institutional efforts to 'socialize' foreign exchange risks. In the late 1970s and 1980s these were limited to exchange rate management via intergovernmental policy coordination; in the late

Table 7.4 European FDI flows and their distribution, 1985-94

	Recipients				Suppliers			
	1985[a]	1990[b]	1992[a]	1994[b]	1984[a]	1990[b]	1992[a]	1994[b]
EU	100	100	100	100	100	100	100	100
Belg./Lux.	14	16	23	12	9.7	18.2	18.2	9
Den.	0	1	2	5	3.3	2.3	2.3	4
Ger.	10	11	4	18	41.3	19.3	19.3	22
Greece	2	1	1	1	0.2	0.0	0.0	0
Spain	21	15	14	17	2.4	0.5	0.5	1
France	22	10	26	20	23.2	25.7	25.7	16
Ireland	5	6	6	4	0.6	0.8	0.8	4
Italy	24	5	5	6	19.5	6.1	6.1	8
Neth.	6	12	6	4	54.3	13.1	13.1	24
Port.	4	3	4	3	0.0	1.0	1.0	1
United Kingdom	-7	21	9	10	-54.6	13.0	13.0	12

Sources: [a] Eurostat (1995), p. 443.
[b] Eurostat (1996), p. 273.

1980s and 1990s they evolved into the institution of a European Exchange Rate Mechanism (ERM). The introduction of the euro is the final step in this process aiming at the elimination of foreign exchange risks from intercountry economic transactions.

The real economic effects which have resulted from the exigencies of the integration process have also had important political ramifications. This is only natural since the four freedoms which are the cornerstones of the single market, namely the freedom of labour, of goods and services, of capital and of establishment, are closely intertwined with the pursuit of fundamental economic and social rights. The free movement of goods, services and capital is intimately tied to the structure of the domestic market and the conditions in which competition takes place; the freedom of establishment impinges on environmental and property rights, on domestic regional development and on social policy; finally, the free movement of labour cannot be divorced from employment and other social rights.

This interdependence of economic and political outcomes directly challenges the basic distinction along 'issue' lines that dominated thinking and theorizing about European integration in the 1960s and 1970s and even the 1980s and the 1990s. It also challenges the fundamental separation between economic and political competencies.

In addition, the 'policy vacuum' that characterizes the workings of present-day European institutional arrangements has increased dissatisfaction with European democracy and has contributed to the emergence of a 'democratic deficit'. To the average citizen, the political system appears to lack accountability, transparency and policy effectiveness. This is made worse by the fact that economic decision-making, entrusted to Community institutions which appear to be incapable to initiate positive legislation or joint fiscal action, is increasingly perceived to be influenced by lobbies and organized commercial and business interests that engage in rent-seeking activities through their influence on legislation or policy guidelines.

In the context of an institutionally weak Europe, dominant elites often present themselves as agents of specific constituencies, resisting the development of horizontal networks among national parliaments or the local authorities. Instead, acting on behalf or the 'wider Community interest', they tend to promote vertical integration as a means of retaining ultimate authority within their domestic subcultures. As Tsinisizelis and Chryssochoou (1997) point out:

> this tendency towards inter-elite accommodation, and controlled pluralism, is conditioned by the extent to which a delicate balance of interests can be struck among the constituent units.

Under 'consociation', as this process has come to be known, democratic deconsolidation can easily occur if the balance of interests among elite cartels is disrupted. This introduces a further element of instability in the present-day functioning of the European polity.

THE CHALLENGES AHEAD

The analysis so far highlights three tentative conclusions:

(1) That economics cannot be separated from politics, since 'welfare issues' directly influence economic and social rights, through their effects on income, employment and opportunities.
(2) That the progressive erosion of member state capabilities in the field of economic policy, without corresponding positive action at the Union level, threatens to increase financial fragility and to promulgate economic stagnation.
(3) That the continuation of a policy deficit runs the risk of bringing about democratic deconsolidation of national and European

institutions as these become institutionally weaker (Gunther, Diamandouros and Puhle 1995).

The risks of prolonged stagnation, of increased financial fragility and of democratic deconsolidation could undermine the process of European integration, unless mitigated by concerted action to expand growth and employment opportunities and to safeguard the social cohesion of the Union, through active policy measures. This will require a major reorganization of competencies across national and Community institutions so that they become empowered to use the necessary economic policy instruments to promote growth, to redistribute income and to guarantee financial governance.

The need for a major restructuring of competencies across European institutions and across regulatory areas – local, regional, national or European – will be increased in the years to come in view of enlargement and the introduction of a common currency which will tend to increase conflicts among the different constituencies.

On the issue of enlargement, industrial capital will thus tend to favour the extension of the market whereas financial capital will be wary of the greater instability that such enlargement might entail. On the conduct of monetary policy, industrial capital and labour will opt for a reduction of interest rates and higher growth, while financial capital will put pressure for greater returns to savers. Finally, on the conduct of exchange rate policy, industrial capital will be in favour of greater European competitiveness in world markets, while financial capital will favour greater monetary stability.

In the light of these potential tensions and sources of friction there is an urgent need to rethink the workings of Europe's key institutions so that a more balanced representation of interests is secured and effective policy outcomes obtained. At the same time, Europe has to provide solutions to the European 'assignment problem' – namely, to devise suitable policy instruments to meet express policy targets: the pursuit of such targets as the maintenance of growth and employment requires the effective exercise of policy instruments by national and supranational institutions.

Fiscal policy provides a good example. If it is decided that it is best exercised at the national level then it follows that the Maastricht criteria need to be relaxed. If, on the other hand, a more coordinated expansion at the European level is chosen, the Community budget needs to be extended, its own funds replenished and redistributive policies adopted.

In the absence of such decisions the Community's financial governance, its democratic consolidation and its social cohesion will be seriously eroded.

Notes

1. For a summary of this debate see Gordon (1987, 1988); Modigliani (1996).
2. The links between the Cohesion Fund and performance criteria on convergence illustrate this point.
3. For an analysis of the Stability Pact, see Katseli (1997a, 1997b) and European Policy Centre, 1997.

References

Eatwell, J. (1997) 'International Financial Liberalization: The Impact on World Development', UNDP Discussion Paper Series.

European Economic Community (EEC) (1962) *Action Programme of the Community for the Second Stage* (Brussels: EEC).

European Community (1962) *Annual Economic Report* (Brussels: EEC).

European Community (1986) *Annual Economic Report* (Brussels, EU).

European Commission (1988) *European Economy* (Brussels: EU).

European Commission (1997) *European Economy* 63 (Brussels: EU).

European Policy Centre (1997) 'Making Sense of the Amsterdam Treaty', *Challenge Europe*.

Eurostat (1995) *Eurostatistics* (Brussels: EU).

Eurostat (1996) *Eurostatistics* (Brussels: EU).

Gordon, R. (1987) 'Wage Gaps vs Output Gaps: is there a Common Story for all of Europe?', NBER Working Paper, 2454 (December).

Gordon, R., J. (1988) 'Back to the Future: European Unemployment Today Viewed from America in 1939', *BPEA*, 1, 271–304.

Gunther, R., N. Diamandouros and H.J. Puhle (1995) *The Politics of Democratic Consolidation: Southern Europe in Comparative Perspective* (Baltimore: Johns Hopkins University Press).

Held, D. (1987) *Models of Democracy* (Polity Press).

Katseli, L.T. (1989a) 'The Political Economy of Macroeconomic Policy in Europe' in P. Guerrieri and P.C. Padoan (eds), *The Political Economy of European Integration* (London: Wheatsheaf), 31–57.

Katseli, L.T. (1989b) 'The Political Economy of European Integration: From Euro-sclerosis to Euro-corporatism', CEPR Discussion Paper, 317 (October).

Katseli, L.T. (1997a) 'The Recent Decisions of Dublin: The Achillean Heel of European Unification?', *Epilogi* (January) 84–89.

Katseli, L.T. (1997b) 'The Greek Economy in the Post-Maastricht Era:

Challenges and Perspectives', *Hellenic Studies*, 5 (Autumn) 109–20.
Keynes, J.M. (1936) *The General Theory of Employment, Interest and Money* (London: Macmillan).
Modigliani, F. (1996) 'The Shameful Rate of Unemployment in the EMS: Causes and Cures', *De Economist*, 144, 363–96.
Triffin, R. (1960) *Gold and the Dollar Crisis* (New Haven: Yale University Press).
Tsinisizelis, M. and D. Chryssochoou (1997) 'The European Union: Trends in Theory and Reform', in P. Schmitter and A. Wheale (eds), *The Political Theory of European Constitutional Choice* (London: Routledge).
Tsinisizelis M. and D. Chryssochoou (1998) 'From Gesellschaft to Gemeinschaft? Confederal Consociation and Democracy in the European Union', Institute of Federal Studies, University Press, Discussion Paper, FS 95/3).
Tsinisizelis M., K. Yfantis and D. Chryssochoou (1999) *Theory and Reforms in the European Union* (Manchester: Manchester University Press).
Tsoukalis, Loukas (1977) *The Politics and Economics of European Monetary Integration* (London: George Allen & Unwin).

8 Capitalist Globalization and Economic and Monetary Union

Gugliemo Carchedi

THE MYTH OF GLOBALIZATION AND THE REALITY OF IMPERIALISM

Usually, the notion of globalization put forward by the majority of both popular and academic publications emphasizes three aspects. First, there is the economic dimension – that is, the further internationalization of capital within which the multinationals play a predominant role. In this view, not only national capitals but even nation-states are no match for global capital, which is often seen only in its financial form. Secondly, there is the political dimension – that is, the epochal victory of capitalism over so-called communism. This makes it possible for capital to penetrate territories from which it had been excluded from the Bolshevik revolution until 1989. For capitalism's apologists this will make it possible for democracy to be spread to all four corners of the world. It is, of course, a specific type of democracy, that which is functional for the development of capitalism, to which they refer. Finally, there is the technological dimension – that is, the new technologies will not only foster further capital internationalization but will also radically change our daily life. The two examples most commonly mentioned are the computer and information technology (IT). These technologies will put an end to human labour (and thus to the working class) thus allowing men (and women?) to become the arbiters of their own destiny.

The dominant role of the multinationals, the great mobility of huge masses of capital on the international financial markets, the fall of the Soviet Union and the constant introduction of new technologies are all real developments. However, the notion which unifies them in one single concept – globalization – is aggressively ideological.

These aspects are seen as elements of a system which, having defeated its mortal enemy, 'communism', puts an end to history itself by opening the doors to general cornucopia and global democracy. It is added with some embarrassment, that unemployment, poverty, wars, ecological disasters, and so on have not disappeared, but these are residues of the past which will be wiped out by the triumphal march of global capitalism. In short, if capital were a person, this would be its rosiest dream.

The reality, of course, is different. To see this, it is not sufficient to stress the class content of the concept of globalization – that is, the glorification of capital inherent in it. One should also analyze those real developments which are perceived by this concept, even though in a distorted way. To do this, one needs a different theoretical framework, one which allows us to see globalization as a partially new form of contemporary imperialism. It is within this alternative framework that the movement towards the EMU can be properly understood.

Let us begin by examining one of globalization's myths, that technological innovation (TI) will bring us generalized employment and welfare, thus erasing the contradictions arising from poverty amidst affluence. Nothing could be further from reality. The reasons are complex but basically can be reduced to the contradiction inherent in capitalist production between use values and (exchange) value. In other words, the introduction of TI usually implies the shedding of labour so that an increasing quantity of output is produced with a decreasing labour force. Given that only labourers can produce value, an increasing number of use values contains a decreasing quantity of value and thus of surplus value.[1] If abstraction is made of the many counter-tendencies, the average rate of profit (ARP) cannot but fall.[2] The way this fall becomes manifest is through the fall in the labourers' purchasing power.

To see this, let us distinguish between the sector producing means of production (sector I) and that producing means of consumption (sector II). Consider first the case of a productivity increase in sector II not followed by reduced employment. The same value is incorporated in more means of consumption. If the monetary expression of value does not change (given that the value produced is the same),[3] the quantity of money is constant and the unit prices of the means of consumption fall. Let us distinguish between purchasing power in value terms (PPv) and in use value terms (PPu). If money wages are constant (and thus with a constant rate of surplus value, given that the labour performed is also assumed constant), the labourers' PPv does not fall while PPu rises to purchase all the extra products. There are no realization problems in sector II.

This case, while theoretically possible, does not correspond to the dynamics of capitalist development, given that all the benefits of productivity increases (PPu) would go to the labourers and not to the capitalists. Capital can, and does, react by increasing the prices of the means of consumption through inflation. At constant money wages, this means a higher rate of surplus value through an increase in absolute surplus value. It is because of this that TI usually implies lower wages and/or the eviction of labour force – that is, unemployment. The outcome is a fall in the masses' PPv (at constant money wage rates). This holds also if money wage rates increase but insufficiently to absorb all the extra products. While the output of means of consumption has grown, the labourers' PPv needed to absorb it falls. Realization problems appear in this sector.[4] To avoid these difficulties, capitalists react by reducing prices and thus the costs of production. They thus invest even more in TI, thus causing more unemployment and worsening, rather than relieving, the economy's realization problems. Orders for means of production to produce means of consumption start falling and this creates unemployment in sector I, too. The economy has fallen into a vicious circle and the ARP falls.[5]

However, the price system redistributes the value produced both by the technologically advanced enterprises and by the technological laggards from the latter to the former. Those enterprises which have introduced new technologies, thus shedding labour force, on the one hand are consequently responsible for the decreased production of value and surplus value and thus for the inevitable tendency towards economic crises, but on the other appropriate a part of the value produced by the technological laggards, which employ more labour. It follows that the technological innovators realize a higher rate of profit at the expense of the rest of the economy and thus of the general rate of profit. In other words, crises hit on the one hand those capitals left behind in the technological race and on the other the workers, the very producers of value and surplus value. Technological 'progress' and unemployment are two sides of the same coin, as the 20 million unemployed in the EU show.

It should be mentioned that TI does not engender unemployment automatically but only tendentially. TI generates unemployment because the variable capital (labourers) employed per unit of capital usually falls (the saving on labour costs is just a powerful incentive to innovate as the increase in efficiency). However, the introduction of new technologies can be accompanied by increased employment if (1) new branches of production are opened, and (2) if the number of labourers shed by each unit of capital is more than offset by an increase in the number of units of capital invested – in other words, by an increase in the total capital invested. In other words, the tendency is for TI to generate unemployment (if the same or a smaller quantity of capital is invested on the basis of 'labour-saving' technologies) but the counter-tendency is the opposite – that is, is given by the creation of more employment for capital as a whole even if each unit of capital uses less variable capital and more constant capital.

While the tendency (technological unemployment per unit of capital invested) is always present, it manifests itself as higher societal unemployment only in periods of crises – that is, of decreased capital accumulation. In periods of economic boom it manifests itself as its own counter-tendency (higher societal employment). In other words TI generates more or less employment according to the phase of the economic cycle. In periods of crises, as less capital is invested, new technologies are accompanied by increasing unemployment, lower ARP and bankruptcies. At a certain point, as sufficient capital has been destroyed, a period of economic recovery and boom starts again.[6] During this period technological unemployment appears at the level of the capital units but total employment usually grows due to an increased mass of total investments. As the labour market tightens and wages rise, profits start falling and total capital invested stagnates or decreases. This total capital is re-invested on the basis of more technologically advanced techniques and unemployment starts reappearing. A new crisis sets in and cycle begins again anew.

It should be stressed that, while it is impossible to determine beforehand whether TI produces an increase or a decrease in total (un)employment, it is possible, and necessary, to distinguish between the tendency and the counter-tendency. Failure to do this leads to the inability to grasp this particular law of movement of the system. Contradictory empirical results do not necessarily, and they do not in this case, imply indeterminacy. In other words, social reality's laws of movement are not mechanical but tendential.

At this juncture, it is necessary to open a parenthesis. The approach just sketched runs counter to the commonly held but mistaken idea that an increased productivity raises the ARP, rather than decreasing it. There are at least six reasons for this misconception. The first three are theoretical mistakes of various types while the last three belong to the same category of mistakes – that is, the inability to distinguish between the tendency and the counter-tendency. Let us consider the first group of theoretical mistakes.

First, most economic theories consider only one aspect of productivity increases, the greater physical output per unit of capital invested. These theories see only physical quantities and disregard the value (labour) dimension. They thus cannot understand how a greater physical productivity can lead to a falling ARP. Second, higher output per unit of capital can be achieved either through TI or through greater intensity of labour and longer working days (absolute surplus value). While in the former case less value is produced (given that labour is shed) so that the ARP falls, in the latter case more value is produced, so that the ARP rises. Usually no distinction is made between these two cases, so that confusion arises as to the effects of the introduction of TI on the creation of value and on the ARP.[7] Third, as stressed above, innovators do realize a greater rate of profit, at the expense of the value appropriated by other producers, thus causing a fall in the ARP. An a-critical extension of the effects of TI on the innovators' profit rate to all capitals leads to the wrong conclusion that TI must increase the ARP.

Resistance to the idea that TI tendentially decreases the ARP is also due to the failure to distinguish between the tendency and its counter-tendencies. Only three such failures will be mentioned here. First, an increased productivity in sector II reduces the unit value of wage goods (a smaller labour force produces more use values). Unit prices fall, too, given that more means of consumption circulate through less money (the quantity of money in circulation falls under the assumption of a constant monetary expression of value). If less labour per unit of capital is employed, less value and less surplus value is produced per capital unit, and the ARP falls.[8] This is the tendency. Now the counter-tendency. We have seen that a smaller labour force now gets a proportionally smaller quantity of consumption goods. This is not the reason for a lower value of labour power; the reason is that, on the basis of that smaller force, since the consumption goods' unit prices have fallen, if PPu remains the same, PPv falls and with it the value of the employed labour power. *Ceteris paribus*, the rate of surplus value rises and with it the ARP rises. Or, while TI cause a fall in the ARP owing to the smaller quantity of living labour employed per unit of capital invested (the tendency), the same TI causes a rise in the ARP due to the fall in the value of labour power and thus due to a rise in the rate of surplus value (the counter-tendency).[9]

Second, a part of the increased quantity of products following the increase in productivity can be exported. What is realized is value produced in other countries, thus realizing a greater ARP in the exporting country (at the expense of the value appropriated by other countries). Third, the fall in prices, and thus in the ARP, can be delayed through inflation. However, if the price of the outputs of this period rise, the prices of the inputs of the next period are also by definition greater (given that the inputs of this period are the inputs of the next period). This reduces the rate of profit in the next period, *ceteris paribus*. The fall in the ARP has been delayed at the cost of the depreciation of money (a fall in money's purchasing power[10]). To conclude, TI, if immersed in capitalist production relations, generates a tendency towards a falling ARP, economic crises and thus poverty amidst affluence. Globalization's claim that TI will generate generalized cornucopia is simply wrong.

Against this backdrop, let us consider three more claims made by the theorists of globalization. First, it is claimed that TI will lead to the disappearance of the working class. Let us begin with some figures. While in the early 1970s there were 7000 multinationals, this figure had risen to 37 000 in the early 1990s. These 37 000 enterprises had 170 000 subsidiaries in the whole world. The greatest 300 multinationals control one-quarter of the world's productive assets and almost half of foreign direct investments. Approximately 70 per cent of international trade is accounted for the largest 500 multinationals. This huge concentration of economic power becomes even more visible in the financial sphere. These, and other similar figures, are a vivid substantiation of Marx's theory of capital concentration and centralization. What does this mean for the working class? The 72 million workers employed by the multinationals are only 5 per cent of the world's labour force. Does this mean that, if we extrapolate this tendency, the working class is melting away? Certainly not. The reason is simply that there cannot be capitalism without a working class. Capitalism's essence is the production of value and surplus value and only labourers can produce (surplus) value. Without labourers there are no capitalists, there would only be petty commodity producers (possibly operating at high technological levels).

Secondly, it is commonly held that TI will lead to labour's radical transformation as well as to a great improvement in people's general life conditions. There is no doubt that the application of TI has a profound effect on the composition and transformation of the working class. As I have argued over the years (Carchedi 1991a, b), one of the fundamental tasks left unfinished by Marx is that of developing his embryonic analysis of mental labour in order to identify new forms of labour as well as of what Marx called, in the third volume of *Capital*, non-labour – that is, the work of control and surveillance. TI, however, while possibly leading to greater welfare, also leads to new forms of labour's subordination to capital. The computer is a great step forward not only in human productivity for example but also in labour's control by capital. But even more dangerous are the great strides in genetic engineering. This on the one hand alleviates human suffering but on the other has already created new forms of life which reflect the capitalist division of labour and are functional for profit-making. One aspect of capital's dream is that of moulding life itself in its own likeness.[11]

A third aspect usually stressed by the theoreticians of globalization concerns financial capital whose power and magnitude would seem to have exceeded that of national states and central banks. It is common knowledge that every day 1200 billion dollars roam the international financial markets in a constant quest for speculative profits: a huge mass, whose movements not only cause the volatility of interest rates but also influence and sometimes dictate national economic policies. This is so. But there are two aspects which the theoreticians of globalization cannot see and which put financial capital's movements in their proper perspective.

First, while capital movements have basically a speculative nature, the source of this enormous mass of financial capital resides in the fact that that capital which cannot find a profitable outlet in the productive sphere tries its luck in financial–speculative operations. Seen from this angle, the magnitude of financial capital looking for speculative profits provides an indication of the gravity of the present economic crisis. It is these figures, together with unemployment figures, rather than GNP figures, which are a reliable indicator of a nation's economic health. It is these figures which reveal to us that the present economic crisis is far from having been overcome.

Second, the so-called globalization of financial markets amounts to a partially new form of appropriation of international surplus value. This, too, is a complex matter regarding both the redistribution of the world's surplus value among capitalists and the consequences of such a redistribution for the world's working class. As far as the first aspect is concerned – that is, the redistribution of surplus value at the international level – the key concept is seigniorage. This means that those nations whose currency is also the international currency (the US dollar but also increasingly the deutsche mark and the Japanese yen) can use their own currencies in order to appropriate the surplus value produced in other countries. Within limits, seigniorage means to be able to print paper money with which real value can be paid (commodities) without having to give back any real value. The nations which can exercise seigniorage are those whose economic power, and in the last analysis their level of productivity is consistently greater than that of other nations. It follows that the result of the globalization of the financial markets, inasmuch as its new form is concerned – that is, the emergence of three rivals competing for the role of the only international currency (just like the US dollar after the Second World War) – is a strife among nations and their capitals for the appropriation of gigantic quantities of the world's surplus value as a reward for having reached a dominant technological position.

EMU AND THE SINGLE CURRENCY

Having criticized some general features of globalization theory and having argued that they indicate, in a distorted way, a new stage of imperialism, let us now focus on the effects of these new developments for a specific geopolitical area, Europe. The thesis to be submitted in what follows is that the European nations have to aggregate in an economic and monetary union in order to compete with the two other major blocks, the United States and Japan.[12] This, however, takes place under the leadership of Germany. This leadership is accepted because it allows for a common advantage, the extraction of greater surplus value. To understand how this takes place concretely, an example will be provided, that of the European Monetary System (EMS), the forerunner of Economic and Monetary Union (EMU).

The two basic features of the EMS are the Exchange Rate Mechanism, or ERM, and the European Currency Unit, or ECU.[13] The

ECU is a composite currency in which all member states' currencies are represented by different quantities (weights). Through this fixed value relative to the ECU, national currencies have a fixed value relative to each other. For example, according to the *Financial Times* (7 March 1995), ECU 1 was equal to Fl 2.152 and to FFr 6.406. These are the bilateral central rates against the ECU, or 'central rates', for short. They imply that Fl 2.152 = FFr 6.406; or, FFr 1 = 2.152/6.406 Fl = Fl 0.3359 and Fl.1 = 6.406/2.152 FFr = FFr 2.976. These are the cross-bilateral central rates, or cross-rates, for short. Up to 1992, the member states undertook to keep their currencies' fluctuations within relatively narrow limits (2.25 per cent above and 2.25 per cent-below the cross-rates – Italy was allowed a ± 6 per cent band but adopted the ± 2.25 per cent band in 1990). These limits of fluctuations are the bands or bilateral limits. After the 1993 crisis, these bands were widened to ± 15 per cent (except for Germany and the Netherlands, which retained the ± 2.25 per cent band).

Consider, by way of example, the maximum fluctuation of the FFr and the Fl relative to each other. Suppose the FFr loses value relative to the Fl (that is, the Fl gains value relative to the FFr). Either the FFr devalues by a maximum of 15 per cent or the Fl revalues by a maximum of 15 per cent. Politically, there is a difference between Holland revaluing relative to France or France devaluing relative to Holland; France will prefer the former option in order to avoid devaluation and the concomitant negative image associated with it. Computationally too these two outcomes are not the same. Then, the average is taken. For example, if the FFr devalues by 15 per cent, it falls to (6.406 + 15 per cent of 6.406) = FFr 7.3669 relative to Fl 2.152. This means that if Fl 2.152 = FFr 7.3669, Fl 1 = 7.3669/2.152 = FFr 3.423. If the Fl revalues by 15 per cent, it rises to (2.152 − 15 per cent of 2.152) = Fl 1.8292 relative to FFr 6.406. This means that Fl 1.8292 = FFr 6.406, so that Fl 1 = 6.406/1.8293 = FFr 3.5021. If the average is taken, (3.5021 + 3.423)/2 = FFr 3.46255. This gives the maximum devaluation of the FFr relative to the Fl (that is, the maximum revaluation of the Fl relative to the FFr). Or, given that the cross-rate is, Fl 1 = FFr 2.976, the FFr is allowed to devalue relative to the Fl (that is, the Fl can revalue relative to the FFr) up to a maximum of Fl 1 = FFr 3.457. Similarly for the case in which the FFr revalues relative to the Fl (that is, the Fl devalues relative to the FFr).

To keep currencies within their bilateral limits, central banks and governments have to intervene. In the case of a weak currency, they resort to a rise in interest rates, to support operations using a diversity of currencies, or to a tightening of fiscal policy. The opposite happens in case of a strong currency. However, central banks do not wait until the bilateral limits have been reached before intervening. Once a country's currency has diverged by three-quarters of its permissible margin above or below its ECU central rate, the *divergence indicator* is reached. There is then a presumption that a government will take remedial action. Notice that a currency, inasmuch as it is a part of the ECU, cannot fluctuate around itself. Thus, for example, if the deutsche mark forms 30.2 per cent of the value of the ECU, it can only fluctuate by 100–30.2, that is 69.8, around the ECU – in other words, against the other currencies forming the ECU. ECU is the maximum fluctuation against the then 0.698 x 15 = ± 10.47.

We can now see how the bilateral bands limit the technological laggards' possibility to use anti-cyclical measures, thus tying them to the dominant country's policy. Consider the example of Germany (higher productivity) and Italy (lower productivity). Germany, given her higher productivity, is more competitive on foreign markets. Also, greater productivity allows German labour's greater material welfare.[14] Germany's pursuance of higher profits, then, is relatively independent of high inflation. Moreover, inflation would dent price competitivity thus requiring devaluation, something Germany is reluctant to use because, as we shall see shortly, this would check Germany's aim to make the deutsche mark an international currency. Inflation, then, is enemy number one in Germany. Italy's situation is the opposite. Lower productivity levels create the conditions for inflationary policies as a means to reduce the level of real wages (that is, to increase the rate of surplus value and thus the rate of profit). To safeguard her international competitiveness, Italy has to resort to devaluation. But the less efficient country's possibility to resort to competitive devaluation is limited by the relative fixity of the exchange rates within the ERM.

Suppose, for example, that the Italian government decides to resort to money creation to stimulate the economy, that is profitability. This will generate inflationary pressures and call for a devaluation of the lira. However, the bilateral bands rule out large exchange rate fluctuations. Consequently, Italy, if she does not want to devalue by modifying the central rate, must either accept a deterioration of the balance of trade or reduce the rate of inflation. In this indirect way – i.e. through the ERM–Germany sets a limit to the Italian rate of inflation thus restricting the (limited) effectiveness of this anti-cyclical measure in Italy. Or suppose that Germany lowers her interest rate in order to check pressures on the deutsche mark. Inasmuch as interest rate differentials play a role in financial capital movements, financial operators sell deutsche mark and buy lire. This tends to revalue the lira and devalue the deutsche mark. If this process threatens to send the lira through the upper limit of the band and Italy has to lower her interest rate in order to relieve the pressure on the lira. But this might have unwanted inflationary effects.[15]

In this way a seemingly neutral mechanism fosters specific economic policies and interests, those of the dominant country, that is Germany, and within it of the German oligopolies. While Germany can compete basically through greater efficiency, technological laggards have to compete basically through higher rates of surplus value. This can be done in one of the following two ways. It can be done at the point of production – that is, through longer working days and higher intensity of labour. The extraction of absolute surplus value increases. This is fostered by the dismantling of social security systems and the increased legal possibility to arbitrarily dismiss labourers, nowadays called labour flexibility. Alternatively, higher rates of surplus value can be achieved through redistribution (inflation). The ERM forces technological laggards to *renounce inflation and devaluation* and to *extract more absolute surplus value at the point of production* rather than through redistribution mechanisms (inflation). This makes it possible for Germany, too, to raise its rate of absolute surplus value, as German entrepreneurs too demand more 'freedom' to deal with labour.

However, the law according to which technological leaders tend to revalue their currencies and technological laggards tend to devalue theirs is stronger than the conscious attempts to check it. In fact, since the EMS has entered into force, the deutsche mark has only been revalued (from 1979 to 1990, the deutsche mark has been revalued six times) and the Italian lira has only been devalued, six times (Swann 1992, p. 211). As for inflation, if 1980 = 100, consumer prices in Germany had risen to 121 by 1987 but to 214 in Italy. Moreover, if the weight of the ERM becomes intolerable for the weaker countries in terms of unemployment, loss of foreign markets and foreign currency, popular discontent, or simply speculative movements, only one solution is left: leaving the ERM. This is indeed what happened to Italy and the United Kingdom in September 1992.[16]

What has been said up to here can now be applied to EMU and the euro. The advantages of EMU and the euro for capital are numerous. According to official economic doctrine, EMU is supposed to create a zone of monetary stability and this in its turn is supposed to contribute to the achievement of a stable, equilibrium and crises-free economy. This, of course, bears no relation to reality which obstinately continues to be in an unstable, disequilibrium and crises-prone state. Official economics also submit that the discipline imposed by EMU will induce greater competitiveness through the introduction of TI. But what has been said above shows that both ERM and EMU force laggard countries to extract more absolute surplus value at the point of production, something which, if anything, slows down the introduction of TI. If these latter countries introduce TI, they do so in spite of, and not thanks to, the EMS. On a less ideological plane, official ideology stresses the euro's common advantages, such as better trade conditions deriving from savings on exchange rate costs and hedging, or the simplification which could be achieved in managing the Common Agricultural Policy (CAP). However, this is not the heart of the matter. Neither is it of decisive importance to know that the computer industry will gain from a greatly increased demand while the car industry will suffer from reduced demand.

The real reasons behind the introduction of EMU and the euro lie elsewhere. Only four will be mentioned here. First, in post-Second World War Europe, high rates of inflation have been a means to increase the rate of surplus value, and thus the rate of profit, in periods of heightened labour militancy. But inflation corrodes not only labour's income but also that of all other classes, including those which are traditional allies of capital, thus being a possible cause of generalized dissatisfaction with the national governments's economic policies. High rates of absolute surplus value at the point of production avoid this drawback. Secondly, high rates of inflation in Europe might call for successive rounds of competitive devaluations and these would leave the relative competitive positions unaltered while weakening the international strength of the European currencies. Again, this is not the case for high rates of absolute surplus value at the point of production. Thirdly, while inflationary measures increase the ARP by redistributing the value produced, higher rates of absolute surplus value at the point of production increase both the ARP and the economic base (the production of value and of commodities). Fourth, contrary to inflationary measures, high rates of absolute surplus value at the point of production foster an increased direct control on labour within the labour process itself and the (ideological, political and organizational) weakening of labour's organizations.

Thus, the economic significance of the EMU and of the Euro for labour *cannot but be negative*. Only a few aspects have been highlighted, that is (1) the creation of more surplus value contained in more commodities (rather than the redistribution of an unchanged quantity of value and of commodities in favour of capital), (2) based on a greatly increased control and surveillance of labour (and on the weakening of its political, ideological and organizational forms) and (3) tied neither to the generalized worsening of the conditions of life of capital's allies nor to the weakening of the national currencies. At the same time, this system appears to be imposed by a distant bureaucracy whereas it is actually the result of conscious anti-labour economic policies.[17] These are at the same time *the common advantages for European capital*. The euro, and thus German leadership, is accepted by the other European countries because the bill is paid by labour.[18]

It follows that the more the EU countries are tied to Germany and to this project, the greater the expropriation of value from labour. This all happens under a double deception. First, an antilabour policy desired by national governments (and by the multinationals) is disguised as if it were an economic policy imposed by some distant bureaucracy, as we saw above, for which the member states are not responsible, and reflecting some socially neutral rationality. Second, an economic policy ultimately in the interest of industrial capital appears as if it were imposed by (German) financial capital. In reality, financial capital forces industrial capital to renounce the competitive instruments of the poor countries (inflation and devaluation), it calls industrial capital to task, and thus is functional for the greater creation of (surplus) value rather than simply for a more favourable redistribution of the (surplus) value created. Supranational financial capital (the European Central Bank or ECB) will enjoy a measure of relative autonomy in the interest of the expanded reproduction of the most advanced European industrial capital. But, of course, this will not be sufficient to hold back future crises.

The common advantages for European capital deriving from EMU and the euro have been stressed above. Let us consider the specific advantages for different countries. For Germany, EMU and the euro are important because they will be the platform from which Germany's economic interests will be best served. Let us first consider the importance of EMU for Germany. EMU is important for Germany because it is supposed to transform the deutsche mark into the euro and this into a world currency. At present, the deutsche mark is only a potential contender for the role of international money; its economic basis is still too restricted. To become a truly international currency, it will have to become the currency used in the whole Community, in a market comparable to that of the United States, served by an efficient and technologically advanced production system. This will propel a volume of euro-denominated international transactions such that demand for the euro will be equal to or surpass that for the dollar. This, in its turn, will facilitate the placing of euro-denominated financial instruments on non-EMU markets, thus increasing the demand for the currency. Inasmuch as this process will be successful, the world's Central Banks and other institutional investors will adjust their portfolios from dollar-denominated to euro-denominated instruments, thus reinforcing this virtuous circle.

But this is not yet sufficient for the euro to become the new form taken by the deutsche mark. This will be the case only inasmuch as the euro is managed according to an economic policy reflecting and fostering the interests of German capital (even though in a mediated and negotiated way[19]) – that is, according to a relatively strict interpretation and application of the Maastricht convergence criteria (at least, as long as Germany retains its dominant position within the EU[20]). It is through these criteria that the other member countries' interests are subordinated to those of Germany.[21] The single currency will erase even the restricted possibility offered by the ERM to resort to devaluation (realignments) while the stability criteria will tie the weaker countries' economic policies to that of Germany even more strongly. Within EMU, the ERM will not disappear but will tie the non-EMU members to the euro. The difference will be that the euro will replace the ECU as the pivot of the central rates of non-euro currencies (European Council, 1996). This will tie the economic policy of the non-euro members to that of the euro area and thus of its dominant country, Germany. In this way, the introduction of EMU and of the euro, a further step towards not only European integration but also towards a strengthening of Germany's dominant position, will be paid by labour both in the euro area and outside it.

As for the *less competitive countries*, by adhering to EMU and to the euro, they definitively renounce inflation and devaluation as independent instruments of anti-conjunctural policy and international competition (right at the moment when they badly need them). These are the disadvantages they have to accept in order to participate in EMU projects – that is, in order to participate in the common advantages mentioned above. But they have other advantages as well, which partially compensate for these disadvantages. First, it has been mentioned that Germany's project is that of transforming the deutsche mark into the euro, thus profiting from seigniorage. In the process, the currencies of the technologically laggard countries will be also converted into the euro. This means that these countries, too, will be able to participate in the gains deriving from seigniorage, inasmuch as the euro does become a rival of the dollar. For these countries, then, the euro on the one hand cancels the possibility of competitive devaluation but on the other offers, together with the advantages mentioned above, the promise of participating in seigniorage. This is a further advantage the laggards share with the leading country.

Secondly, there are specific advantages for these countries inherent in EMU and the euro project. Only three will be mentioned here. First, in a common market, given the free movement of goods, the effects of demand stimulation through inflation might be lost to other member states. The disadvantage of renouncing inflation might be smaller than otherwise. Second, the ERM (and EMU and euro) deprive individual countries of the possibility to use competitive devaluation but on the other hand makes generalized competitive devaluations impossible. These would leave all countries concerned with an unchanged competitive position relative to each other, would create commercial and political tensions with Germany and would ultimately endanger their membership in the European project. Third, a common currency by definition eliminates monetary crises and speculative movements against the weaker currencies. These crises can have a disruptive effect on the real economy as well.

Finally, *common advantages do not imply harmony of interests*. France, for example, is unable to match Germany's leading role in the formulation of common policies. France is thus interested in the single currency because through it common monetary policy, including Euro devaluations if needed can be influenced. This is why France advocates a flexible interpretation of the Maastricht criteria and of the stability pact which will follow the creation of EMU. It is in this light that the French–German disagreement on the nomination of the ECB's president and the creation of a Stability Council should be seen.

CONCLUSIONS

To conclude, while the concept of globalization celebrates the defeat of so-called communism, the end of an epoch in which capitalist development was inhibited by the 'evil empire', the concept of imperialism shows that, after this historic defeat of the international working class, we are on the verge of a new phase in which capital's contradictions emerge again both in their time-honoured forms and in new, but perhaps even more dangerous, forms. While the notion of globalization stresses the speculative aspects of capital movements, the notion of imperialism perceives such movements both as one of the effects of a crisis which has not yet been overcome and as a gigantic redistribution of value and surplus value. While globalization perceives new technologies as the source of a new, generalized, cornucopia and as the great social equalizer, imperialism sees these technologies as one of the factors transforming and recomposing, but not erasing, the working class. While globalization theorists see the end of ideology, the theory of imperialism sees in these transformations and recomposition the objective basis of a new subjectivity, truly international and internationalist.

Notes

1. For the purposes of this chapter, 'value' can be defined as human labour performed under capitalist production relations and necessarily taking a monetary form. Surplus value(s) is that part of total value (in its monetary form) which is appropriated by the owners of the (material and mental) means of production. Variable capital (v) is that part of total value (also in its monetary form) going to the collective labourer. The rate of surplus value is s/v. If constant capital (c) is that part of total value invested in means of production (in its monetary form), the rate of profit is $s/(c + v)$.
2. What follows in this section deals with some aspects of a theory of

economic crises, but is far from providing a full account of such a theory.
3. Throughout this chapter changes in the quantity of money are assumed to correspond to changes in the value produced for reasons of theoretical comparison. In reality, of course, this need not be the case.
4. Prices must fall more than the increase in productivity. In fact, if less labour has been expended and less value produced (due to the unemployment caused by TI), less value can be realized. It follows that, for less value to be realized, prices have to fall more than the increase in productivity.
5. It has been argued that crises need not manifest themselves as lack of purchasing power for means of consumption first, and then for means of production. The argument runs more or less as follows. Let us split sector I into Ia (means of production to produce means of production) and Ib (means of production to produce means of consumption). The system could become relatively insulated from realization difficulties in sector II (the masses' purchasing power) if capitalists invested more and more in Ia (investment in Ib would only postpone the fall in the masses' purchasing power). Then, that labour power which would be expelled by Ib and II could be absorbed by Ia. High productivity in sector II would ensure sufficient means of consumption both for the whole of the labour force and for the capitalists.

The problem with this hypothesis is twofold. First, sector Ia too introduces TI, thus expelling labour power. The scale of investments in Ia would have to be such as to absorb the whole of the economy's technological unemployment; this might or might not be the case but is certainly not sustainable in the long run. Secondly, the role adjudicated to Ia assumes that all capitals would behave in such a coordinated way, that they would migrate from Ib and II to Ia and that no capital would move in the opposite direction. This assumption is groundless. Capitals move to where the (expected) rate of profit is higher, thus back and forth between sectors I and II. If, for example, TI is introduced in sector II so that the innovators realize a higher rate of profit, capitals in sector I realizing a lower profit rate will move to sector II and adopt those new technologies. In so doing, they improve their own profitability at the cost of the rest of the economy, thus causing a fall in the ARP. As long as TI is introduced in Ia, the lower ARP does not appear as difficulties of realization in sector II and the masses' purchasing power does not fall. But there is no reason to assume that capitals will invest more and more in Ia and less and less in Ib and II. At some times they will and at others they will not.

It should be stressed that the masses' lack of purchasing power is not the cause but it is the manifestation of the falling profit rate. This would seem to clash with Marx's quotation that

> The ultimate reason for all real crises always remains the poverty and restricted consumption of the masses as opposed to the drive of capitalist production to develop the productive forces as though only the absolute consuming power of society constituted their limit. (Marx 1971, III, p. 484)

As I have argued elsewhere, this quotation is taken out of Marx's discussion of the relation between commercial credit and real crises and thus refers to realization crises (Carchedi 1991a, pp. 181–3). It is clear that realization crises are ultimately determined by lack of purchasing power. However, realization crises are themselves determined by production crises – that is, less can be realized because less has been produced. To explain crises of realization on the basis of insufficient demand would be tautological or to take refuge in psychological 'sentiments'. On the tendency for the ARP to fall, one should consult A. Kliman's work (see Freeman and Carchedi 1996, for a bibliography). The works in Freeman and Carchedi are part of what has come to be known as the 'temporal single system approach' (TSS).
6. Higher rates of profit are a necessary but insufficient condition for recovery to start again. Capitalists must also foresee a greater market for their products, something which presupposes the disappearance of a sufficient number of their competitors through a chain of bankruptcies. If this has happened, more investments and employment follow. The money (value) needed for the initial steps of economic growth comes from the reserves and savings accumulated during the previous period of crisis.
7. While more surplus value is created, difficulties of realization emerge. In case of greater intensity and longer days in sector II, more labour is expended and thus both more value and more use values (means of consumption) are produced. A higher rate of surplus value implies that money wages are not raised (let us disregard for the sake of simplicity the case in which they rise less than the increase in productivity). If the monetary expression of value is constant (as it should be, to make comparison possible), more money must be put into circulation in order to represent the greater quantity of value produced. Assuming that this extra quantity of money affects only the prices of the means of consumption, these goods' unit prices can be kept constant. Then, a constant money wage can purchase a smaller proportion of the total quantity of means of consumption. Labour's PPu is constant but PPv has fallen and realization difficulties appear. However, the assumption that the increased quantity of money affects only the prices of consumption goods is unrealistic, given that a greater quantity of money will affect all prices (even if in different measures). The prices of the means of production will then rise and those of the means of consumption will fall. Labour's PPv falls less and PPu increases. Realization problems persist unless all the extra value (and use values) are appropriated by the labourers as higher wages. But this, as said above, cannot be the principle upon which capitalism rests. Consider now greater intensity and longer days in sector I (which produces the means of production). The quantity of means of consumption does not change, while more means of production are produced. Here, too, the quantity of money in circulation must increase (for reasons of comparison), given that more value has been produced. If all the extra money affects only the prices of the means of production, the unit prices of the means of consumption do not change. At constant wages,

there are no realization problems. But the greater quantity of money affects the prices of both the means of production and the means of consumption. In this case, the unit prices of the means of consumption increase and, at constant wages, the masses's purchasing power (both PPv and PPu) falls. Realization difficulties appear.

8. Realization difficulties follow inasmuch as a part of the greater output is not appropriated by labour – that is, inasmuch as PPu falls, remains constant, or increases but PPv falls.
9. Here, too, difficulties of realization will arise.
10. Inflation is beneficial for the ARP if the price of the means of consumption increases more than money wages. But then the rate of absolute surplus value increases. Realization problems in sector II follow. Notice that inflation changes the monetary expression of value, not the value produced. However, if more (less) value is appropriated by labour as wages, in the next period the value of labour power rises (falls) so that the surplus value produced falls (rises).
11. 'The first genetically engineered lamb, named Polly... was born two weeks ago. She was cloned from a fetal cell that had a human gene... Cloning experts say the work is a milestone. Animals with human genes could be used, in theory, to produce hormones or other biological products to treat human disease. They could also be given human genetic diseases and used to test new treatments. And genetically altered animals might also produce organs that could be transplanted into humans with less chance of rejection than now exists... Genetic engineering of human beings is now really on the horizon' (G. Kolata, Dolly's creators take next step, *International Herald Tribune*, 26–27 July 1997). One can only shiver at the idea of what kind of 'human beings' can emerge from profit-driven laboratories.
12. Actually, we witness a double process. On the one hand the aggregation of nation states in the EU as a step towards a United States of Europe but on the other a tendency towards secessionism within the existing nations-state, as in the case of Northern Italy and in Bavaria. This theme cannot be pursued here.
13. Up to now the ECU has been basically a unit of account and a major currency of denomination of Eurobond issues. The ECU is increasingly being used for private transactions, but this is still a much more restricted role than that to be attributed to the euro, the ECU's successor.
14. Which does not necessarily mean that Germany's rate of surplus value is lower than that of the other less advanced countries.
15. Incidentally, the above highlights the reason why exchange rates within the ERM cannot be stable: the member states' unequal development. But there is also a second reason. Investors, when moving out of dollar positions for fear of a fall in its value, seek a safe currency. They usually do not purchase other European currencies but prefer the deutsche mark, which is in no (or less) danger of being devalued. This extra demand for deutsche marks affects the exchange rate between the deutsche mark and the other European currencies putting the bilateral bands under strain and possibly forcing a realignment. In this way, a large influx of dollars threatens the working of the ERM, whose aim is to avoid realignments.

16. Italy was re-admitted to the ERM in August 1996. The asymmetry in terms of value appropriation is hidden by terms such as 'symmetric adjustments', which refer to equal obligations to intervene by the Central Banks of both the weak and the strong currencies. But even in this limited meaning, adjustments are asymmetric because caused by a policy predominantly influenced by the strong country.
17. The conditions of life of society at large are also damaged by the 'austerity measures' necessary to launch EMU and the euro. But in this case these sacrifices seem to be imposed by some distant logic coming from Brussels rather than by national governments through an inflationary economic policy. For a lucid analysis, complementary to the present one, of this and related points concerning Britain's membership of the ERM, see Bonefeld and Burnham (1996).
18. Within labour, some strata, as women, children, foreign workers, racial and other minorities, and so on are penalized more than others. This important point cannot be pursued here. (See Gill 1997.)
19. Contrary to some commentators' opinion (for example Bladen-Hovell 1994, p. 337), the 'German leadership hypothesis' does not imply Germany's absolute power to impose its policies.
20. These are: deficit must not be greater than 3 per cent of GDP, debt must not be greater than 60 per cent of GDP, inflation cannot be higher than 1.5 per cent of the average of the inflation rates of the three countries with the lowest rates, long-term interest rates cannot be higher than 2 per cent of the rates of the three countries with the lowest rates and the exchange rates must be within the ERM. While these criteria are meant to transform the future euro into the new form of the deutsche mark, it has been pointed out repeatedly that, quantitatively, they are arbitrary (why 3 per cent and not any other figure?) and irrational: Japan, for example, would not be allowed membership in EMU owing to its high level of debt.

These criteria are not limited to the accession to EMU. They are meant to continue to play a role also after its inception. On 8 November 1995, the German minister of finance Waigel spelled out his proposal for a 'Stability Pact', approved at the Dublin summit of 13 and 14 December 1996. Basically, after joining EMU, member countries will have to aim at a budget deficit of 1 per cent in normal times and of no more than 3 per cent in difficult times. Countries failing these requirements will have to pay a deposit (of between 0.2 per cent and 0.5 per cent of GDP) which, if the deficit will not be corrected within two years, will be turned into a fine, although there are also escape clauses (Bureau Van de Europere Commissie 1996).
21. This is the meaning of Article 3a(3) of the EC Treaty which lays down the EMU's guiding principles: stable prices, sound public finances and monetary conditions and a sustainable balance of payments.

References

Altvater, E., B. Blanke and C. Neusüss (1971) 'Kapitalistischer Weltmarkt und Weltwährungskrise', *Probleme des Klassenkampfs*, 1, 5–117.
Artis, M. and N. Lee, (1994) *The Economics of the European Union* (Oxford University Press).
Bladen-Hovell, R. (1994) 'The European Monetary System', in Artis and Lee, 329–45.
Bonefeld, W. and P. Burnham (1996) 'Britain and the Politics of the European Exchange Rate Mechanism 1990–92', *Capital and Class*, 60 (Autumn), 5–38.
Bureau Van De Europese Commissie in Nederland (1996) *Europa van Morgen*, 26e jaargang, 20.
Business Week (January 9 1995; January 16 1995; January 30 1995; 13 February 1995; March 6 1995; March 28 1995).
Carchedi, G. (1984) 'The Logic of Prices as Value', *Economy and Society*, 13, 431–55.
Carchedi, G. (1991a) *Frontiers of Political Economy* (London: Verso).
Carchedi, G. (1991b) 'Technological Innovations, International Production Prices and Exchange Rates', *Cambridge Journal of Economics*, 15 (March), 45–60.
Carchedi, G. (1996) 'Non-Equilibrium Market Prices,' in Freeman and Carchedi (eds).
Carchedi, G. and De Haan, W. (1996) *The Transformation Procedure: A Non-Equilibrium Approach*, in Freeman and Carchedi (eds).
Coakley, J. (1988) 'International Dimensions of the Stock Market Crash', *Capital and Class*, 34, (Spring), 16–21.
Deubner, C., U. Rehfeldt, F. Schlupp, and G. Ziebura (1979) *Die Internationalisierung des Kapitals. Neue Theorien in der Internationalen Diskussion* (Berlin: Campus Verlag).
European Council (1996) 'Conclusies van het Voorzitterschap', Annex 2 to Annex I, in Bureau Van Der Europese Commissie.
Evans, T. (1988) 'Dollar is Likely to Rise, Fall or Stay Steady, Experts Agree', *Capital and Class*, 34 (Spring), 10–15.
Financial Times (21 December 1994; 22 December 1994; 23 December 1994; 24–25 December 1994; 28 December 1994; 29 December 1994; 30 December 1994; 31 December 1994–1 January 1995; 9 March 1995; 1 November 1995; 22 January 1996).
Freeman, A., (1988) 'The Crash', *Capital and Class*, 34, (Spring), 33–41
Freeman, A. and Carchedi, G. (eds) (1996) *Marx and Non-Equilibrium Economics* (Aldershot: Edward Elgar).
Gaveau, G. (1982) 'Turmoil in the International Monetary System', *World View* (London: Pluto Press).
Gill, S. (1997) 'The Global Political Economy and the European Union: EMU and Alternatives to Neo-liberalism', unpublished paper.
Glyn, A. (1988) 'The Crash and Real Capital Accumulation', *Capital and Class*, 34, (Spring), 21–4.
Grahl, J. (1988) 'The Stock Market Crash and the Role of the Dollar', *Capital and Class*, 34, (Spring), 24–32.

International Herald Tribune (1995) (March 18/19).
Kolata, G. (1997) 'Dolly's Creators Take Next Step', *International Herald Tribune*, 26–27 July.
Marx, K. (1971) *Capital*, vol. III (New York: International Publishers).
Robinson, J., (1962) *Economic Philosophy* (Harmondsworth: Penguin).
Senf, B. (1978) 'Politische Ökonomie des Kapitalismus', *Mehrwert*, 18.
Siegel, T. (1980) 'Wertgesetz und Weltmarkt. Eine Kritik am Theorem der Modifizierten Wirkungsweise der Wertgesetzes auf dem Weltmarkt', *Mehrwert* (21 July).
Siegel, T. (1984) 'Politics and Economics in the Capitalist World Market', *International Journal of Sociology*, 14.
Swann, D. (1992) *The Economics of the Common Market* (Harmondsworth: Penguin).
The Economist (1995) (4 March).
Whalen, C. (1997) 'Divided Economy', *Financial Times* (14 January).

Discussion
George Liodakis

Although I am in agreement with most of the work published by Carchedi over many years, and the present chapter is in many respects interesting, I shall dare a few comments for the sake of discussion. It should be noted, in the first place, that the critique of the dominant notion of globalization is well taken. This notion reflects some real developments, which tend partly to legitimize it theoretically. It is seen, however, as Carchedi correctly points out (p. 173), through an 'aggressively ideological' frame. Carchedi himself interprets these real developments in the world economy, correctly, as elements of a new stage of imperialism. Incidentally, this new stage has recently and tentatively been called 'totalitarian capitalism'.

Although a growing critical stance on the notion of globalization has recently begun to develop, an extreme trend should be recognized, which tends essentially to disregard these real developments of the world economy, overemphasizes some renationalization trends and advocates a return to the national economy (and nation-state), or to social formation which is usually identified with the national economy, as the main component of (and actor on) the world economy. It seems that those espousing this approach tend to throw out the baby with the bath water, and thus miss the rapid trend toward internationalization of capital. This, of course, does not so much concern Carchedi's approach; it seems, however, that the discussion in his chapter is somewhat influenced by a realist approach, which sees not capitals and social classes but rather nation-states or imperialist blocs as the main actors in the world economy, despite the critique of this approach by other authors and Carchedi himself elsewhere (see Shaikh 1979-80; Carchedi 1988, p. 54).

These two approaches may refer to a different level of analysis, but it seems to me that class structures, international class contradictions and the international operation of the law of value are of crucial importance in determining specific state policies and institutional structures. The relationship, therefore, between the international expansion of capital and operation of the law of value, on the one hand, and state regulation or the specific formation of economic and monetary institutions, on the other, needs to be specifically delineated, as a precondition for a better understanding of both the internationalization–globalization debate and the class implications of the ERM and EMU in the context of the EU. Unfortunately, this problem is not addressed in Carchedi's chapter, nor is the associated and controversial issue regarding the modification of the law of value in the international context (see, however, Carchedi 1988, pp. 50–1, 1991a, Chapter 7; Siegel 1984, pp. 56–7).

In terms of method in general, a partial analysis cannot, I think, be a substitute for a truly dialectical analysis. This is also the case with the investigation of the character and implications of technological innovation (TI). Instead of examining the effects of a TI for a particular capital, or confronting a tendency (implying labour substitution and a decline of employment) with a counter-tendency (implying an increase of employment), in a linear fashion as Carchedi does, it might be more appropriate to focus on the dialectical relationship of the part (the innovator) to the whole (social capital). On this terrain, one can more fully examine the process of dissemination of a particular innovation, as well as its impact on the rate of surplus value and the average rate of profit (ARP). While it is correctly noted that 'technological "progress" and unemployment are two sides of the same coin' (p. 175), it is rather misleading to consider that it is impossible to determine beforehand whether TI produce an increase or decrease in employment, or to argue that 'TI generates more or less employment according to the phase of the economic cycle' (p. 176). I would argue that TI undertaken by capitalist firms *always* result in a decline of employment and an increase of unemployment, insofar as the motive for innovation is the increase of the firm's rate of profit, which can be achieved partly by disciplining labour and reducing its cost. So, even in periods of economic boom, increasing employment (on an aggregate, social level) is not generated by TI, but rather by the expansion of production and the rapid accumulation of capital.

Carchedi's more general conclusion, that 'TI, if immersed in capitalist production relations, generates a tendency towards a falling ARP, economic crises and thus poverty amidst affluence' (p. 178), is unquestionable. It is rather misleading, however, to perceive the fall in the ARP as manifested 'through the fall in the labourers' purchasing power' (p. 174). The problem of this approach is manifested by the repeated appearance of the 'realization problem' (underconsumption) as a decisive check on the accumulation process, while there is also an occasional retreat to a profit-squeeze interpretation of crisis (p. 176). An alternative and perhaps more relevant interpretation, of course, perceives the falling ARP as the main determinant of overaccumulation, which may in turn be manifested as an overproduction and a realization problem. It is moreover remarkable that the introduction and the character of TI, as well as the falling ARP, appear to be primarily determined, not by the specific capitalist character of productive relations, but rather by the distributional struggle for income between capital and labour. Another determinant of the ARP, also an issue of class struggle – namely, the increasing accumulation of constant capital which is associated with the free appropriation of natural resources and the partial externalization of production cost – is completely disregarded. This, however, is not a weakness only of Carchedi's interpretation of the falling ARP; it is rather a common omission.

Coming to international relations, the increasing globalization of financial markets and the contradictions between the major imperialist blocs are correctly seen as 'a strife among nations and their capitals for the appropriation of gigantic quantities of the world's surplus value' (p. 180). On a European plane, it is submitted that 'the European nations have to aggregate in an economic and monetary union in order to compete with the two other major blocs, the United States and Japan' (p. 180). It may indeed be in accordance with the strategic interests of the capitalist class in Europe, insofar as it can be considered sufficiently integrated and to have common interests, despite the extensive and deep involvement of American and Japanese capital in the European area, to aggregate in an economic and monetary union. The working class of the European nations, however, does not have to do so, and it is indeed contrary to its interests to consent to such a European unification in accordance with the terms and the particular interests of capital.

The requirements of EMU and the Maastricht Agreement will have a severe deflationary effect and a heavy cost will be imposed on the working class of the European countries, and especially of the less developed ones, as Carchedi has adequately demonstrated. It is rather misleading, however, to focus, as any neoclassical economist could, on the restricted use of competitive instruments by poor countries, such as inflation and devaluation, imposed by EMU. Although these additional restrictions may have some significance, and some negative effects may trickle down to the working class, they concern the capitalist class more. At the same time, it should be stressed that inflation in LDCs is largely a structural phenomenon resulting from an external (trade) imbalance and not so much an intended policy to reduce real wages. Moreover, devaluation may be primarily in the interest of industrial and merchant classes, but may also have certain often disregarded negative effects on the working class and the national economy at large (reduction in potential command of value and use values in the world economy), not to mention its direct and indirect inflationary impact (see also Carchedi 1997).

As the exchange rates between national currencies play a definite role in the monetary expression of international values and prices, and the state may, in general, have some influence on the determination of exchange rates, a short reference to the determination of exchange rates, their impact on the formation of international prices of production (and hence the international competitiveness) of particular industries, may be in order here. Despite a long disregard of exchange rates in the context of Marxist literature, considerable analyses have recently contributed to this issue (see Carchedi 1988, 1991a, 1991b, 1997; Bryan 1995a). These analyses demonstrate the objective determination of exchange rates, on the basis of the production-determined structure of competitive advantage. More generally, it has been shown that exchange rates are not simply determined by natural resource endowments or the accumulated forces and the corresponding specialization of production but also, in a more comprehensive way, by international capital flows determined by the specific valorization conditions of capital. The volatility in the monetary and exchange sphere and the subjective determination of speculative capital flows need not lead to an indeterminacy of exchange rates, as Bryan (1995a) implies (see also Bryan 1995b). The determination of exchange rates is, in the final analysis, influenced only by international flows of productive capital (in the capitalist economic sense). It follows, therefore, that although exchange rates constitute an additional factor potentially leading to a divergence between price competitiveness and productivity advantages, they should not be expected, for all that, systematically to affect the fundamental determination of international prices of production. Hence any exchange rate movements should not be expected to modify fundamentally or upset the relative competitiveness of particular countries.

What is perhaps more relevant here is the structural development imbalance and its negative employment and welfare impact, which will most likely be exacerbated with the onset of EMU and the even greater free flow of commodities and capital within the European plain. A. Shaikh (1979–80) has, in a seminal paper, demonstrated that free trade by itself, and independently of any capital flows or international transfers of value, produces or reinforces uneven capitalist development. Capital flows and transfers of value will most probably further reinforce this development imbalance (see Shaikh 1980; Liodakis 1996). Such uneven development within the European plane, apart from its employment and welfare implications, may lead, along with the international flows of financial capital and the increasing confrontation with the other imperialist blocs, to a disruption of the adjustment process towards EMU, and undermine the course of European unification.

Contrary to globalization theorists, Carchedi correctly points out that the current transformations of imperialism create 'the objective basis of a new subjectivity, truly international and internationalist' (p. 188). However, the chapter simply examines the impact on labour of the capitalist strategy for EMU in Europe, without indicating any specific strategy for labour. Such a strategy, of course, cannot but oppose the current process towards EMU and any further capitalist integration in the EU, while at the same time posing the question of a radical transformation, and an alternative socio–political unification, in Europe.

References

Bryan, D. (1995a) 'The Internationalization of Capital and Marxian Value Theory', *Cambridge Journal of Economics*, 19, 421–40.
Bryan, D. (1995b) *The Chase Across the Globe: International Accumulation and the Contradictions for Nation States* (Boulder: Westview Press).
Carchedi, G. (1988) 'Marxian Price Theory and Modern Capitalism', *International Journal of Political Economy*, 18, 1–111.
Carchedi, G. (1991a) *Frontiers of Political Economy* (London: Verso).
Carchedi, G. (1991b) 'Technological Innovation, International Production Prices and Exchange Rates', *Cambridge Journal of Economics*, 15.
Carchedi, G. (1997) 'The EMU, Monetary Crises, and the Single European Currency', *Capital & Class*, 63.
Liodakis, G. (1996) 'Terms of Trade, International Transfers of Value and Uneven Development' *The University of Macedonia Scientific Record*, 12, 360–84.
Shaikh, A. (1979–80) 'Foreign Trade and the Law of Value', *Science & Society*, 43, 44.
Siegel, T. (1984) 'Politics and Economics in the Capitalist World Market', *International Journal of Sociology*, 14.

Discussion
John Milios

Charchedi's chapter is an important one. It presents an incisive criticism of mainstream approaches to international economic relations and to the process of European integration from the perspective of the third stage of Economic and Monetary Union (EMU). The myths surrounding the 'buzz-word' 'globalization' and the intimations of an approaching 'end of labour' are duly refuted. The chapter correctly attributes low economic performance as well as the explosion of international speculative financial operations to a fall in the average rate of profit in capitalist economies.

However, this analysis in terms of the falling rate of profit requires more detailed elaboration. If all other factors remain unaltered, technological innovation as such leads to a fall in the rate of profit only under certain circumstances – (1) where the technical composition of capital increases at a higher rate than labour productivity, thus causing an increase in the value composition of capital, and (2) where the rate of this increase in the value composition of capital is higher than that of the increase in the productivity of labour.

By contrast, in all cases where technical innovation and the subsequent increase in the technical composition of capital are able to induce an even higher increase in labour productivity, the value composition of capital decreases and the rate of profit subsequently increases. The same effect occurs in cases of productive re-organization linked to increases in the time and intensity of utilization of the means of production (at a given level of production technology), such as the extension of the working day, the reduction of stocks and so on, which constitute cases of what Marx described as 'economy in the use of constant capital'.

The rate of profit also increases where the value composition of capital increases, but at a lower rate than the labour productivity.

In order to further elucidate these theses, I will make use of Marx's analyses in *Capital* of the factors influencing the rate of profit. I will not restrict myself only to his famous 'law of the tendential fall in the rate of profit' (Marx 1991, III, Part 3), where Marx examines the effects on the profit rate of increasing labour productivity due to *technical innovation*, but I will also consider the other parts of his work (particularly Marx 1991, III), where Marx analyses on the one hand the influence of the surplus value rate on the rate of profit and on the other the change in the value composition of capital (and thus in the profit rate) due to factors other than technological innovation. Marx's analytical method was based on the study of the change of a specific quantity under the influence of a change of another quantity, given that all other factors remain constant.

If the profit rate is the dependent variable (R), then the rate of exploitation of surplus value (S/V) and the value composition of capital (C/V) will be the independent variables, in accordance with the following formula:

$$R = \frac{S/V}{(C/V) + 1} \tag{8.1}$$

where S stands for surplus value, V for the variable part of capital (value of labour force), and C for constant capital (value of the means of production).

Marx studies the influence of (S/V) on R by considering (C/V) as a constant quantity (1991, III section 3, Chapter 15, where he defines overaccumulation; see also Ioakimoglou and Milios 1993). On the other hand, when Marx studies the 'nature of the law' of the tendential fall in the profit rate (in III, Chapter 13), he considers (S/V) as a constant quantity. He therefore studies the influence of all the independent variables in succession on the dependent one, endeavouring in this way to cover all possible cases and isolate all factors that determine change in the dependent variable.

Let us consider the following equations:

$$\frac{C}{V} = \frac{C}{Y} * \frac{Y}{V} = \frac{C}{Y} * \frac{(S+V)}{V} = \frac{C}{Y} * \left(\frac{S}{V} + 1\right) \tag{8.2}$$

This means that:

$$R = \frac{S/V}{C/Y\,[(S/V) + 1] + 1} \tag{8.3}$$

where Y is the net product – that is, the sum of surplus value and value of labour power (variable capital).

Relation (8.2) shows that the factors influencing the value composition of capital (C/V) can be analyzed into the factors that influence the surplus value rate, on the one hand, and those that influence the quantity (C/Y), on the other.

This latter quantity expresses the value of constant capital which is necessary for the production of one unit of product. The increase or decrease of this quantity illustrates, therefore, the ability of the capitalist class to economize on constant capital. Marx himself devoted the whole of III, Chapter 5 to this subject ('Economy in the Use of Constant Capital'). In this chapter we find the enumeration of all factors related to the ability of capitalists to economize on constant capital.

In Chapter 5, Marx once again follows the abstraction method noted above. He postulates that the surplus value rate is 'given' (that is constant), 'in order to avoid needless complications' (Marx 1991, p. 171). He then describes the factors which ensure or limit economy in the use of constant capital. Let us attempt to summarize the main points of the Marxian analysis:

(1) Lengthening of the work day or work year (1991, p. 170).
(2) Concentration of the means of their production and employment 'on a massive scale' (1991, p. 175).
(3) Economy in the conditions of work at the expense of the workers (1991, p. 179).
(4) Socially combined labour (concentration and cooperation of workers, social character of labour) (1991, p. 172).
(5) Economy designated as the experience of the collective worker (1991, pp. 198–9).
(6) Economy as a result of the appropriate education of the collective worker and his subordination to factory despotism (1991, p. 176).

Through these practices, capitalists economize on constant capital without changing the labour productivity *due to technical innovation* and the technological status of the economy.

There are, of course, other forms of 'economy in the use of constant capital' connected with an increase in labour productivity due to technical innovation:

(7) Re-cycling of waste products (1991, pp. 173–4).
(8) Productivity increase in sector I, (which produces means of production) (1991, p. 175).

Marx's analysis shows that the ability of the capitalist class to economize on constant capital is not a 'technical aspect' of the production process, but an outcome of the social relation of forces – that is, a product of class struggle. Increasing economy in the use of constant capital presupposes increasing power of the capitalist class over the production process itself; it is often connected with a deterioration in the workers' economic and social status, as Marx showed.

An increase in the factor illustrating the use of constant capital (factor C/Y) over a certain period (that is a fall in the 'constant capital efficiency,' Y/C) – that is, the declining ability of the capitalist class to economize on constant capital – can again be the result of either a decrease in (Y/N) or an increase in (C/N), since:

$$C/Y = (C/N)(N/Y)$$

where N is the number of workers, (Y/N) is the 'apparent labour productivity', assuming that the length of the work year is constant and (C/N) is the capital intensity.

It is worth mentioning at this point that since the end of the 1970s the process of restructuring the capitalist economy through the introduction of microelectronic applications in capitalist production (automation of production) has not been designed only to increase labour productivity and thereby the rate of exploitation. It has also sought to introduce considerable economy in the use of constant capital, through the reduction or even the elimination of all kinds of stocks ('JIT delivery', and so on).

The thesis that technological innovation may cause a fall in the rate of profit is correct, but it does not complete the analysis. A more concrete examination of the variety of factors affecting the profit rate is also needed, focusing on the different forms of economy in the use of constant capital, along with a study of the effects of technological innovation on the value composition of capital, on the one hand, and on labour productivity, on the other.

Concluding my comments on the chapter, I must note that I find very pertinent and original the interpretation of Germany's hegemony in Europe as a means imposing the strategic interests of all European capitalist classes over the European labouring classes. In this context, however, I think that the analysis of the effects of the EMS on the competitive position in the world market of unequally developed national capitals (economies) should be based on an analysis of the trend in *real* (not nominal) currency parities. It may well be that what appeared as a gradual nominal devaluation was actually a real revaluation, especially in the 1970s and 1980s, when inflation differentials among the EU countries were significant.

References

Ioakimoglou, E. and J. Milios (1993) 'Capital Accumulation and Over-Accumulation Crisis: The Case of Greece (1960–1989)', *Review of Radical Political Economics*, 25, 81–107.

Marx, K. (1991) *Capital*, vol. III (Harmondsworth: Penguin).

9 Central Bank Independence: Problematic Theory and Empirical Evidence*

Costas Lapavitsas

INTRODUCTION

The trend towards central bank independence appears to have gathered unstoppable momentum in recent years. It is sustained by an ever-expanding literature, which attempts to demonstrate welfare benefits and superior inflation performance resulting from central bank independence, and has attracted support from unexpected quarters (Goodhart 1994). In view of this, it is truly surprising to realize how precarious, narrow and unconvincing are the theoretical underpinnings of central bank independence. It is even more surprising to realize how tendentious is the empirical evidence that seeks to demonstrate the superior performance of independent central banks. The present chapter argues that these theoretical and empirical weaknesses originate in the literature's treatment of the central bank as a monetary planner in command of the supply of fiat money rather than as an institution embedded in the financial system and sustaining the supply of credit money.

THEORETICAL SUBSTANTIATION OF CENTRAL BANK INDEPENDENCE

The theoretical literature on central bank independence originates in Kydland and Prescott's (1977) influential analysis of rules vs. discretion, further developed by Barro and Gordon (1983a, 1983b). Systematic presentations of the theory can be found in Blanchard and Fischer (1989) and Cukierman (1992) (with several extensions). The core of the theoretical model comprises the following three macroeconomic relationships. First, the existence of equilibrium natural output is postulated, from which current output can only temporarily diverge. Thus, given nominal wage contracts set at the beginning of each period, disparity between current and expected inflation implies that real wages and output will change. If, for instance, current inflation is above expected inflation, real wages will fall and current output will rise above the natural level; however, in equilibrium, output returns to the natural level, for reasons that will become clearer below. Of course, current output can also diverge from natural output because of purely random shocks. Second, it is assumed that current inflation depends simply on the rate of growth of the money supply; indeed, for simplicity, it is equal to the later. Third, it is hypothesized that macroeconomic policy is formulated on the basis of minimization of the policy-maker's loss function. The latter contains two 'bads' – namely, current inflation and the difference between current output and the policy-maker's desired output.

Given that the only policy instrument is the supply of money, which determines current inflation, the policy-maker's problem amounts to choosing current inflation to minimize the loss function. It follows immediately that the policy-maker's chosen level of current inflation depends on the economic agents' expected inflation. Moreover, under rational expectations, in equilibrium, expected inflation equals current inflation, ensuring the economy's return to natural output. The mathematical implication is that the policy-maker's chosen current inflation varies positively with natural output and negatively with the random shocks affecting current output (the intuition behind this result is explained below). The former represents positive inflationary bias while the latter stands for macroeconomic stabilization that uses inflation to counter random output shocks. Quite clearly a positive inflationary bias is less socially desirable than equilibrium with expected inflation equal to zero, given that output cannot ultimately diverge from the natural level. The first-best, socially optimal, rate of current inflation contains no positive bias and simply varies negatively with the random shocks on output.

The reason for the existence of positive bias in the choice of current inflation by the policy-maker is the 'time or dynamic inconsistency' inherent in all 'rules'-based monetary policy. Since the policy-maker's loss function is minimized given the agents' expectations of inflation, the policy-maker has an incentive to cheat by accelerating current inflation after the setting of nominal wage contracts, thus lowering real wages and temporarily raising output above the natural level. One possible explanation for such action by the policy-maker might be that natural output is below desired output due to 'distortions', such as trade unions, though the precise manner in which 'distortions' might result in such discrepancies is rarely specified. More broadly, if the policy-maker is the government, recourse might be sought to monetary policy because fiscal policy has reached some limit in expanding output and employment (Alesina and Tabellini 1987). Finally, the government might simply be bribing the electorate by generating unexpected inflation, a process that can generate a 'political business cycle'.

Nevertheless, after a few repetitions of the government's action (in the theoretical model, a few repetitions of the game between policy-maker and economic agents), people will cease to be fooled. To prevent the government from lowering their real wages (which is the effective cause of the rise in current output and employment), agents will adjust their inflation expectations upwards until these are equal to current inflation. At that point, it will become impossible for the government to generate temporary gains in employment. Discretionary monetary policy run by a policy-maker (the government) who has an incentive to generate temporary gains in output thus forces agents to adjust their inflationary expectations upward, and results in permanent positive inflationary bias. Social welfare is consequently less than would have been had the bias and expected inflation been zero.

Into this framework Rogoff (1985, 1989) incorporated the 'conservative' central bank. The distinguishing characteristic of this institution (frequently personified by its governor) is to assign a relatively greater weight than the elected government to the 'bad' of inflation, though why this should be so is not explained in the literature. In all other respects the structure of the macroeconomic model remains the same – hence the repetitive game played between policy-maker and economic agents also remains unchanged. Given the greater weight now attached to inflation, central bank interventions to raise current output by raising current inflation are smaller, thus leading to smaller upward adjustment of inflation expectations and lower inflationary bias at equilibrium; social welfare thus increases. By the same token, stabilizing interventions in the face of random shocks on output are also smaller; hence output variability under a 'conservative' central bank is greater.

An important issue in this connection is whether the policy-maker (government or central bank) can become committed to a particular monetary policy rule (inflation or money supply) prior to the decision-making period. Such a commitment would be credible only if it were dynamically consistent (credibility measured by the difference between actual and expected inflation); no other commitment is credible. However, with asymmetrically distributed information regarding shocks to output, the all-or-nothing aspect of credibility disappears. If the central bank possesses more information about such shocks than the public, and signals it to the public through the actual rate of inflation (hence imparting uncertainty to it), there can be gradations to credibility (Canzoneri 1985). Thus, the central bank's private information on shocks gives it certain room to undertake stabilization and expansionary policy, but the policy-maker must be careful not to disturb inflationary expectations too much lest credibility be considerably reduced. Loss of credibility reduces the effectiveness of future policy, since people's inflationary expectations adjust appropriately in advance of the policy-making period. Concern about credibility is the closest society comes to ensuring the commitment of policy-makers to particular monetary policies (though no mechanism exists that can enforce such a commitment). It is generally assumed that a 'conservative' central bank whose decision-making powers have been rendered independent of the government is better able to increase its credibility (improve its reputation).

The most influential recent extension of this literature has been to devise optimal contracts that might make central banks choose rates of current inflation without any positive bias – that is, limit monetary policy purely to responses to random shocks on output. This is basically a principal–agent approach, developed by Persson and Tabellini (1993) and (mainly) Walsh (1995), based on the notion that the central bank's receipt of transfer payments from the government (budgetary allowances, salaries, and so on) should be made conditional on the current rate of inflation. Consequently, the first-best result for inflation (no bias) can be obtained by designing a contract that sets the transfer payments to the central bank according to the observed value of inflation. The central bank is, thus, penalized according to the level of current inflation and is given an incentive to opt for zero inflationary bias. In theory, such contracts could allow for stabilizing responses to random output shocks.

IS THIS A CENTRAL BANK?

It cannot be overemphasized that the 'central bank' to which this literature copiously refers has no banking functions at all, the theoretical framework contains no financial system and there are no credit flows. Money, moreover, is purely state fiat money created at the whim of the policy-maker. What these models call 'the central bank' is a monopolist in control of the supply of legal tender, ultimately determining (passively or actively) the rate of price inflation and assumed to have no ability to influence output and employment in the long run.[1]

However, modern money is largely credit money created through the complex interaction of loan demands emanating from output production, lending operations of financial institutions and generation of reserves of financial institutions. The distinctive analysis of modern money as credit (rather than fiat) money is captured by the classical tradition often referred to as 'the endogenous supply of money', that goes back to Steuart, the banking school and Marx, and has been revived in recent years by post-Keynesianism.[2] Based upon the arguments of this tradition (particularly its Marxist component), it will become evident below that to posit the central bank as simply a monopolist of fiat money constitutes weak and misleading theory. In short, the central bank's controlling operations over the supply of credit money are inseparable from its organic role in the financial system of a capitalist country.

The character of the central bank as an integral part of the financial system comprises three elements: the bank of banks, the bank of the state and the holder of the reserve of international money, all of which are analyzed in a distinctive way in Marxist monetary theory (Itoh and Lapavitsas 1998, Chapter 7). Thus, the bank of banks emerges spontaneously as commercial banks participating in the money market tend to centralize their banking reserve. The central bank, in the first instance, is the holder of the centralized reserve of the banking system. The presence of a centralized reserve ensures economies in the size of the reserve for the individual banks and the banking system as a whole, and allows greater flexibility in the lending operations of individual banks. By this token, access to central bank liabilities ensures access to the centralized reserve, and sustains the supply of individual bank liabilities (and hence the supply of credit money).[3]

The bank of the state also emerges necessarily, as long as the rise of a national state, which taxes, spends, borrows, and assigns nationality to money, accompanies the rise of industrial capitalism. To meet its borrowing needs the state needs regular access to the money market; a bank with a strong presence in that market is well placed to become the manager of the state's borrowing needs. There is no bank better able to do so (and also lend to the state on its own account) than the bank of banks. On the other hand, the existence of state debt gives greater fluidity and depth to the money market, allowing the bank of the state more easily and flexibly to intervene in the money market. Thus, the public character of the bank of the state strengthens its ability to function as the bank of banks.

The bank of banks and the bank of the state becomes fully a central bank when it emerges as the guardian of a nation's reserves of international money. The world market comprises units of capital competing in commodity and financial markets but within a system of national states with their own laws, tariffs, subsidies, work practices and money. A national bourgeoisie seeks to secure a place in the international division of labour and to defend the interests of its component parts, including the ability to import, export, borrow and lend. Defending these interests need not only imply narrowly economic measures, such as buying and selling goods and currencies or borrowing and lending, but also diplomacy, bribery, coercion and war. Effectively to undertake this broad role a nation-state needs to possess reserves of internationally acceptable means of payment. Thus, the centralized reserves held by the central bank tend to acquire an international as well as a domestic role, confronting the pressures of persistent and acute balance of payments deficits. The overlapping of domestic and international functions of the central bank's reserves is ultimately the reason for the frequently observed incompatibility between the aims of domestic and international monetary policy. Typically, defending the international reserves could imply unnecessarily restricting the supply of bank credit to the domestic economy.

Of particular importance for our purposes is that the liabilities of the central bank emerge spontaneously as the pre-eminent form of a country's credit money. The mechanism that underpins the pre-eminence of central bank money is the role this money plays in the clearing processes of the financial system, thus increasing the flexibility and efficiency of the flows of bank credit money and of commercial credit among firms. Central bank liabilities, since they give access to the centralized money reserves, have an advantage over other forms of credit money in providing the main means of payment in the clearing process. Nevertheless, the conscious intervention of the state is also necessary for central bank liabilities to become legal tender – that is, a means of payment with obligatory acceptability. The political economy of how and why such a step takes place is not particularly important for our purposes; suffice it to note that the state acknowledges (and underscores) the pre-eminence of central bank money already established by the operations of the financial system. Despite its elevation into legal tender, central bank money remains distinct from pure fiat money – that is, from valueless paper money created at the whim of the state. Contemporary legal tender credit money is still created as a bank liability, its supply being linked to the supply of reserves to the individual banks. Unlike pure fiat money, the supply of which is largely exogenously determined by the state, the supply of legal tender credit money rests on loan demand by the real sector, on the flexibility of lending by banks and on the institutional structure of the financial system. It is simply incorrect to assume, as the literature of central bank independence does, that the enormous structure of pure credit money resting on central bank money is an instrument in the hands of the central bank.

In the light of the above, it is evident that the concept of central bank 'independence' is rather meaningless. Decision-making by the central bank cannot be 'independent' of the rest of the credit system since the central bank is the bank of banks, regularly and extensively intervening in the money market. Stable and long-existing markets are characterized by a dense web of professional, informational, training and even personal relations, all of which are present throughout the financial system. Similarly, decision-making by the central bank cannot be 'independent' of the mechanisms of industrial production and trade, though it is naturally more remote from those than from the financial system. The central bank inevitably becomes exposed to the institutional and personal influence of industry and trade, since it ultimately underpins the supply of credit to them and can thus materially influence their performance. Put differently, the central bank might have the mantle of a public institution, but remains a spontaneously arising economic entity, the range, type and manner of operations of which are determined by its underlying character as a bank. It is a creature of the financial system in terms of its personnel and large parts of its activities. Analogously, the bank of the state, even if it does not itself lend directly to the latter, necessarily becomes entangled with the state personnel which oversees and plans revenue collection, expenditure and borrowing. Finally, but no less significantly, the central bank can scarcely become 'independent' of other state mechanisms in taking decisions regarding the reserves of international money, given the importance of the latter for the defence of the international interests of the national bourgeoisie.

It is, thus, apparent that the 'independent central bank' of the theoretical literature is not a central bank at all. It is, rather, a social planner armed with a single instrument of economic policy – fiat money – in pursuit of one aim – price stability. With this in mind, 'independence' acquires meaning: it is, above all, the independence of the social planner from the executive branch of the state, the periodically elected government. Given that the latter is inherently mendacious and untrustworthy, social welfare is greater when the social planner achieves greater independence from the electoral process. From the perspective of price stability alone, it is ultimately desirable to appoint a benevolent monetary dictator. The following four related but separate points are important in this connection.

First, the internal consistency of the theoretical work on central bank independence is problematic, as McCallum (1995, 1997) has already claimed. If the independent central bank is indeed concerned about inflation, and realizes, as it must, that monetary policy cannot shift long-run output away from the natural level, why should it accept the inferior outcome of a smaller positive bias and not aim for the first-best of no bias at all? Analogously, if no means exist of forcing the elected government to adopt the optimal monetary policy (the lack of these being, presumably, the root of the problem), who is going to enforce the 'optimal contract' between the government and the central bank? McCallum considers his argument to be in support of central bank independence (despite identifying weaknesses in the theory), since it implies that outcomes could be enforced which are even better for society than those achieved by Rogoff's 'conservative' central bank. However, if McCallum's argument supports the theory it does so only by pointing out that a monetary dictator might as well act as one.

Second, it is deeply paradoxical for theorists within the neoclassical tradition, who typically proclaim the welfare and efficiency optimality of free markets, to advocate assignation of complete control over money to a planner. If systematic disharmony and disequilibrium at the macro-level originate in the misuse of monopoly over legal tender, it seems more consistent to demand the abolition of this monopoly and the determination of the supply of credit money via the competitive issue of liabilities among banks. That such a proposal might not be practicable under present political conditions is not a decisive consideration in the realm of theory.[4] If, as the literature claims, systematic disturbances to equilibrium output are caused by inflation emanating from the misuse of monopoly of legal tender, it appears more congruent with neoclassical analysis to demand market freedom rather than a benevolent social planner with dictatorial powers over money.

Third, if indeed society is to have a planner in command of monetary policy and the issuing of money, why should the planner's remit be limited to price stability? The view that it is impossible to effect permanent shifts in output by means of demand management, despite its overwhelming popularity in contemporary economics, is merely an assumption. A social planner, who has complete control of money and significant influence over the generation and allocation of credit, possesses considerable powers to promote capitalist accumulation in certain areas and restrict it in others. There is no *a priori* reason for the planner to abdicate the power over capitalist accumulation afforded by command over money and credit. At the very least, and even if it were accepted that production and accumulation should be left alone, there is no reason why the planner should not attempt to influence the distribution of income. Money and credit afford considerable influence over the distribution of income through preferential rate loans, consumption-smoothing advances, housing advances, and the like. If the creation of a public institution with monopoly powers over money and credit is advocated, there is no reason why it should not avail itself of these opportunities for policy.

Fourth, the appointment and democratic accountability of such a planner are considerably more complex issues than allowed for in the literature. As we have seen, central bank independence is posited largely as a matter of making the planner independent of the elected executive, given that to win elections governments have to placate, bribe, and deceive the electorate. Monetary policy is best left in the hands of experts with sufficient stability of tenure and freedom to pursue what is 'optimal' for society. Here we have a clear example of what Marxists call the 'reification' of economic activity. The economy is not a set of social relations based on the reproduction of material life, over which humanity ought to be able to exercise conscious control in its own interest; rather, it is a mechanism that obeys its own logic and movement, over which the democratic process exerts a disturbing influence. Hence the planner ought to be independent of electoral expressions of popular will. That is a remarkably narrow view of economic activity in general and monetary policy in particular. Monetary policy is a powerful instrument to influence production and distribution: why refuse society the opportunity to employ it consciously and in its own democratically ascertained interests? There is no *a priori* reason why a monetary planner could not be subject to mechanisms of election and accountability in which broad swathes of people can participate.

EMPIRICAL SUPPORT FOR CENTRAL BANK INDEPENDENCE

Irrespective of the theory's weaknesses, a trend towards some kind of central bank independence has materialized in recent years, drawing support from the literature's empirical offshoots. Typically these studies construct indices of central bank independence and econometrically test their relationship to price inflation. Grilli, Masciandaro and Tabellini (1991), for instance, find that for a group of developed industrialized countries there is a significant negative relationship between the two for certain periods. Similarly, Alesina and Summers (1993) find that a clear downward-sloping relationship exists for industrialized countries. Not only this but, contrary to theory's analytical results, Alesina and Summers cannot identify a positive relationship between output variability and central bank independence. Instead of treating this result as problematic, however, the literature typically welcomes it as an unexpected bonus: independent central banks somehow deliver lower inflation and stable output.

The empirical studies suffer from several weaknesses in addition to the perverse result on output variability. The construction of indices of independence is an ad hoc exercise fraught with profound difficulties (Cukierman 1992, Chapter 18). The empirical literature naturally distinguishes between legal (or formal) and actual independence: the former is mostly a matter of the law governing the operations of the central bank while the latter is a matter of informal arrangements with the government, other centres of economic decision-making, the analytical capacities of the central bank, and even its governor's personality. The need to employ this distinction in empirical work is apparent in view of our discussion on pp. 209–12: an actual central bank, as opposed to a monetary planner, is inevitably embedded in a set of social and economic relations that leave the notion of actual independence largely devoid of content. In view of the complexity of the relationships in which actual central banks find themselves, and given the absence of theoretical analysis of those (since theory in effect takes central banks to be monetary planners), the empirical literature avoids employing indices of actual in preference to those of legal independence.

Even so, it is practically impossible precisely to specify the point at which legal restrictions in the influence of government over policy render a nominally independent central bank substantively independent of the government. Should there be no government officials on the monetary policy committee? Should there be complete goal independence granted to the central bank?[5] Should the elected authority legally abrogate all powers to intervene in monetary policy in all contingencies? Again, it is impossible precisely to resolve these issues – and measure independence in practice – because of the qualitative difference between an actual central bank and the all-powerful monetary planner assumed by theory. The bank of the state is inevitably a public institution that cannot avoid a degree of entanglement with the elected government and the rest of the state apparatus in the course of its interventions in the money market. Consequently, the empirical work resorts to grossly unsatisfactory expedients – such as using the actual turnover of governors or the ratio between actual and legal tenure of governors – as proxies for the disparity between actual and legal independence. Even worse, empirical work often relies on questionnaires that basically ask central bankers how independent they feel at a particular moment in time. The problem with the latter is apparent: when inflationary performance is good, governors are likely to feel that they face no serious problems of political interference.[6]

Be that as it may, Cukierman (1992, Chapter 20) reports that the vaunted negative econometric relationship between inflation and central bank independence for industrialized countries becomes positive when the sample expands to developing countries; that is, perhaps, not surprising when one bears in mind the relative absence of deep and fluid money markets in developing countries. In such situations, and given the weaknesses of revenue collection characteristic of their tax systems, direct lending by the central bank (often a bank found to be 'independent' by the empirical indices) is essential to balancing the government budget. The concept of central bank independence once again appears to lack meaning in practice. Last, but not least, even for the group of industrialized countries for which a negative relationship is shown to exist for significant periods of time in the post-war era, causation is by no means demonstrated. It is perfectly plausible that broader factors account for satisfactory inflation performance as well as the particular institutional outlook of the central bank. For instance, the historical experiences of hyperinflation together with the system of collective bargaining, might have made counter-inflationary policy more acceptable to German society regardless of the relatively high degree of Bundesbank independence. Similarly, the rapid increases in productivity, the nation-wide system of collective bargaining and a relatively small state, might have limited the effect of inflationary pressures in Japan despite the relative lack of independence for the Bank of Japan.

CONCLUSION

Central bank independence is a deeply problematic notion in theory and in practice. The extensive body of theory on central bank independence is, rather, not at all concerned with central banks but with a social planner in charge of monetary policy. If society is to have such a powerful monetary institution, however, establishing its instruments, goals, process of appointment and accountability ought to be undertaken in a suitably broad and socially aware context. The assumptions of continuous market clearing and a natural rate of unemployment, and the narrow concern with inflation, are very poor guidelines for such a pursuit. The actual trend toward greater central bank independence, on the other hand, suffers from considerable ambiguity concerning what 'independence' is. Such ambiguity is inevitable: a central bank holds an organic position in the financial system as a private institution that necessarily acquires the mantle of a public one. It cannot be independent either of the private sector or of the state.

Notes

* I wish to thank Ben Fine and Alfredo Saad-Filho for comments on the manuscript, and Fanis Papadatos for excellent research assistantship. Some of the ideas of this essay were also discussed in Lapavitsas (1997), and Itoh and Lapavitsas (1998, Chapter 7).

1. The intellectual origins of this literature clearly lie in Lucas' (1972) reformulation of Say's Law for the modern era. The underlying approach is fundamentally monetarist. However, the failed experiments of the late 1970s, and financial innovation throughout the 1980s, have made it clear that the demand for money is not stable: the older monetarist suggestion of a 'rule' to regulate the rate of growth of the money supply is clearly unworkable. Consequently, faith is now placed in the hands of the 'conservative' monopolist of legal tender that could regulate the supply of money and keep inflation in check, if freed from the influence of politicians.
2. This is not to suggest that there is unanimity on the process of creation of credit money among the writers of this tradition. Among post-Keynesians, for instance, there are some who believe that the central bank has no option but to continue providing all the reserves required by the banking system – banks having already fully satisfied the demand for loans by the real sector. Thus, the supply of money is perfectly elastic and the central bank can only manipulate the rate of interest (Moore 1988). Others maintain that the banking system can procure reserves by its own actions (that is, through financial innovation and liability management). The supply of credit money is thus upward-sloping and it is possible for the central bank to limit the quantity of credit money (Pollin 1991; Rousseas 1986).
3. The proportion between central bank liabilities and centralized reserve reflects no material realities of production and reproduction – such as real wages, rate of turnover of capital, and technological composition of capital. The most that can be said about this proportion is that it is determined empirically, relying critically on the stage of the business cycle and the institutional structure of the financial system
4. In this respect, the Free Banking school, the modern literature on which originates with Hayek (1976a, 1976b), seems to abide more closely by the underlying assumptions of neoclassical economics regarding the welfare properties of free markets, regardless of the feasibility of its main proposal that free competitive issue of credit money should replace legal tender.
5. The distinction between goal independence and instrument (operational) independence for the central bank is discussed in more detail in Fischer (1994, 1995).
6. Forder (1996) rightly claims that legal measures of independence (that is, those based on interpretations of the statutes of central banks) are entirely valueless for the purposes of testing the theory. The empirical literature is, therefore, largely worthless.

References

Alesina, A., and L.H. Summers (1993) 'Central Bank Independence and Macroeconomic Performance: Some Comparative Evidence', *Journal of Money, Credit, and Banking*, 25.

Alesina, A. and G. Tabellini (1987) 'Rules and Discretion with Noncoordinated Monetary and Fiscal Policies', *Economic Inquiry*, 24 (August 24).

Barro, R.J. and D.B. Gordon (1983a) 'A Positive Theory of Monetary Policy in a Natural-Rate Model', *Journal of Political Economy*, 91 (August).

Barro, R.J. and D.B. Gordon (1983b) 'Rules, Discretion and Reputation in a Model of Monetary Policy', *Journal of Monetary Economics*, 12 (July).

Blanchard, O.J. and S. Fischer (1989) *Lectures on Macroeconomics* (Cambridge, Mass: MIT Press).

Canzoneri, M.B. (1985) 'Monetary Policy Games and the Role of Private Information', *American Economic Review*, 75 (December).

Cukierman, A. (1992) *Central Bank Strategy, Credibility, and Independence* (Cambridge, Mass.: MIT Press).

Fischer, S. (1994) 'Modern Central Banking', in F. Capie, C. Goodhart, S. Fischer and N. Schnadt (eds), *The Future of Central Banking* (Cambridge: Cambridge University Press).

Fischer, S. (1995) 'Central Bank Independence Revisited', *American Economic Review, Papers and Proceedings*, 85.

Forder, J. (1996) 'On the Assessment and Implementation of "Institutional" Remedies', *Oxford Economic Papers*, 48.

Goodhart, C.A.E. (1994) 'central bank Independence', *Journal of International and Comparative Economics*, 3.

Grilli V., D. Mascianduro and G. Tabellini (1991) 'Political and Monetary Institutions and Public Financial Policies in the Industrialized Countries', *Economic Policy*, 13.

Hayek, F.A. (1976a) *Denationalisation of Money* (London: The Institute of Economic Affairs).

Hayek, F.A. (1976b) *Choice in Currency* (London: The Institute of Economic Affairs).

Itoh, M. and C. Lapavitsas, (1998) *Political Economy of Money and Finance* (London: Macmillan).

Kydland, F.E. and E.C. Prescott (1977) 'Rules Rather than Discretion: The Inconsistency of Optimal Plans', *Journal of Political Economy*, 85 (June).

Lapavitsas, C. (1997) 'The Political Economy of Central Banks: Agents of Stability or Source of Instability?', *International Papers in Political Economy*, 4.

Lucas, R. (1972) 'Expectations and the Neutrality of Money', *Journal of Economic Theory*, 4 (April). 103–24.

McCallum, B.T. (1995) 'Two Fallacies Concerning Central Bank Independence', *American Economic Review, Papers and Proceedings*, 85.

McCallum, B.T. (1997) 'Crucial Issues Concerning Central Bank Independence', *Journal of Monetary Economics*, 39.

Moore, B. (1988) *Horizontalists and Verticalists: The Macroeconomics of Credit Money* (Cambridge: Cambridge University Press).

Persson, T. and G. Tabellini, (1993) 'Designing Institutions for Monetary Stability', *Carnegie–Rochester Conference Series on Public Policy*, 39 (December).

Pollin, R. (1991) 'Two Theories of Money Supply Endogeneity: Some Empirical Evidence', *Journal of Post Keynesian Economics*, 13 (Spring).

Rogoff, K. (1985) 'The Optimal Degree of Commitment to an Intermediate Monetary Target', *Quarterly Journal of Economics*, 100 (November).

Rogoff, K. (1989) 'Reputation, Coordination, and Monetary Policy' in R. Barro (ed.), *Modern Business Cycle Theory* (Oxford: Blackwell).

Rousseas, S. (1986) *Post-Keynesian Monetary Economics* (Armonk: M.E. Sharpe).

Walsh, C. (1995) 'Optimal Contracts for central bankers', *American Economic Review*, 85 (March).

10 Is There any Alternative to the Current EMU Project?

Jörg Huffschmid

INTRODUCTION

When we speak of Economic and Monetary Union (EMU) we are not dealing with the basic structure of modern capitalism – classes and the production of surplus value – nor with a rapidly changing political superstructure with no particular relation to economic laws and tendencies. EMU is something in between: it is on the one hand a particular form, in which the production of surplus value is organized and, on the other, it is the result of a variety of other – political, ideological, historical – factors which may be of equal or even greater importance for its concrete shape than the economic basis.

Looking backwards, concrete economic and political situations and projects like EMU are the results of logic, structures, interests, movements and the relationship between different forces. Unfortunately, such plausible explanations do not allow conclusions for the future. Whereas with hindsight history is closed, it is open in a forward-directed perspective. However, that does not mean that anything could happen at any time. Economic structures and past history shape the basis and influence the perspectives for future developments, as potentials which can be used or constraints which can be overcome. In either case – the process will be time consuming and require individual and social activity. In rejecting the reduction of history to a deterministic view of the pure logic of capital, we should also beware of voluntarism which will often result in ill-guided activity, with ensuing defeats – and, very often, resignation, which is more or less equivalent to determinism.

In my understanding, the question of an alternative to EMU is not that of an alternative to capitalism as the basic economic and social structure in contemporary Europe. But it should also not be reduced to the question of whether or not the introduction of the euro should be postponed or not. It is a question of potential and perspective as well as the constraints for an alternative type of economic development which is not dominated by the Neoliberal paradigm but controlled by a set of socially defined objectives and instruments. Seen from that perspective, an alternative to EMU obviously requires more than better conceptions; it requires social and political movements. But when I say 'more than', I am also implying that alternatives *also* imply better conceptions of how to shape the process of European integration and unity starting from their prevailing circumstances.

The following chapter is divided into three sections. In the first, I will show that European integration has always been a contested area in which alternative approaches and concepts were at stake and the concrete form of development was a result of political interests and forces rather than the outflow of the logic of capital – which, nevertheless, in the mid-1970s imposed upon the economic and political agents a choice between strategic alternatives with very important consequences. In the second, I shall present a brief outline of the main elements of an alternative to the EMU project: a short-term employment initiative and a medium- to long-term institutional and economic policy reform, both necessary to bring Europe on to the path towards an alternative type of economic development. In the concluding and considerably shorter third section, I will argue that rising opposition could indicate the beginning of the decline of the Neoliberal project and that economists have to contribute to the possibilities of this process.

EUROPEAN INTEGRATION AS A CONTESTED AREA

Historical Development of European Integration: Shifts and Alternatives

Speaking of EMU does not even mean speaking of European integration as such, that is developing according to the laws of integration and has reached a certain necessary stage now – dictated, for instance, by the state of production technology or productive forces in general. The development of European integration itself is a sequence of economic and political processes, measures and shifts in orientation, which cannot be explained by the underlying development of productive forces; it was in no way inevitable, but was shaped by a certain constellation of forces and interests. I will mention three processes to demonstrate this.

After 1945

The overwhelming interest at the beginning of European integration after the Second World War was the desire for peace in Europe following the experience of fascism and German aggression (Loth 1991, pp. 9–27, Pinder 1991, pp. 1–18). There was also a determination to bind Germany into an all-European political structure and thus prevent her from any new military adventures. This was the basic content of the famous Schuman Plan which led to the European Community for Coal and Steel (ECSC) at the beginning of the 1950s (Statz 1975, pp. 123–51). There were also other forces and interests at work: the beginning of the Cold War, which made it desirable to build a strong European bloc against the perceived expansionist policy of the Soviet Union and caused the United States to support the process of West European integration; this meant the failure of a comprehensive European unification and the establishment of a Western and an Eastern bloc. On the other hand, nationalist interests were so strong that the attempt to build a joint European political and/or military structure could not be realized and economic integration – first in the sense of a joint administration of the basis of any military production (iron, coal and steel) and afterwards expanding to the economy as a whole – was established instead. The proponents of further-reaching all-European unification believed that the pressures emerging from economic integration would create spillover effects leading at last to political unification. So, there were alternatives at the time – all-European integration, political integration, military integration – which were not realized because various interests and forces – and not the logic of capitalist accumulation nor the state of production technology – pushed the development in a specific direction which, of course, was not only compatible with but even conducive to capitalist accumulation.

1970s and 1980s

The various enlargements of the EEC in the 1970s and 1980s were not without alternatives and were not even realized under overwhelming economic or systemic pressure (Pinder 1991, pp. 43–59): the accessions of Greece (1981) and of Spain and Portugal (1986) were mainly driven by political considerations – namely, to stabilize the recently established civilian democracies and to prevent a regression to dictatorship. The immediate economic reasons and interests of the then EEC did not require enlargements by small and economically weak countries, thus making the economic structure of the EEC more heterogeneous and raising the problem of intra-EEC transfers and compensation measures. This is, by the way, the reason why the negotiations with these countries took so long – almost 10 years. Of course, one could always invoke a general systemic interest in enlargement and hegemony underlying these accessions, but these were not the driving political forces at the time.

Economic Integration

Speaking more narrowly of economic questions, one must note that there have always been alternatives in the process of European economic integration: the ECSC was (and is!) a highly interventionist set of regulations and the EEC treaty provides – apart from the establishment of a Single Market – for the approximation of economic policies of the member states. In 1970 a report (the so-called Werner Report, Europäische Kommission 1970) commissioned by the Council, recommended the creation of an economic and monetary union within 10 years – that is by 1980! This recommendation was welcomed by the Council but disappeared a couple of years later under the pressure of crisis and nationalism in Europe. Interestingly, the Werner Report recommended the establishment of a European Central Bank (ECB) and of an additional institution in charge of European economic policy (cf. the recently discussed idea of a 'European economic government', see Europäische Kommission 1970, p. 5). Even the Delors Report of 1989, upon which the decisive parts of the Maastricht Treaty were built, envisaged an approach much more comprehensive than the one which eventually was decided in Maastricht and the economic policy which followed (Committee 1989, pp. 34–40). The negotiations for Maastricht and the conference itself give a clear indication of the different alternative conceptions and interests leading to partly contradictory and partly chaotic provisions. There is neither a theoretical argument nor any empirical evidence that the present course of European integration follows a design to which there are no alternatives.

Structural Pressures and Constraints and the Question of Strategic Alternatives

Having said this, and having put some emphasis on the proposition that there is no iron logic in history which led to the EMU project and left no room for any alternative developments, I hasten to add that this is only one side of the picture. The other side is that the strategy behind the current EMU process is embedded in, and reflective of, economic structures created under economic pressures which cannot be disregarded and neglected, neither in explaining the shape of EMU nor in developing viable and reasonable alternatives to the prevailing policy course. Economic pressures confronted economic agents and policy-makers with certain options and choices, which when taken can have very severe consequences. The decade of the 1970s, when the basic choices for a thorough turnaround in economic policy were taken in Europe, was as a demonstration of this.

The pattern of capital valorization which had been established under the impact of the great depression, the experience with the link between capital and fascism, the emergence of a socialist camp and the new force of the labour movement – all these factors resulted in an economic policy pattern with widely uncontested priority for domestic growth and employment and in an international monetary framework designed to protect these priorities and maintain a stable international framework for capitalist growth (Panić 1995, pp. 37–45). This framework was definitely not a democratic, but a hegemonic one and it suffered from inherent contradictions (which finally led to its collapse), but it served for more than two decades as a functioning institutional basis for the accumulation of capital and the growth of profits. Only after the domestic potential for expansion on the basis of the existing set of regulations was exhausted in the second half of the 1960s and the constraints of overaccumulation became an obstacle for further valorization did the international monetary order come under pressure. This was the time when strategic alternatives were put on the agenda: one was to continue with priorities on domestic growth and employment (which did not impede international expansion but gave it an orderly framework). Under the prevailing economic circumstances, this choice would have required a reinforcement of the framework of regulations and guidance for economic development – for instance, by a stronger control of private or an enhancement of public investment, an income policy favouring domestic final demand, and so on. The alternative was to reverse the economic policy priorities towards more rapid internationalization, to abandon the cooperative monetary framework and try to make profits on the world market which were increasingly hard to realize at home. This change of strategic option would require the subordination of all domestic aspirations and claims for employment and welfare to the imperative of the world market. 'International competitiveness' would become the magic mantra and guideline for corporations and governments, and would of course also result in a thorough change in the role of the nation-state, not its abandonment.

Today we know which strategic alternative was chosen: that of uninhibited international expansion and competition, which is now bouncing back under the cover of globalization as a mystified fetish of modern capitalism (Hirst and Thompson 1996, pp. 1–7). With hindsight, one can state that the labour movement and the left and reformist political forces were not aware of, or at least not living up to, the challenge. The alternative to the development path which was subsequently followed would have been to extend the scope and the reach for reforms and economic control, which would have required the will to fight for both. This was not there and therefore the alternative was not realized. Instead, the Neoliberal option became more and more a reality: in the United States, in Great Britain, Germany and by and large in all major and most minor countries. It was supported by a change in the economic 'paradigm': from Keynesianism to Neoliberalism, instead of Keynes-plus-Marx approaches.

On this basis, Neoliberalism has also taken over the process of European integration and it is using – or, better, abusing – the appealing rhetoric of European unification, democracy and peace in order to instal a regime which generates the exact opposite: social polarization, hegemony – domination and conflict (European Economists 1997, pp. 4–12). In the meantime, the Neoliberal strategy has acquired the status of supranational law, a rather unique promotion of a very shaky economic doctrine, full of risks and contradictions which in themselves are a strong basis for the rise and development of alternatives to this economic and political course.

The 'Strong euro' – A Risky Option

The foundations and internal consequences of this strategy have been analyzed and criticized in Chapters 6, 8 and 9 of this volume and I am not going to repeat this material. I would like, however, to discuss briefly the underlying concept of external expansion which is often disregarded in the discussions. In public statements we often find the reassuring assertion that monetary union will be a strong union with a strong euro at its heart. It remains mostly unclear what is meant: what is a 'strong euro'? Is it a euro which everybody wants to have and to invest money in? In this case, the exchange rate of the euro would more or less continuously move up with damaging effects for export oriented countries – for instance, Germany and the Netherlands. The strong euro would weaken the export sectors of the economy. That may be desirable in an alternative development conception but is certainly not intended by those advocating a strong euro. Or is a strong euro a currency with a very low inflation rate, lower than other currencies? That would of course be favourable for exports and lead to trade surpluses and additional employment. But, in the next phase, it would also lead to a tendency of the euro to appreciate, which would be harmful to exports. The solution of this problem is expected to come from the Central Bank and monetary policy (see Chapter 9 in this volume). They could restore the price advantage lost by appreciation through a deflationary austerity policy, putting domestic prices under increased pressure by a very restrictive monetary policy, thus keeping the domestic currency externally undervalued in spite of nominal appreciations. This is exactly what the Bundesbank did with regard to Germany's neighbours, and this policy of artificially generated undervaluation resulted in the 'strong deutsche mark' and permanent trade and current account surpluses in Germany and equally permanent current account deficits in the main European countries (Herr 1991, pp. 236–9). My assumption is that the policy of the strong euro is aiming at a new edition of this rather aggressive strategy as European policy. The strong euro will be – in real terms – an undervalued euro, on the basis of which the EU seeks to conquer additional shares of the world market. This looks very elegant and tricky, and it has worked for Germany for two decades. But as a strategy for Europe it is a very risky and, in my opinion, not viable conception, for three reasons (Huffschmid 1998):

- The price differentials (and the underlying differentials in productivity fundamentals) between the EU and the United States (or NAFTA) and Japan in the 1990s are not as large as they were between the members of the EEC in the 1970s and 1980s.
- The economic policy differentials have almost been eliminated: most countries are following the Neoliberal course and would follow a deflationary path: artificial depreciation would be answered by artificial devaluations, leading to a wave of competitive devaluations.
- The power relations between the EU, on the one hand, and the United States and Japan, on the other, in years to come will be significantly different from the ones prevailing between Germany and most other countries in the EEC during the last two decades. An attempt to sterilize the pressure to appreciate the euro resulting from gains of world market shares via restrictive monetary policy would undoubtedly – and correctly – be regarded as an element of economic warfare, provoking retaliation which could easily escalate into dimensions beyond political control and could end up in political warfare or even worse. This does not necessarily have to happen, but it cannot be excluded either.

The abandonment of a – however imperfect and hegemonic – frame of international cooperation and its replacement by uninhibited international competition, the replacement of growth and employment by international competitiveness and world market superiority as primary economic policy goals is therefore a very risky strategy. Domestically, it requires cost-cutting and subordination of all social claims and aspirations under the imperative of competitiveness, creating permanent unemployment, social polarization and political instability. Externally, it creates exclusion of most countries from the potential benefits of the international division of labour and increasing confrontation and conflicts emanating from economic competition. In short, the Neoliberal pattern of capitalist development is internally and externally inconsistent and generates contradictions. That does not mean that it is not viable at all, or for a long time. The contradictions generated require solutions, and the best – and in fact only – method to resolve contradictions is to develop them. And there we are again confronting the question of alternatives as to the direction towards which the contradictions are developed: either the Neoliberal strategy is extended further into domestically more authoritarian regimes of austerity (abolishing more and more political democracy and replacing it by the rule of 'independent experts' – as Friedrich Hayek recommended) and externally into a more aggressive pattern of conquest, utilizing more political pressure and, in the last instance, military power instead of cooperation. Or, alternatively, the contradiction is developed into a reversal of priorities, putting employment and welfare – and a number of other goals to which I will come below – at the heart of an economic policy concept which imposes domestic and external constraints upon the freedom of capital, taking up and carrying further the concept of reform which was developed after the Second World War. The idea that such reforms can be developed and realized only after a complete catastrophe like a war should not be acceptable, however.

Intermediate Summary

The history of European integration has been a history of continuous contests about development patterns and of the impact of different conceptions and forces on the concrete institutional and economic shape of the EEC and the EU. There is no reason to assume that this process has come to an end nor that it should have no impact on the concrete development of the EMU project in the future. The currently dominant Neoliberal policy conception and pattern underlying the EMU project is one such alternative, pushed forward by strong interests and forces of capital, made possible by the lack of alternative concepts and the will to fight for them on the side of the left, reversing the priorities established in the post-war development pattern under strong pressure of left and reformist forces. But it generates conflicts and contradictions which in turn require solutions in one or the other direction. This puts once again – and with enhanced force – the question of the alternatives on the agenda.

AN ALTERNATIVE TO THE CURRENT EMU PROJECT: PRINCIPLES AND MAIN ELEMENTS[1]

Four Starting Points

Re-embedding the Rules of the Market
An alternative to the essentially Neoliberal EMU project requires a re-embedding of the rules of the market into a broader political

and social context. While private property, competition, profit orientation, and so on can serve as efficient instruments of resource allocation and stimulation of productivity, they cannot in themselves define or generate the basis of coherent economic and social development. Disembedded or unconstrained capitalism leads to social contradictions, polarization and self-destructive tendencies in society and is not viable in the long run. The re-embedding is, however, no technical matter: it requires social movements and political action, defining the economic objectives and aspirations, by which private property and the profit orientation are constrained and guided. This underpinning of the economy by basic social agreements and a politically set framework is a case for public discussion and decision-making. In short: the economy has to be taken out of the exclusive competence of private property and market regulation and brought into the public space, opening it to public regulation, intervention and control.

Objectives of Public Intervention

The second starting point concerns the objectives which public intervention for an alternative to the Neoliberal EMU project should follow. In the first place it would be required to broaden the perspective beyond the exclusive goals of price stability and free markets and develop a concept of economic stability and development which comprises other essential aspects of economic and social reproduction as well – raising, of course, the problem of conflicts between them and how to manage them.

In a memorandum of European economists for an alternative economic policy in Europe we defined four such objectives or cornerstones of an alternative type of economic development (cf. p.14):

- *Full employment* in the sense that every person who is able and willing to work can find a job at wages which are sufficient for a decent living, and in which they can unfold and further develop their productive capabilities.
- *Social equity* in the sense of a fair distribution of income and wealth and strict non-discrimination in the workplace or elsewhere in the economy.
- *Social welfare and security* in the sense that nobody shall be left to poverty or helplessness in old age, sickness, accidents or other adverse circumstances.

– *Ecological sustainability* in the sense that the exploitation of natural resources does not go beyond the limits of their renewability and the emission of waste into the environment does not transgress the limits of its absorption capabilities.

The enumeration of such goals appears trivial because they are very general and the difficult question is how to concretize them and how to design instruments for their realization. With regard to the Neoliberal doctrine in power, however, it seems to me that it is not trivial to designate the cornerstones and principal objectives of a rational economy and not leave employment to the discretion of the employers and social security as a remainder which can be cared for after all profit claims have been met, and so on. Of course this does not dismiss the desirability and necessity of high productivity, technical progress, efficiency and price stability as guidelines along which a rational economy should work in order to function properly. It does also not reject the idea of markets, private property and competition as potentially efficient mechanisms for organizing production and reproduction processes in a highly complex economy. But the question is who controls whom: do the markets control policy in order to maximize profits or does public intervention control markets and profits in order to fulfil the above defined goals?

I would like to mention that each of the four cornerstones of an alternative type of economic development stands for itself and is not subordinated to one of the others: full employment is not more or less important than a proper environment or social security and equity, for example. However, under the present circumstances in Europe it appears that employment plays a particularly crucial role insofar as persistent mass unemployment is also a material and a political obstacle to the fulfilment of the other goals. In material terms, it diminishes the resources available for organizing a solid system of social security, and in political terms, it creates a general atmosphere of intimidation and resignation in which it is extremely difficult to implement necessary ecological regulations or measures to improve social equity, and so on. Employment policy must probably, in the short run, therefore be the centre of an alternative to the current direction of development in Europe.

The Question of Europe

The third starting point refers to the question of Europe. An alternative to the current EMU project should not dismiss the idea of

European unity and the road to it. I am therefore far from any EMU criticism from a nationalist standpoint (which is, however, much more common in Germany than a left critique). The challenge of European unification remains, although its concrete form should be altered with respect to the changed circumstances since 1990. After the end of the Cold War it seems quite appropriate to return to the perspective of an all-European cooperation and unification – for reasons of overcoming nationalist competition and in order to organize a European division of labour beneficial for all participating parties. Under the present circumstances and with regard to the leading role of the EU in Europe, it is reasonable to accept the EU as the core of a united Europe and to open it to the accession of other countries. The way this is done presently is not very conducive to the goal because it submits the Eastern countries to rules which they cannot meet without severe damage for their people. An alternative to the current EMU project must therefore slow down the process of core-building, loosen the set of rules (the *acquis commmunitaire*) and adapt it to the perspective of a substantial enlargement.

It should, however, not be overlooked that a united Europe is of no value in itself and under any circumstances desirable: if the 'United States of Europe' followed a domestic and external policy similar to that of the United States, this would certainly be no progress in the sense of an alternative to EMU according to the goals defined above. As an aggressive superpower Europe would certainly be still more dangerous than a powerful Germany or France alone, and a Neoliberal European bloc would probably leave less room for internal manoeuvre than that existing in the different countries today. The pursuit of European unity should therefore be narrowly linked to the pursuit of a change in the prevailing policy course.

An Alternative Strategy for Europe

The fourth starting point is a methodological one and concerns the question of implementation and transition from the present Neoliberal to an alternative strategy for Europe. It is obvious that a viable alternative to the present EMU course requires not only short-term measures on the basis of the existing set of institutions and legal bases and frameworks, but far-reaching institutional changes including the amendment of the Treaties of Maastricht and of

Amsterdam, to which I will turn below. However, such changes require time and they will be possible only if the general political and economic situation is influenced in such a direction that it becomes more open to a thorough change than at present. My central thesis in this respect is, then, that the immediate and short-term outlook should be a concerted and forceful attack on the present level of persistent unemployment, using all instruments of traditional macroeconomic policy in order to stimulate growth and employment and complementing them with new measures such as working-time reduction (see below). This is of predominant importance because unemployment is not only a personal catastrophe and a crucial economic waste, but also a political obstacle to any progressive political change, intimidating workers and pushing people into the arms of reactionary, xenophobic and aggressive political parties.

An Immediate Initiative for More Employment

Employment policy in Europe does not have to invent or discover anew the instruments at its disposal. Although the structure of the workforce and the production process has changed substantially during the last four decades, some basic macroeconomic arguments and instruments are not obsolete today, but can be applied – and should be adapted to new conditions and complemented by new instruments such as working-time reduction, structural and regional as well as labour market policies, and so on. The core of an immediate policy initiative for more employment should be a change in monetary and fiscal policy and an initiative for working-time reductions. In each of theses cases, the question for the EU must be answered as to what can be done on the EU level itself (that is, Commission or Council, since the European Parliament has no effective powers to do anything), what can be coordinated and stimulated by the EU in the member countries and what must originate there. A problem will also be to protect such immediate EU-wide programmes from external shocks or speculative attacks. Such an initiative requires enormous political energy, but from a purely economic and technical point of view it is feasible. It could be started at the official yearly coordination meetings on employment policy, which were decided at the Employment Summit in November 1997.

Monetary Policy

In the first place, monetary policy in the EU should be loosened further in order to facilitate employment-creating investment. In spite of recent reductions, capital market interest rates remain far too high (cf. pp. 16–17). While this is probably not so much a factor of cost-related deterrence against investment (whether the interest rate is in this respect of major importance can be questioned), it makes financial investment in bonds more attractive. In a situation, in which a considerable degree of overcapacity exists, there is no danger of inflation, if money supply were increased. The transition to a more accomodating monetary policy which supports a generally more expansionary economic policy will be of vital importance for the EU.

If this coordination takes place, it would not be particularly difficult to shield the new monetary stance against speculative attacks by coordinated Central Bank interventions *and* by formulating credibly recourse to Article 73f of the Treaty, which enables the Council to take protective measures with regard to capital movements from or to third countries if they threaten to impede the proper functioning of EMU. Decisions to this effect require a qualified majority and can last only for six months, but they may be taken several times. Alternatively, a currency transaction tax can be levied to deter speculative movements.

Fiscal Initiative

Secondly, a fiscal initiative for more jobs should be undertaken, as both an investment programme and an expansion of employment in the public sector or as a publicly financed and controlled employment initiative (cf. pp. 20–4). There is no shortage of need for such programmes, be it in restructuring the transport and energy provision, initiatives to develop industrial structures, or improve child, old age or health care and education, and so on. One could also easily take up some of the proposals made by the Commission in the 'White Paper on Growth, Competitiveness and Employment' (1994) which was generally approved, but subsequently buried by the Council. The needs for such programmes are usually not denied, but cuts are nevertheless carried out and justified with reference to the lack of money. The question of financing employment programmes is, however, not such a problem, provided that they really lead to more employment. In this case value, which otherwise would not have been created, is generated and can serve as a basis for debt-financing. This self-financing effect of new jobs is impressive: in Germany the official employment agency estimated it to be in the range of 70 per cent for the early 1990s. The reason is easy to understand. Unemployment leads to a fall in tax revenues and in social security contributions on the one side, and to more public expenditure for unemployment and welfare benefits, on the other. A successful employment policy would reverse this trend: generating more income for the public budget and the social welfare systems and reducing the payments they have to make. In this sense, successful employment policy should, from a purely economic standpoint, be regarded as an income-generating investment – which consequently can be financed by government debt, the philosophy being that the debt can be serviced and repaid out of the additional income generated by more employment. Of course, under the present circumstances additional government debt will also entail additional burdens in the form of interest payments to the capital markets. To change this requires the institutional changes discussed below, which will, however, need time to be implemented.

Apart from this general direction of publicly financed employment programmes, the question arises as to who can do what. It must be clear that at present the EU cannot finance any programmes of relevant size because her budget is so small – 1.24 per cent of EU–GNP. The EU could and should, however, take up loans from the capital market (Eurobonds). But even then the resources at the disposal of the Community remain very small and by no means sufficient. If employment policy is to be successful, it therefore very urgently requires tight coordination and cooperation amongst member countries, putting more employment at the top of their economic policy agenda. Actually this coordination could be organized on the basis of the present institutional structure of the EU (Article 103) which could be interpreted and filled out in a more rigorous way and in a direction different from that at present.

Reduction of Working Time

Initiatives for the reduction of working time are still more difficult to undertake on a European level, since there are no instruments pertaining to this in the EU Treaty (cf. pp. 25–30). Nevertheless, it would be helpful and in fact indispensable to synchronize and coordinate such initiatives on a European level, trying to avoid the dismantling of social security via working-time reductions and avoiding the transformation of part-time into precarious jobs. The main issue of an energetic employment initiative in the EU is the question of cooperation and coordination. This is so not only for reasons of mutual solidarity (which are nevertheless important) but also for economic and social reasons. While isolated growth policies in a contractionary environment will always be threatened by external drains (additional internal import requirements not matched by additional export opportunities), coordinated efforts in Europe to promote growth and employment will largely trigger off a mutually reinforcing dynamic via two-way import/export stimulation. Coordination will also be needed to agree to the necessary transfers in order to compensate for the disadvantages created in some countries.

Medium-term Institutional Reforms: Macroeconomic Aspects

While short-term measures to fight unemployment have the highest priority to initiate a relevant move for change in Europe, they are by no means sufficient, either to realize full employment or to bring the EU on the path towards an alternative type of economic development, not to speak of keeping it there. For this purpose further and more profound changes are necessary, which concern the institutions and the instruments of economic regulation and control in Europe (I am not – yet – speaking of social movements and the change of power relations necessary in order to achieve such changes). I see such necessities in three fields: *macroeconomic policy*, *social policy* (including working-time reduction and labour market policy) and the whole complex of *structural policies*. In the following, I will concentrate on macroeconomic aspects, for reasons of space and of personal competence.

Re-embedding Independence: A 'European Economic Government' (cf. pp. 13–15)

The name is off-putting, but the idea behind it quite rational and reasonable. It is the idea that if European integration is not left to the market and policy is not left to a restrictive money supply, then a European place for discussing and controlling European economic policy is needed. Since the relevance of monetary, fiscal and exchange rate policies for the development of the EU are more or less equivalent, there is no reason not to organize European policies on equally relevant levels. One could argue whether the Commission as such would not be the proper place for this common policy, and this would be reasonable if the Commission were elected by the European Parliament, which is not the case. But wherever the economic policy institution is located, the essential feature is its comprehensive competence: it should discuss and decide the main orientations and directions of economic policy as a whole, the concretization and execution of which could then, of course, be delegated to member countries and regional authorities. There are two crucial aspects to this conception:

First, the idea of Central Bank independence as advocated in the Neoliberal concept and laid down in the Treaty of Maastricht should be modified by re-embedding monetary policy into the general framework of economic policy, the general orientations of which must be decided by a politically responsible and not by an independent body. There is no good reason to exempt monetary policy from the process of democratic decision-making and parliamentary control; the argument that monetary matters are too important to be left to the ups and downs of changing political priorities and governments, and should instead be delegated to independent experts is somewhat strange, assuming first that experts have the truth and second that governments behave in an irresponsible way. The latter may very often be the case, but that should be a reason for parliaments to intervene and for the people to vote for another government. Central bankers do not have the truth in their hands nor are they free from political and economic biases and interests – certainly not more than a responsible government. This does not mean that particular tasks and competences in economic policies should not be assigned to separate institutions with particular expertise and a considerable freedom for the execution of their tasks. But the general line of their tasks should be clearly defined by democratically controlled political bodies. This applies equally to monetary, fiscal and exchange rate policies.

Secondly, there is the crucial question of how much power should be assigned to a centralized European economic policy institution at all, bearing in mind the inclination to bureaucracy of centralized political institutions. Democracy certainly requires much decentralization, but on the other hand it is equally true that social and political cohesion – and this is the aim of European unity – requires a certain amount of redistribution and internal transfers, which are not possible without prior institutional and – to a certain extent – economic (and therefore also economic policy) centralization. The European economic policy institution could and should be so designed that it decides the general lines of the relevant macro-economic policies which are necessary to keep the economies of the member countries on a path of development which comes 'ever closer' to the realization of the four main objectives of an alternative to the EMU project. It would therefore have to be something quite different from the EURO-X council, which the summit of December 1997 agreed to establish and which became the EURO-11 council after the decision to start monetary union with 11 members. As an informal meeting of the economic and finance ministers, this council has no decision-making powers whatsoever.

The Central Bank as a Political Instrument: Monetary Policy (cf. pp. 15–20)

Being integrated in a politically controlled process of development means that monetary policy – in a EMS or a MU – should generally be conducted in a more accommodating way than under Neoliberal rule. This should have two consequences:

First, monetary policy could by regional modification of interest rates and/or asset reserve requirements, take into account the different situations in different countries (north–south) and regions. Here, monetary policy would overlap with structural and regional policies.

Secondly, the strict denial of governments' access to Central Bank money – national or European – does not make sense. In the long run, it makes sense to raise as much tax revenue as is needed to meet the expenditure of the EU. In a shorter perspective, the possibility of deficit spending in order to stabilize the overall development may arise, or specific temporary expenditures may become necessary and may be accordingly decided by the institutions. In these cases, governments have to incur debt – and at present they have to do that on the capital markets – by paying interest and thus increasing the amount, they have to borrow. As long as the additional amount which is needed is not larger than the expansion of the money supply – which the government or the Central Bank were envisaging anyway – it can be raised interest-free from the Central Bank: Instead of giving additional liquidity to the commercial sector in a first phase, the Central Bank gives it to the government (resulting in a lower Central Bank profit) which subsequently spends it and, thus, transfers it to the accounts of commercial banks. This has no inflationary impact whatsoever; governments would just not have spent so much taxpayers' money for bankers' profits. By the way, the position that public deficits can be easily – and more efficiently – financed by way of money creation (i.e. the issue of zero interest public debt) rather than by borrowing on the capital market used to be in the theory of public finance less than 40 years ago, following Musgrave's seminal book (Musgrave 1959). The reason why it disappeared from textbooks and discussions has nothing to do with progress of economic knowledge, but much to do with the changing 'paradigm' and changing power relations.

EU-wide Stabilization and Redistribution – The Case for Fiscal Federalism (cf. pp. 20–5)

There has been, and still is, an extensive discussion about the extent to which the EU needs its own resources to fulfil her economic policy tasks. Before Neoliberalism took over the European agenda there was widespread – though not uncontested – agreement that these resources should be enlarged with tighter integration. At the end of the 1970s, a report commissioned by the EEC (the so-called McDougall Report, European Commission, 1977) recommended that 5–7 per cent of EC GDP should be assigned to the Community budget. Federal resources are necessary for stabilization of symmetric and asymmetric shocks and for ameliorating the large differences in productivity, unemployment and welfare – in short, of living standards – amongst member countries and regions. It has been shown that even in countries with a very market oriented approach, such as the United States, a substantial amount of resources is used for these purposes and that it is used with considerable effects on stabilization as well as transfer and redistribution processes. It is the material basis for the creation and strengthening of social cohesion, without which unity cannot be reached – otherwise, perhaps only by creating an external enemy against which the people must unite – which is a very dangerous, though not uncommon, alternative.

If an increase of EU own-resources from its present size of 1.24 per cent of GDP by a factor of about five seems reasonable to enable the EU to organize economic stability and social cohesion more effectively than at present, the question arises where the money should come from. Theoretically, it could come from transfer payments of the member countries to the EU and from taxes raised directly by the EU (including a shift from existing national taxes to EU taxes). The latter option is in the long run probably more viable; the willingness of governments to increase transfer payments is very low, and will probably not be raised substantially by convincing arguments in favour of higher EU spending. EU taxes therefore appear to be more appropriate. In strengthening the fiscal basis of the EU one could additionally pursue regulatory objectives: it makes good sense, for instance, to introduce common new taxes upon energy consumption and currency transactions throughout the union, thus contributing to the objectives of energy saving and currency stabilization and at the same time avoiding tax competition, which is one of the main reasons – apart from unemployment – for the erosion of public finances. The same is, of course, true for capital income or corporate profits taxes – although taxation should not be overestimated as a factor in locational decisions.

Exchange Rate Stability: A Modified European Monetary System (EMS) (cf. pp. 17–18)

In an alternative economic policy approach, the rapid establishment of a monetary union is not an issue of high priority – at least not for some years to come. It is true that EMU and a Single Currency are attractive and desirable in order to eliminate transaction costs and speculation between currencies of different countries, and also – beyond mere economic considerations – as a symbol of political unity. However, after the decision for a monetary union with 11 members, nobody can say whether the speculative movements amongst the three big currencies – the euro, the US dollar and the yen – will not become more volatile, in which case the related risk and transaction economic benefits of monetary union may well shrink considerably and when measured against the increased costs for hedging, may well be reversed to a net loss.

Even after the decision for an 11-member EMU, a reasonable approach to exchange rate policy has to deal with the two problems of stabilizing intra-European currency relations between members and non-members of EMU (and designated future members of the EU: the Eastern European countries), on the one hand, and of protecting such a zone of European monetary stability against external shocks from the US dollar or yen area – be it as spontaneous inflows, or outflows, or as speculative attacks – on the other.

The first problem can be resolved by a renewed and modified

EMS. Renewed insofar as it operates on the basis of narrower bands and with unconditional obligation on the side of the ECB and the Central Banks of the non-members of monetary union to intervene in the currency market, in order to stabilize the central rate. Modified in three respects: first, the bands could be determined differently for different countries; secondly, the obligation to intervene could be limited in size; and, thirdly, there should be the possibility of more and dedramatized realignments, which would be used as a technical instrument of adjustment instead of a symbol of national pride and prestige. The working of the system could be so arranged that the Eastern European countries could be a part of it from the beginning, benefiting from special concessions (for instance, broader bands and higher intervention ceilings) and at the same time being integrated in the same framework of obligations and adjustment pressures.

The best solution for the second problem would, of course, be a global agreement for monetary cooperation, such as the one which was discussed (though subsequently only very imperfectly implemented) in Bretton Woods in 1944. Such an agreement does not seem very likely in the foreseeable future, and therefore the second-best solution must be envisaged: the protection of a European monetary zone by economic and administrative measures. The most famous economic instrument for this is the much discussed Tobin tax, which is really well suited to fight and largely prevent short-term capital flows for arbitrage reasons and herd-like speculation. Against fundamental speculative attacks, such taxes would, however, not be viable and therefore the toolkit of capital controls should be credibly revitalized in the EU. Strangely enough, this does not require new legal rules, but only the determined and credible announcement that the EU will – if necessary – really make use of the provision in Article 73f of the Treaty which allows it to take protective measures, if capital flows to or from the EU threaten to impede the functioning of EMU (not only in stage III!). The implementation of both taxation and the possibility of capital controls would undoubtedly raise reactions from those concerned, loopholes and methods of circumvention may be developed, but that does not make such measures futile or nonsensical. Here, too, almost all depends on the political energy to implement a reasonable regulation.

Such protective measures will be efficient and cannot simply be rolled over by the 'global financial markets'. These markets work only to the extent to which power-based political decisions let them do so. It is an absurd conception that modest measures to protect monetary stabilization should turn one of the three big financial and economic centres of the world into a financial desert. After all, Europe remains attractive in many other aspects – and the profit perspectives in other places will not become better by a strong inflow of financial capital. In this sense, a European initiative to constrain the uninhibited flow of (short-term) capital could well exert pressure on other countries and be a big step towards an international monetary reform.

RESISTANCE AGAINST A NEOLIBERAL EUROPE: A NEW ROUND OF THE CONTEST BEGINS (cf. pp. 35–7)

The foregoing very schematic outline of one part of institutional and political reforms, in and of the EU, in order to bring it on to an alternative path of economic and social development (other parts, which have not been dealt with here, concern European social policy and the whole range of structural policies), could lead – and among the left often does lead – to a long and passionate discussion about the question of whether its implementation is still possible in capitalism, or whether it requires a completely different social formation, a new socialism. I find this question not only unanswerable but also not particularly interesting or relevant. Neither answer would lead me to drop the project of an alternative to the present EMU. The challenge instead – apart of course from the never-ending task of further developing the arguments and proposals – is to find ways to get it started. The outlook for this is not promising, having to do with the economic, social, individual and political implications of the catastrophic employment situation. Any serious attempt to change the course of the European development for the better – there are also possible roads to the worse – should therefore concentrate on the task of fighting unemployment and increasing employment, with imagination, determination and political energy. In a situation where stock exchanges plunge deeply at the announcement of positive employment figures and soar if unemployment increases, in which the 'natural rate of unemployment' and the NAIRU govern the political and the majority of the scientific discussions, this appears to be a huge and almost unrealistic task and one must ask who is prepared to cope with it.

However, we do not have exclusively bad news and depressing

outlooks. During the last few years we have witnessed rising protest and resistance in all countries of the EU – not against Neoliberalism in general, or for a new pattern of economic policy orientation, but against specific policy measures (mostly social cuts and layoffs) which were regularly justified with reference to the constraints of EMU convergence requirements. The justification of the anti-social policy as necessary for the achievement of European unity has, on the one hand, led to a certain hostility against Europe in general. On the other hand, we find a growing rejection of the close link between European unity and Neoliberal policy. In France and Great Britain, governments were ousted in elections because of their austerity policy and new governments were elected with the perspective of a new, more employment and welfare oriented economic policy. Of course, attempts like the French one to put employment at the top of government priorities have been met with resistance and hostility by Neoliberalism in governments, the media and the scientific community, and industrial and employers' associations regard them – in part, correctly – as attacks against the dominant position which they have occupied over the past two decades. Moreover, it is by no means clear that a new orientation in economic policy will gain hegemony in Europe in the next three–five years. The French situation is revealing in relation to the complications which a political turnaround will generate; the government signed the deeply Neoliberal Stability Pact in Amsterdam but also announced a government programme which will have exactly opposite effects. It is hard to say which side will be victorious or – more precisely – what the compromise between the two will look like. In any case, it seems to me that we can safely say that the situation today is more open than it was five years ago; a new round in the struggle for the development of the economy and the orientation of economic policy in Europe has begun.

In this situation the possibilities of social scientists in general and of economists in particular, are limited, but not unimportant.

- We can and should support and reinforce the critique of Neoliberalism in its different forms, revealing its extremely individualistic basis, its inherent contradictions and authoritarian implications, as well as its empirical fallacies and failures.
- We can and should – on the basis of a solid theoretical and empirical analysis of modern capitalism – engage in the exploration and concretization of the cornerstones of, and political

instruments for, an alternative economic development path which promotes European unity on the basis of full employment, social cohesion and solidarity amongst the European people and with regard to the underdeveloped world.

- We can, with our competence as professional economists, support practically the concrete movements against dismissals, social cuts and other forms of Neoliberal policies, wherever and in whatever form they emerge.

I find it very encouraging that critical economists all over Europe have been recently facing the challenge in that, at various occasions and in various places, they have been publicly formulating their opposition against the mainstream economic discourse, an opposition based equally on scientific knowledge and on social concerns. In the new round of struggle over Europe, we have to say something and we should do so more than before – and, whenever possible, we should do it jointly.

Note

1. The following remarks are a summary and explanation of the proposals which were published by a group of European economists to whom the author belongs (cf. European Economists 1997). References to this text are given by page numbers in brackets.

References

Committee for the Study of Economic and Monetary Union (ed.) (1989) *Report on Economic and Monetary Union in the European Community* (Delors Report) (Brussels: Office for Official Publications of the European Communities)

Deppe, F. (ed.) (1975) *Europäische Wirtschaftsgemeinschaft. Zur Politischen Ökonomie der Westeuropäischen Integration* (Hamburg: Rowohlt).

Europäische Kommission (1970) 'Bericht an Rat und Kommission über die stufenweise Verwirklichung der Wirtschafts- und Währungsunion in der Gemeinschaft', in *Amtsblatt der Europäischen Gemeinschaften*, C136, (11 November 1970), (Werner Report), 1–38.

European Commission (1977) 'Report of the Study Group on "The Role of Public Finance in European Integration," chaired by Sir Donald MacDougall,' *Economic and Financial Series*, A13, (Brussels).

European Commission (1994) *Growth, Competitiveness, Employment. The Challenges and Ways Forward into the 21st Century* (Brussels–Luxembourg).

European Economists (1997) 'Full Employment, Social Cohesion and Equity for Europe – Alternatives to Competitive Austerity. A Declaration and a Memorandum of European Economists' (Bremen), manuscript.

Herr, Hansjörg (1991) 'Der Merkantilismus der Bundesrepublik in der Weltwirtschaft', in Voy, Polster and Thomasberger (eds), 227–61.

Hirst, P. and G. Thompson (1996) *Globalization in Question. The International Economy and the Possibilities of Governance* (Cambridge: Polity Press).

Huffschmid, Jörg (1998) 'Hoist with its Own Petard – Consequences of the Single Currency for Germany', in J. Michie and B. Moss (eds), *Domestic Consequences of the Single Currency* (London: Macmillan), 87–104.

Loth, W. (1991) *Der Weg nach Europa, Geschichte der Europäische Integration 1939–1957* (Göttingen: Vandenhoeck & Ruprecht).

Musgrave, R.A. (1959) *The Theory of Public Finance. A study in Public Economy* (London: MacGraw Hill, Kogakushor).

Panić, M. (1995) 'The Bretton Woods System: Concept and Practice', in J. Michie and J. Grieve Smith (eds), *Managing the Global Economy* (New York: Oxford University Press), 37–54.

Pinder, J. (1991) *European Community. The Building of a Union* (New York: Oxford University Press).

Statz, Albert (1975) 'Zur Geschichte der Westeuropäischen Inegration bis zur Gründung der EWG', in Deppe (ed.), 110–74.

Voy, K., W. Polster and C. Thomasberger (eds), *Marktwirtschaft und Politische Regulierung. Beiträge zur Wirtschafts- und Gesellschaftgeschichte der Bundesrepublik Deutschland (1949–1989)* (Marburg: Metropolis).

Discussion*
Panos Tsakloglou

I wish to start my comments by stating that I am very sympathetic to many of the ideas developed in the chapter. Nevertheless, I should also add that, for reasons I explain below, I consider some of these ideas as rather utopian, at least in the present political climate. The chapter first provides a survey of the developments that led to the current state of affairs regarding EMU, emphasizing the main dangers resulting from the current Neoliberal EMU project, and then outlines the principal elements of an alternative to it.

With respect to the first part of the chapter, unlike Huffschmid, I believe that after the completion of the Internal Market, a common currency was a sensible step with respect to the internal logic of capital regarding the process of European integration. Nevertheless, this point is not central to the main arguments I present below. For the long run, I believe that EMU can facilitate higher growth rates through lower and less variable interest rates. The gains may be higher precisely in those countries which have suffered from high and variable inflation rates in the past, owing to both lower transactions costs and lower risk premia. However, in the short and the medium term there are a number of factors – to some extent, interlinked – which may well derail the entire EMU project. If the EMU is not accompanied by the appropriate institution-building, some of these factors may have negative long-run effects, too. These factors and the corresponding dangers for the EMU project are only briefly, if at all, discussed in the chapter. In my opinion, the most important of these are the following:

(1) The European Central Bank (ECB) is going to be an 'untested quantity' in its early stages. Taking into consideration, first, the fact that the public opinion in a number of low-inflation EU member states seems to be unconvinced about the ability of the ECB to keep inflation low and, secondly, that the international financial markets seem to share this perception, in the early stages of the implementation of EMU the ECB is likely

to adopt a very tight deflationary monetary policy in order to convince them that it is at least as 'tough' as the Bundesbank (Goodhart 1996a, 1996b). Such a policy is likely to result in unnecessarily high rates of unemployment, thus providing grounds for public resentment against the EMU project. Moreover, if the analysis put forward by the proponents of the 'hysteresis hypothesis' (Layard, Nickell and Jackman 1991) is correct, the impact of such policies on unemployment may not be just a temporary one.

(2) Taking into consideration the relatively low level of flexibility in European labour markets, in the short run the loss of exchange rate flexibility that will result from the participation in the EMU may lead to some erosion in competitiveness in a number of (mainly peripheral) EU countries. This loss of competitiveness is likely to create the need for some sort of 'compensation' in the form of fiscal transfers. However, no corresponding transfer mechanism is in place at the European level at the moment – the Cohesion and other Structural Funds should be deemed as rather insufficient and badly focused for such purposes. Hence, once again, despite possible long-term benefits, in the short run participation in EMU may be associated with higher rates of unemployment and, possibly, popular dissatisfaction. Moreover, if in the longer term the EU does not behave as a unitary economy, the above costs may have a permanent rather than temporary character (Bean 1992, and the references cited there).

(3) Recent research points out that business cycles are not synchronized in EU member states (Dickerson, Gibson and Tsakalotos 1997, for opposite evidence, see Christodoulakis, Dimelis and Kollintzas 1995). A particular type of (common) monetary policy may therefore be appropriate for one set of countries but exacerbate the cycle in others. The outcome is likely to be higher unemployment in the latter countries and, once again, there is no compensatory fiscal mechanism in place at the European level to mitigate the resulting negative effects. Similar outcomes may result if a common monetary policy is applied when the EU countries experience an asymmetric external shock (Bayoumi and Eichengreen 1993; Krugman 1993) – or even a symmetric one if, owing to institutional factors, the propagation mechanisms differ across countries (Carruth, Gibson and Tsakalotos 1997).

The rise in unemployment that is likely to be associated with the above factors may lead to justifiable protests and, perhaps, abandonment of the whole EMU project. Even though this scenario is not the most likely one, it cannot be considered as completely unrealistic. The chaos that may follow in such a case is not difficult to envisage – strong appreciation of non-EU currencies such as the US dollar and the yen and run on the weaker EU currencies. Both the economic and the social costs of such a scenario are likely to be extremely high. Moreover, it should be noted that the danger of a popular upheaval against the EMU project may be fuelled by the tendency of a considerable number of politicians across the continent to blame the EMU for the adoption of long overdue but painful reforms.

In the second part of the chapter, Huffschmid offers an alternative to the current EMU project. In a nutshell, this is a 'Keynes-plus-a-little-Marx' recipe for the whole continent. This is not a bad idea, since the experiences of both large countries (France in the early years of the Mitterrand presidency) and small countries (Greece under Papandreou) in the 1980s show convincingly that, in the present international economic environment, Keynesianism in a single country simply does not work. The author's basic idea is that such an alternative project should promote full employment, social equity, social welfare and security and ecological sustainability, although emphasis is primarily placed on full employment. These aims are to be realized within a more or less federalist framework. Regarding the means to achieve these objectives, Huffschmid recommends the coordination of a number of policies across EU member states (especially fiscal policy, which gains crucial importance in the framework of his analysis), the creation of some sort of central European economic government and, interestingly enough, a fivefold increase in the EU budget.

In my view, the validity of a number of assumptions that are crucial for the author's analysis is doubtful (especially those related to 'balanced budget multipliers'). Further, at the political level, the governments of the member states do not seem to be even remotely willing to surrender to supranational bodies functions that constitute important parts of national sovereignty – perhaps for good reasons. Such a transfer of powers, however, is crucial for the alternative project recommended by Huffschmid. Two questions therefore arise:

(1) As with so many nice ideas coming from the left, there is no price tag in the chapter's proposals. This is not to say that they are necessarily unrealistic, or even so, undesirable; it may also be beyond the scope of the chapter to provide detailed cost estimates. However, almost all the policy measures recommended are likely to lead to higher costs. Within an open international economic environment, these higher costs are likely to lead to lower competitiveness, balance of payments problems, stagnation and rising unemployment. What can the EU do in this case? One can think of several alternative scenarios but, certainly, there will be a lot of pressure for the creation of a 'fortress Europe' (Klein and Hong 1993). The European market is large enough to sustain such a move but, no doubt, this will lead in the longer term to retaliatory measures by the United States and Japan and lower living standards for EU citizens. Furthermore, the creation of a 'fortress Europe' is likely to have negative unintended consequences on the really disadvantaged citizens of the world – that is, the citizens of poor third world countries.

(2) One may also wonder how realistic at the political level is the alternative recommended. At a superficial first sight, the answer to this question may be positive. Elections in 1997 brought into power left-of-centre parties in a number of EU countries. However, most of them were elected on almost Neoliberal economic manifestos and they are very unlikely to adopt the measures necessary for the successful implementation of the alternative strategy outlined by Huffschmid. Further, how realistic is the recommended substantial increase in the resources of the EU, even in the medium to long run? Even though, for the reasons mentioned above, I think that a substantial increase in the EU budget is essential for the successful implementation of EMU, in my opinion and to the extent that long-run predictions can be made, the answer to the above question is: 'not at all'. A European federalist movement that could support such proposals is almost non-existent and the events of the early 1990s seem to suggest that in many EU countries there is strong popular resistance to expanding the powers and the resources available at the central European level. In addition, the decision of the EU to expand by accepting new members from the former COMECON block rather than deepen cooperation among existing member states does not augur well for the policies recommended.

Suppose the title of the chapter is slightly rephrased: 'Is there an alternative to the current EMU project for the labour movement in Europe?'. In my opinion, such an alternative does, indeed, exist and Huffschmid's chapter outlines a number of its basic components. Nevertheless, if we wish to be realistic, the whole alternative project must be redrafted on a far less ambitious scale.

Note

* I would like to thank Euclid Tsakalotos and Heather Gibson for useful comments and suggestions.

References

Bayoumi R. and B. Eichengreen (1993) 'Shocking Aspects of European Monetary Transition', in F. Torres and F. Giavazzi (eds), *Adjustment and Growth in the European Monetary Union* (Cambridge: Cambridge University Press for the CEPR).
Bean C. (1992) 'European Monetary Union', *Journal of Economic Perspectives*, 6, 31–52.
Carruth A., H.D. Gibson and E. Tsakalotos (1999) 'Are Aggregate Consumption Functions Similar across the EU?', *Regional Studies*, 33 (forthcoming).
Christodoulakis N., S. Dimelis and T. Kollintzas (1995) 'Comparisons of Business Cycles in Greece and the EC: Idiosyncrasies and Regularities', *Economica*, 62, 1–27.
Dickerson A.P., H.D. Gibson and E. Tsakalotos (1998) 'Business Cycle Correspondence in the EU', *Empirica*, 25, 51–77.
Goodhart C.A.E. (1996a) 'European Monetary Integration', *European Economic Review* 40, 1083–90.
Goodhart C.A.E. (1996b) 'The Transition to EMU', *Scottish Journal of Political Economy* 43, 241–57.
Klein L.R. and P. Hong (1993) '"Fortress Europe" and Retaliatory Economic Warfare', in D. Salvatore (ed.), *Protectionism and World Welfare* (Cambridge: Cambridge University Press).
Krugman P.R. (1993) 'Lessons of Massachusetts for EMU', in F. Torres and F. Giavazzi (eds), *Adjustment and Growth in the European Monetary Union* (Cambridge: Cambridge University Press for the CEPR).
Layard R., S. Nickell and R. Jackman (1991) *Unemployment: Macroeconomic Performance and the Labour Market* (Oxford: Oxford University Press).

Discussion
Guglielmo Carchedi

Huffschmid's chapter is, in the words of its author, 'a schematic outline of one part of institutional and political reforms, in and of the EU, in order to bring it on to an alternative path of economic and social development' (p. 241). The chapter accomplishes this task competently. It submits four objectives of an alternative European policy – full employment, social equity, social welfare and ecological sustainability, and also submits alternatives, both short-term and of a more institutional nature, to achieve these objectives. In doing so, Huffschmid raises many important issues and provides a number of stimulating answers – the discussion of the strong euro and of alternative monetary and fiscal policies, to name but two.

It would take too long to discuss all of the detailed points raised by the chapter. Rather, I would like to mention two general matters of a more methodological nature. The first is whether this EU is the only possible outcome, given that it responds to the needs of capitalist development. Huffschmid is certainly right in denying the inevitability of this type and form of European integration. Those who hold an opposite view subscribe to a mechanical, rather than to a dialectical, interpretation of capitalist development. Capitalism creates a variety of conditions of its own reproduction (as well as of its radical change), the concrete, specific, form of which depends on the interrelation between all the determinant and determined elements of social reality. There is, thus, no pre-determined form of appearance of social phenomena. Moreover, the dialectical view stresses that what is born as a condition for reproduction of this system can change into a condition for its radical transformation and vice versa. From this angle, social reforms are thus a contested terrain, between the forces functional for the reproduction and those functional for the radical change of capitalism.

The second and related point is that it is one thing to ask for more employment and social justice. These and other similar demands and alternative policies should be enthusiastically supported, however, it is another to see them as corrective of a system – capitalism and the market – whose merit is that of serving 'as efficient instruments of resource allocation and stimulation of productivity' (p. 229). To fight for labour's Europe implies a fight for reforms and, at the same time, a debunking of Neoliberalist policies at the theoretical level – a task which, in its turn, implies a radical critique of the neoclassical theory upon which Neoliberalism is founded. But it is exactly neoclassical economics which provides the theoretical underpinning for the myth of the efficiency of the market as an allocative system. The question as to whether these measures can be implemented, how and when (that is, to whose advantage), is a question which only the power relations among classes will decide. Unfortunately, in the EU at present, in spite of the great strikes witnessed in 1997, these relations are in favour of capital rather than of labour.

Economists can contribute to a reversal of these relations, not only by submitting and working out alternative schemes of economic and social development, but also by clearly stressing and supporting theoretically the thesis that these alternative schemes should not be seen as a trade-off between greater social justice and the efficiency of the market. Rather, they should be seen as measures against an irrational system, a system which might be rational in terms of profit-making but which is irrational in terms of human development and of the allocation of the natural resources needed for it. In my opinion, to argue for more employment and greater social justice within an interpretative scheme stressing the rationality of the system which originates these social evils, cannot but be self-defeating.

Index

accumulation rate 100, 101, 102
Adaman, F. 138–9
Albert, M. 114
Albert–Hahnel horizontal planning 116
Alesina, A. 207, 214
analytical Marxism 115
Artis, M. 92, 93
autonomy 134, 138, 139, 141
average rate of profit 174, 175, 176–7, 178, 184, 196, 197

Baldwin, R. 21
bank-based system 56
Barro, R.J. 2, 5, 6, 205
Bayoumi, R. 246
Bean, C. 27, 28, 30, 246
Belgium 150, 168
Belkin, D. 113
benefits 72, 73
Bennett, A. 93, 96
Berliner, J. 137
bilateral limits 181, 182
Blanchard, O.J. 205
Blinder, A. 4, 7, 10, 11
Bretton Woods system 162, 240
British Telecom 58
Brus, W. 139
Bryan, D. 198
budget deficits 25, 27–8, 29, 92, 94, 167
Busch, K. 17
business cycle 7, 14, 96

Canzoneri, M.B. 208
capital 3, 43, 99, 168, 176, 179
  accumulation 70
  concentration and centralization theory 14, 178
  constant 197, 202, 203
  financial 70, 179, 185
  human 10, 24
  industrial 185

markets, internal 30
  physical 24
  restructuring 68
  stocks 100
  value composition 200, 201, 202
capitalism 229, 250
  contemporary 14, 82
  control 117
  critical issues 12, 13, 15, 16, 18, 20, 24–5
  economy 92
  free market 86
  inflation and unemployment 89, 91, 98, 102, 106
  internationalization 16
  managed market 86
  Neoliberal 128
  private 76, 77, 78, 79, 80, 81, 86
  privatization: United Kingdom 42, 43, 69
  rethinking socialism 113, 122, 124, 126, 127, 133, 134, 137, 140
  state 14–16, 76, 77, 78, 80, 81, 82, 86, 133, 134
  state limiting versus expansion 77, 80, 81, 82, 87
  system 90
  totalitarian 195
  Western Europe 17
  Western-type 137, 138
capitalist crisis theory 14–15, 33–4, 116
capitalist globalization *see* Economic and Monetary Union and capitalist globalization
car industry 57
Carchedi, G. 173–92, 250–1
Carruth, A. 246
Cassis de Dijon case 166
Cecchini Report 21

Central bank 29, 153, 154, 182, 186, 226, 232, 240
  Board of Governors 162
  'conservative' 207, 208, 212
  independence 205–17, 236;
    empirical support 214–16;
    theoretical
    substantiation 205–8
  as political instrument 237–8
  see also European Central Bank
central planning 114
central rates 181
centralized reserve 209
Cherry Esplanade Conjecture 126, 127
  see also pi curve
Christou, G.K. 1–34
Christoudoulakis, N. 246
Chryssochoou, D. 160, 169
Churchill, W. 156
civil service 53
class 12–13, 18, 77–8, 86–7, 134, 195–6, 203–4
  issue 81
  structure 77, 78, 82
  working class 178, 180
coalmining industry 56
cobweb theorem 120
Cockshott, W. 128
Cold War 222
combined and unequal development 17
commercial banks 153, 209
Common Agricultural Policy 184
communism 18, 76, 77, 78, 79, 80, 81, 127, 133, 134
comparative advantage 22, 23, 24, 151
competition 4–5, 13–14, 21–4, 28, 106, 225, 227
  international 17
  monopolistic 9
  oligopolistic 24
  perfect 47
  privatization: United Kingdom 48, 49–55, 58–9
  quantity theory 49
computer and information technology 173

consensualization 114, 128
Conservative government 57
consumption 45, 175, 177
control 116
  ceiling 117
  over production 116–17
convergence criteria 147
conversion rates 151, 152, 153
cost–benefit measurement 81, 82
costs 72, 73
Cottrell, A.F. 128
Council for Mutual Economic Assistance 248
credibility 208
credit 98
Cripps, F. 93
crises 14
  Marxist theories of 14, 33–4
critical issues 1–34
  Economic and Monetary unification of Europe 18–31
  neoliberal theory 2–8, 9–18
cross-bilateral central rates or cross-rates 181
Cukierman, A. 205, 214–15
current-account imbalances 23
Cutler, T. 19

Delors Report 25, 223
delta curve 119–22, 124, 125, 127, 140, 141
demand 3, 4, 11, 96, 98, 99
democracy 114
democratic consolidation see financial governance and democratic consolidation
democratic deficit 29, 159
denationalization 54
  see also privatization
Denmark 26, 146, 168
deregulation 23
deutsche mark 180, 186, 187, 226
devaluation 150, 182, 187, 188, 197, 198, 227
Devine, P. 114, 138–9
devolution ratio 117
dialectical method 13
Diamandouros, N. 170
Dickerson, A.P. 246

Index 255

Dimelis, S. 246
divergence indicator 182
division of labour 23, 90
Dobb, M. 138
dollar 154, 160, 180, 186, 239, 247
Earley, J.S. 98
Eastern Europe 114, 133, 134, 135, 239, 240
Eatwell, J. 163, 164
EcoFin 151
economic dimension 173
Economic and Monetary Union 8, 18–31, 155, 159, 167, 220–51
  alternative: principles and main elements 228–41; fiscal initiative 233–4; monetary policy 233; public intervention objectives 229–30; re-embedding rules of the market 228–9; working time reduction 234–5
  and capitalist globalization 173–204; globalization myth and imperialism reality 173–80; single currency 180–8
  integration as contested area 221–8
  internal market 19–25
  medium-term institutional reforms 28–30, 235–41; central bank as political instrument: monetary policy 237–8; exchange rate stability: European Monetary System 28–30, 239–41; re-embedding independence 235–7; stabilization and redistribution: fiscal federalism 30, 238–9
  neoliberalism, resistance against 241–3
  single currency 145, 147, 151, 153, 154, 155
  treaty 17

economic shocks 28
economies of scale 45, 50, 51
effective demand theory 89
efficiency 3, 72, 73, 76, 77, 79, 82, 86
  calculus 87, 88
  –equity trade-off 140
  wage theory 117
Eichengreen, B. 27, 28, 246
electricity industry 57, 59
employment 3, 4, 93, 159, 196, 209, 229, 230, 233
Employment Summit 232
Engels, F. 114–15, 122
engineering industry 56
equilibrium natural output 205–6, 207
Euro 150–5, 167–8, 184–8, 221, 226–8, 239
EURO-X council 237
EURO-11 council 237
Eurobonds 234
Europe 6, 237
  see also Economic and Monetary unification of Europe; European; single currency
European Central Bank 20, 25, 28, 29, 150–1, 152, 153, 155, 185, 188, 223, 240, 245
  Governing Council 26
European Commission 21, 23, 145, 150, 164–6, 232, 236
  Action Programme for the Second Stage 161
European Community for Coal and Steel 222, 223
European Council 147, 148, 151, 165, 223, 232
European Court of Justice 165, 166
European Currency Unit 152, 180–1, 182
European Directives 21, 23
European Economic Community 18–19, 222, 223, 227, 228
European Exchange Rate Mechanism 162

European Monetary Institute 26
European Monetary System 27, 29, 180, 183, 204, 237, 239–41
European Monetary Union 25–31
 expected benefits 26–8
 expected costs 28–31
European Parliament 145, 236
European Reserve Union 160
European Union 228, 231, 232, 234, 235, 248, 250
 enlargement 170
 Treaty 148, 149, 150, 152, 165, 223, 232, 234, 240
 see also financial governance and democratic consolidation
exchange rate 25, 27–8, 148, 151–4, 161–2, 164, 166–7, 170, 198, 226
 fixed 26
 stability 239–41
Exchange Rate Mechanism 147, 149, 152, 168, 180, 182–3, 184, 186, 187, 196
exchange value 12, 174
expansion 156, 225
exploitation 106
externalities 4, 45

Federal Republic of Germany 80
federalism, fiscal 238–9
Feldstein, M. 96
fiat money 209, 211, 212
financial activity growth 163
financial governance and democratic consolidation: European Union 159–71
 challenges 169–71
 integration, dynamics of 160–5
 integration, evaluation of effects of 166–9
financial institutions 59
financial liberalization 20
financial sector 42
Fine, B. 15, 33, 41–64, 68, 69, 70
Finland 146, 147
fiscal federalism 238–9
fiscal initiative 233–4
fiscal policy 7, 155, 167, 170, 232

fiscal rules 30
Fischer, S. 205
Fitoussi, J.P. 24
Fleming, J.M. 92
Folbre, N. 116
foreign direct investment 167, 168
foreign exchange 153, 162, 163, 167, 168
France 22, 52, 146–7, 150, 168, 181, 187–8, 242, 247
Franks, J. 22
free market conservatism 113
Friedman, M. 5, 6, 91, 93
fulfilment–democracy–equality–autonomy 118, 119–20, 121, 122, 123, 125

gathering information cost 10–11
general equilibrium models 9
Germany 18, 22, 79, 147, 166, 168
 Bundesbank 216, 226, 246
 capitalist globalization and Economic and Monetary Union 180, 181, 182–3, 185, 186, 187, 188, 203–4
 Economic and Monetary Union alternatives 222, 225, 226, 227, 231, 234
 see also deutsche mark
Gibson, H.D. 246
globalization 1, 42, 55, 225
 of production 68, 69
 see also Economic and Monetary Union and capitalist globalization
Godley, W. 93
Goodhart, C.A.E. 205, 246
goods and services 168
Goodwin, R.M. 91
Gordon, D.B. 205
Gordon, R. 10, 96
government intervention 22–3, 67, 79, 80, 182
Grahl, J. 11, 19–20, 24
Gramsci, A. 78
Gray, J. 138
great depression 78–81, 87

Index

Greece 22, 23, 26, 108–11, 146, 152, 168, 223, 247
Greenwald, B. 10, 11
Grilli, V. 214
gross domestic product 25, 26, 27, 100, 109, 161, 238
gross national product 167, 234
growth 106, 107, 109, 159
Gunther, R. 170

Hahnel, R. 114
Harris, L. 15, 33, 55, 68, 69
Harrod, R. 99, 104
Hayek, F. 228
Hayri, A. 61
Heilbroner, R. 7
Held, D. 160
Helm, D. 22, 24
Henderson, J. 4
Herr, H. 226
Hirst, P. 225
historical factors 53–4
Hong, P. 248
horizontal ties 127–8
Huffschmid, J. 220–43
human nature 13
Hunt, L. 57
hysteresis hypothesis 10, 246

imperialism 173–80, 188, 195, 199
incentives 15, 116, 117, 118
income 3
  distribution 4, 45
  –expenditure model 91
  inequality 58
independence 212, 213
  see also central bank independence
India 80
industrial economics and policy 49–55, 56
ineffectiveness 8
inflation 5–8, 15, 25, 27–9, 31, 167
  central bank independence 206, 207, 208, 209, 212, 213, 214, 215
  financial governance and democratic consolidation 175, 178, 182, 183, 184, 187, 197–8, 204
  single currency 146, 147, 148, 149
  tax 166
  see also inflation and unemployment; non-accelerating inflation rate of unemployment
inflation and unemployment 5–7, 89–111
  classical Marxian economics 106
  conventional theory versus empirical patterns 94–6
  empirical evidence 96–102
  theory and history 91–4
  throughput coefficient and inflation rates in Greece 108–11
innovation 13, 14
insider–outsider theories 10
institutions 50
integration 8, 159, 225, 228
  dynamics 160–5
  evaluation of effects 166–9
  see also integration as contested area
integration as contested area 221–8
  Euro 226–8
  historical development: shifts and alternatives 221–4
  structural pressures and constraints and strategic alternatives 224–5
interest rates 6, 25, 146, 147, 149, 154, 155, 182, 183
internal market 19–25, 27, 28, 30, 164, 166, 245
  critical questions 22–5
  gains 21–2
Internal Market Project 164
intra-industry trade 21
investment 24, 56, 57, 99, 111, 155
'invisible hand' 3
Ioakimoglou, E. 201
Ireland 146, 168

Italy 79, 146, 150, 168, 181, 182–4
Itoh, M. 209

Jackman, R. 246
Jacquemin, A. 23–4
Japan 18, 56, 160, 161, 164, 180, 197, 227, 248
  Bank of Japan 216
job search model 6
joint ventures 22, 42

Kalecki, M. 89–90, 96, 103
Katiphoris, G. 145–56
Katseli, L.T. 159–71
Keynes, J.M. 79, 91, 163, 247
Keynesian theory 5, 6–7, 89, 90, 92
Keynesianism 1, 11, 15, 225, 247
  inflation and unemployment 93, 94, 96, 98, 100, 102, 103, 107
  privatization: United Kingdom 45, 67, 69
  state limiting versus expansion 78, 79, 80, 87
  see also New Keynesianism
Klein, L.R. 248
Kollintzas, T. 246
Kornai, J. 138
Krugman, P.R. 24, 246
Kydland, F.E. 8, 205

labour 3, 7, 12, 15, 20, 42–3, 98, 168, 175, 177–9
  contracts 9
  flexibility 183
  market flexibility 20, 68
  mobility 29
  productivity 18, 203
  surplus 12, 77–8, 80, 81, 86
  theory of value 106
Laibman, D. 18, 113–31
Lapavitsas, C. 205–17
Laski, K. 139
Law of Nature 124
law of the tendential fall in the rate of profit 200–1
Layard, R. 246

Lenin, V.I. 118, 133
Leontief, W. 99
Liberals 77, 79, 80
limitation of the state versus expansion 72–84, 86–8
  change, understanding of 77–8
  example 78–81
  problem 72–4
  reasons for problem 75–7
  solutions 81–2
Liodakis, G. 195–9
Loth, W. 222
Lovejoy, D. 126
Lucas, R.E. 4, 6, 11, 12
Luxembourg 146, 147, 151, 168
Lynk, E. 57

Maastricht Treaty 19, 23, 25, 26, 27, 30
  capitalist globalization and Economic and Monetary Union 188, 197
  convergence criteria 186
  Economic and Monetary Union alternatives 223, 231, 236
  financial governance and democratic consolidation 166–7, 170
  preconditions for entry 25
  single currency 145, 147, 155
  timetable 26
McCallum, B. 5, 6, 212
McDougall Report 238
McLaughlin, A. 57
macro-policy 166
macroeconomic theory 5–8, 91
Maler, H. 115
Maloney, W. 57
managers 59–60
Maniatis, T. 16, 106–11
Mankiw, N.G. 7, 8, 9, 10
Mannheim, K. 115
market
  allocation 73, 76
  –based system 56
  –clearing model 12
  competitive 4
  economy 48
  failure 45, 46, 48, 49–55

imperfections 4,
institutions 47
mechanism 78
planning 77
socialism 113, 137
Marshall, A. 2
Marx, K. 12, 76, 77–8, 82, 87, 91, 99, 106, 114, 122, 138, 178–9, 200–1, 202–3, 209, 247
Marxism 19, 20, 22, 24, 31, 113, 114, 134, 198, 213
analytical 115
classical 106
economic theory 12–18
inflation and unemployment 14, 15, 90, 96, 102, 107
privatization 16
privatization: United Kingdom 68, 69
state limiting versus expansion 78, 79, 80
Mascianduro, D. 214
Mathews, K. 93
Mavroudeas, S. 67–70
maximum sustainable growth rate 99
Mayer, C. 22
means of consumption 174
means of production 12, 174, 175
Mencken, H.L. 116
mergers 22
microeconomic basis 2–5
microfoundations 5, 9
Milberg, W. 7
Milios, J. 200–4
Milonakis, D. 137–42
Mitterrand, F. 247
Monetary Committee of the Union 162
monetary policy 6, 9, 11, 207, 208, 226, 232, 233, 237–8
monopoly 9, 14, 106
natural 50–1, 55
pricing 23
Moore, B. 98
moral incentives 141
Moseley, F. 68
motivation 118, 125, 140–1
multinationals 173, 178

Mundell, R.A. 28, 92
Musgrave, R.A. 238

National Health Service 52–3
nationalized industries 52, 55
see also state firms
natural rate of unemployment 6, 7, 93, 96
neo-Austrianism 46–8, 50
neo-functionalist school of thought 161
neo-Ricardian 140
Neoclassical approach 19, 22, 70, 251
central bank independence 212–13
inflation and unemployment 89, 90, 93, 94, 96, 98, 100, 102, 107
rethinking socialism 121, 138
state limiting versus expansion 78, 79, 80, 81, 82, 86–7
Neoclassical Economics, Neoclassical theory see Neoclassical approach
neoliberal theory 1, 2–8, 9–18
macroeconomic basis 5–8
Marxist economic theory 12–18
microeconomic basis 2–5
New Keynesian theory 9–12
Neoliberalism 12–16, 18–19, 26, 28, 31
capitalism 128
Economic and Monetary Union alternatives 221, 225, 227–31, 236, 238, 245, 248, 251
paradigm 72
privatization: United Kingdom 41, 43
resistance 241–3
rethinking socialism 113, 121, 124, 127, 137
state limiting versus expansion 73, 77
see also neoliberal theory
Netherlands 146, 168, 181
Neven, D. 21–2
New Classical approach 5, 6, 8, 9, 11, 28, 31, 93

Index

new institutional economics 46–8
New Keynesianism 9–12, 19, 28, 31
Nickell, S. 246
'1992' programme 17, 18, 20, 21–2, 24
non-accelerating inflation rate of unemployment 6, 241
non-market institutions 47
non-tariff barriers 19, 21
normal capacity utilization path 99
North American Free Trade Agreement 227

Oil Producing and Exporting Countries 96
Ollman, B. 114
Organization for Economic Cooperation and Development 91, 94, 95, 97, 100, 102, 107, 108
output 69, 94, 100, 209, 214
overdetermination 13

Panić, M. 224
Papandreou, A. 247
Pareto optimality 3, 4, 31
Parsons, R.J. 98
partial equilibrium 47
Persson, T. 208
Petralias, N. 106–11
Phelps, E.S. 93
Phillips, A.W. 92
Phillips curve 7, 11, 92–3, 106
pi curve 118–19, 120, 121, 122, 123, 124, 125, 126–7
Pinder, J. 222, 223
plan–market dilemma 141
planning process 114
planning or programming system 140
Poletti, C. 56–7
policy rule, fixed 8
policy-making 8
political dimension 173
political economy 46–8
Portugal 22, 23, 146, 152, 168, 223
post-Keynesianism 209

poverty 17, 31
Prescott, E.C. 8, 205
principal–agent approach 47, 208
private property 4, 5, 73, 77, 82
privatization 16, 23, 50, 73
  mainstream approaches 43–6
  market failure, competition and industrial economics and policy 49–55
  political economy, new institutional economics and neo-Austrian economics 46–8
privatization: United Kingdom 41–64, 67–70
production 122
  functions 3
  of value 175
productivity 18, 54, 56, 175, 177–8
  rethinking socialism 118–26 *passim*, 119–20, 121, 123, 125, 133–4, 139
profit 14, 60, 68, 70, 99–102, 106–7, 178, 200–1, 203
  decline 15
  rate, profit rate and crises, 33
  speculative 179
  see also average rate of profit; law of the tendential fall of the rate of profit
programming-planning system 128
property ownership 78
property rights 44, 46, 47, 51–2, 58, 60
Prosser, T. 52
protectionism 24
public finance criteria 146–7
public intervention objectives 229–30
public utilities 58
Puhle, H.J. 170
purchasing power 174, 175, 178

Quandt, R. 4
quantity theory of competition 49

random shocks 207

Index

rational expectations hypothesis 5, 9
Rawls, J. 138
Reaganism 41
real business cycle theory 7, 14
recession 31, 107
redistribution 238–9
rent-seeking 46–7, 48, 50
reserve currency 161
Resnick, S. 3, 15, 76
resource allocation 4
resource endowments 3
Ricardian Equivalence Theorem 32,
rigidities, nominal 10
Roemer, J.E. 113, 115, 137, 138
Rogoff, K. 207, 212
Roosevelt, F. 113
Rowthorn, B. 3, 93

savings function 99
scale economies 22
Schuman Plan 222
Schwartzman, D. 113
science 114–15
seigniorage 29, 180, 187
Semmler, W. 14
Shaikh, A. 68, 86–8, 89–103, 195, 199
Shaked, A. 10
Shapiro, C. 10
share-ownership 60–1
shocks 6, 28, 29, 30, 107, 206, 208
short-run equilibrium 96
Siegel, T. 196
single currency 26–7, 30, 146–56, 180–8, 239
 criteria and fulfilment 145–7
 problem and solution 147–8
 prospects 154–6
 sustainability 148–50
 transition problems 150–4
 see also euro
Single European Act 19, 22, 23, 27, 30
Single Market 223
Single Market programme 21
Smith, A. 2, 4, 67

social effects 73
social equity 229, 230
social welfare and security 229
socialism 18, 77, 78, 79, 80, 113–42
 classical 137, 138
 Cuban 116
 delta curve 119–22
 market 138, 139
 pi curve 118–19
 wider perspectives 127–9
socialization of production 69
socioeconomic factors 54
soft budget constraint 138
solar communism 126
Solow, R. 10
South Africa 52
Soviet Union 17, 79, 80, 173, 222
 rethinking socialism 113, 114, 127, 128, 133, 134, 137
Spain 22, 23, 79, 146, 150, 168, 223
Stability Council 188
Stability Pact 151, 155, 166, 167, 188, 242
stabilization 238–9
Stadler, G. 7
state allocations 73, 76
State Capitalist Right 79
state firms (enterprises) 16,
state ownership 80, 82
state planning 77
state property 73, 77
state, role of 15–16, 69
statists 81
Statz, A. 222
steel industry 57
Steuart 209
Stiglitz, J. 10, 11
stranded assets 59
structure–conduct–performance 49
subcontracting 42
subjectivity 13
Summers, L.H. 214
supply 3, 4, 96, 98
 curve 11
 shocks 6
surplus value 68, 174–5, 177–8, 180, 183–5, 196, 201–2, 220

sustainability 148–50, 230
Sutton, J. 10
Swann, D. 183
Sweden 26, 149

Tabellini, G. 207, 208, 214
takeovers 22, 57
tax 7, 16, 240
Teague, P. 11, 19–20, 24
technical change 14, 106
technological innovation 42, 68, 173–9, 184, 196–7, 200–3
Thatcher, M. 59
Thatcherism 41, 44
Thompson, G. 225
throughput coefficient 99–100, 101, 102, 103, 107, 108–11
time inconsistency of optimal policy 8
Tobin tax 240
Tonak, A. 68
trade unions 15
transaction costs 46
transfer payments 208
Treaty of Amsterdam 19, 25, 232
Treaty of Rome 23
Triffin, R. 160
Tsakalotos, E. 246
Tsakloglou, P. 245–9
Tsinisizelis, M. 160, 169
Tsoukalis, L. 161
Tsoulfidis, L. 67–70

unemployment 6–7, 10, 12, 15, 17, 19, 24–6, 31, 42
 capitalist globalization and Economic and Monetary Union 175, 176, 179, 196
 Economic and Monetary Union alternatives 230, 232, 234, 246–7
 financial governance and democratic consolidation 160, 161, 164
 involuntary 14
 voluntary 11, 14
 see also inflation and unemployment; natural unemployment rate; non-accelerating inflation rate of unemployment
unification 17–18, 231
United Kingdom 22, 26, 149–50, 154, 168, 184, 225–6, 242
 see also privatization
United States 11, 17, 18, 30, 57, 222, 225, 227, 238, 248
 capitalist globalization and Economic and Monetary Union 180, 186, 197
 financial governance and democratic consolidation 160, 161, 164
 inflation and unemployment 91, 96, 98, 99, 100, 101, 102, 103, 108, 111
 state limiting versus expansion 80, 86
 see also dollar
use values 174, 175, 177
utilities 22–3
utility 3
utopia 114–15

value 177, 178
 law of 195, 196
Vietnam War 100
Vlachou, A. 1–34
von Neumann, J. 99

wage 3, 4, 51
 efficiency 10
 flexibility 29
 low 56
 nominal 6, 7, 9
 –price spiral 93
 rates 175
 real 7, 15, 117
Walras, L. 2
Walsh, C. 208
Walters, A. 58
water industry 57
wealth redistribution 52
welfare states 79, 80
Werner Report 223
Wolff, R.D. 3, 15, 72–84, 133–6
work-life quality 126

working class 197, 198
working-time reductions 232, 234–5
workplace 116
World Bank 41

Wright, E.O. 113, 115

yen 180, 239, 247
Yfantis, K. 160
Yilmaz, K. 61